PLAYING WITH THE BEST

Walter French. *United Newspictures*, October 24, 1925. (Courtesy of Author)

PLAYING WITH THE BEST

One Man's Journey Through the Golden Age of Sports

LENNY WAGNER

BROOKLINE
books

Havertown, Pennsylvania

Brookline Books is an imprint of Casemate Publishers

Published in the United States of America and Great Britain in 2024 by
BROOKLINE BOOKS
1950 Lawrence Road, Havertown, PA 19083
and
47 Church Street, Barnsley, S70 2AS, UK

Copyright 2024 © Lenny Wagner

Hardback Edition: ISBN 978-1-955041-35-5
Digital Edition: ISBN 978-1-955041-36-2

A CIP record for this book is available from the British Library

All rights reserved. No part of this book may be reproduced or transmitted in any form or by any means, electronic or mechanical including photocopying, recording or by any information storage and retrieval system, without permission from the publisher in writing.

Printed and bound in the United Kingdom by CPI Group (UK) Ltd, Croydon, CR0 4YY

Typeset in India by Lapiz Digital Services, Chennai.

For a complete list of Brookline Books titles, please contact:

CASEMATE PUBLISHERS (US)
Telephone (610) 853-9131
Fax (610) 853-9146
Email: casemate@casematepublishers.com
www.casematepublishers.com

CASEMATE PUBLISHERS (UK)
Telephone (0)1226 734350
Email: casemate@casemateuk.com
www.casemateuk.com

To Cheryl and Carrie

Contents

Prologue: Escape from Death in the Jungle — ix

1 The Golden Age of Sports — 1
2 Football Education, Rutgers Days, Paul Robeson, March Madness, 1917–1920 — 5
3 The Big Game: Army vs. Notre Dame, Knute Rockne, and George Gipp, 1920 — 27
4 Hans Lobert and Army Baseball, 1921–1922 — 49
5 Connie Mack and the Philadelphia Athletics, 1923–1925 — 61
6 The Pottsville Maroons and the Stolen NFL Championship of 1925 — 79
7 1926 and the Dutch Leonard Affair — 99
8 1929 and the Team that Time Forgot — 113
9 The Stock Market Crash, Dizzy Dean, and the Dixie Series of 1931 — 145
10 Outlaw Ballplayer — 159
11 Coach French — 167
12 Captain French and the War Years — 177

Epilogue — 189
Acknowledgements — 203
Endnotes — 205
Bibliography — 217
Index — 219

PROLOGUE

Escape from Death in the Jungle

It was June 6, 1974, and Jack Glickstein, a World War II Navy veteran, was at his home on Stratford Avenue in Philadelphia. He was watching a documentary on the 30th anniversary of D-Day. The program got over at around midnight, but Jack was not ready to turn in for the night. His mind was taking him back some 30 years to the jungles of Brazil. He went down to his basement and pulled out his old flight logs. It was all there, the place Belem, Brazil, the action, rescue mission on Navy Airship K-114.

In February of 1944, Glickstein was stationed at the naval air base in Amapá, Brazil. He served aboard the Navy Airship K-114, a dirigible housed at Amapá which was located in the Amazon jungle about 250 miles northwest of Belem which was home to one of a network of bases the United States maintained along the coast of Brazil.

Because they could fly low at slow speeds and had an endurance capability of 24 hours, Navy blimps, like the ones housed at Amapá, were perfect for search and rescue. A call came into Jack's crew for one such mission. It was only their second in a span of two months. He later recalled "if it were not for Army planes going down and us going in for rescue work, I guess us blimp men would have gone stir crazy with inactivity." The crew of an Army B-24 was missing after bailing out of their plane which had been caught in a thunderstorm when attempting to land near Belem. The whereabouts of the crew was discovered the next day and Glickstein's team was dispatched to pick them up.

Glickstein's airship set down in a clearing in the jungle where the crew of the B-24 was awaiting rescue. As they boarded the aircraft, Jack thought that he recognized one of the crew members. After thinking about it for a few minutes, he was able to place the man as Walter French, who he had seen play baseball for his beloved Philadelphia Athletics in 1928.

In the excitement of the rescue and perhaps being a little starstruck, he never said anything to French that morning, and soon the men were on another flight out of Belem headed to Africa and then Italy. But on that night in June of 1974, recalling an article written about Walter in the *Sporting News*, which mentioned that he was living in La Selva Beach, CA, Jack sat down and wrote a letter to him. When the old ballplayer died 10 years later, the letter from Glickstein was found among his papers and correspondence.

The fact that Glickstein remembered having seen French play in 1928, when Jack was a very young boy, speaks volumes about how rabid of an A's fan Jack must have been. Walter saw limited action that year, for reasons which we will examine later, that were not of his own making, as he had just come off two very good seasons in 1926 and 1927. It also would have been easy to overlook him on a team as loaded with stars as was the case with the 1928 Philadelphia Athletics. The team included seven future Hall of Fame players: Ty Cobb, Tris Speaker, Al Simmons, Jimmie Foxx, Mickey Cochrane, Eddie Collins, and Lefty Grove, in addition to the team's legendary manager, Connie Mack.

Jack's level of devotion to the A's was only part of the reason that seeing Walter French play stuck in his head so many years later. How does a ballplayer that appeared in only 49 games in 1928 leave such an impression on an eight-year-old boy that he would have remembered seeing him play after all that time, much less recognize him? Certainly, part of the reason was that Walter French was a local product, having been born and raised only about 15 miles from Philadelphia, in Moorestown, NJ. A bigger factor, however, was that Walter French was not only an outstanding baseball player but a great football player as well, and throughout the 1920s, a period known as the Golden Age of Sports, he found himself front and center in some of the period's biggest games, events, and controversies. He also found himself playing with, for, and against some of the biggest stars of those sports in that period. From his days playing football for Army against the likes of Notre Dame's George Gipp, to sharing the outfield with Ty Cobb while going up against Babe Ruth, or facing down the great Walter Johnson, he successfully battled with and against some of the greatest players the sports of baseball and football have ever seen, and often excelled. Some of those encounters and relationships were one-time opportunities like when he knocked in a winning run against an up-and-coming minor league pitcher named Dizzy Dean, or when he played against future Chicago Bears owner George Halas when French was at Rutgers and Halas played for the Great Lakes Naval Air Station football team in 1918. There were encounters with other American icons, not normally thought of in association with sports. Some were fleeting like crossing paths with Thomas Edison, while others were extended and more intimate like his interaction with Gen. Douglas MacArthur, whose tenure as Superintendent of the United States Military Academy at West Point overlapped, as we shall see, not coincidentally, with Walter French's time there.

Also, in order to follow Walter's journey through the Golden Age of Sports, it will require that we learn about the origins of the great football rivalry between Army and Notre Dame, the stolen NFL championship of 1925, the Dutch Leonard Affair, the baseball team that *Sports Illustrated* would label as "The Team That Time Forgot" and the impact of the Great Depression on professional baseball because all of these and more are an integral part of his story.

Although few today know of Walter French, that was not the case in his day, especially in the 1920s. His versatility as an athlete, although not unique to him, certainly set him apart from other sports stars at that time. He was constantly in the news during the period from 1918 through 1936, when his playing days ended. Even then his coaching career was widely covered by the media. He was written about by all the top sportswriters of the time, from Grantland Rice in the 1920s right up to Ed Sullivan in the 1940s.

In 1912, Adolph Ochs, owner of the *New York Times*, introduced readers to a section of the newspaper made up of just pictures. These sections were printed in a style known as rotogravure which utilized a printing process invented in Germany, where circular metal plates could print up to 3,500 pages, from a continuous roll of paper in one hour. Within a few years, a number of newspapers were featuring a rotogravure section, usually in their Sunday edition. In the *New York Times* published on Sunday, May 10, 1925, a five-page rotogravure section was inserted just before the regular sports section. It was a sports who's who of the 1920s and featured a number of the decade's biggest sports stars. There was a photo of President Calvin Coolidge presenting a wristwatch to Bucky Harris, manager of the Washington Senators, the previous year's winners of the World Series. Babe Ruth was shown resting comfortably in a hospital bed as he recovered from an injury and promised his fans that he would be back soon. A picture of future Hall of Famer Mickey Cochrane, catcher with the Philadelphia Athletics, is shown with a caption touting him as one of Connie Mack's top young star players. There is a picture of heavyweight boxing contender Gene Tunney as he trained for his next bout by chopping wood. Golfing greats Bobby Jones and Walter Hagan are shown together as they prepare for an exhibition match. Swimming's Olympic Gold Medalist from the 1924 Paris Olympics, and future star of several Tarzan movies, Johnny Weissmuller is shown getting ready for the 1925 World Championships. At the bottom of the first page of the section with the biggest stars of that period, is a picture of Walter French along with the caption "Former Gridiron Star after Diamond Honors" and announcing that he had made it to the big leagues with the Philadelphia Athletics. The promising Athletics' rookie was keeping fine company on the pages of the *New York Times*.

CHAPTER I

The Golden Age of Sports

In the presidential election of 1920, the first after the end of World War I, Republican candidate Warren G. Harding took as his slogan "A Return to Normalcy." He summed up exactly what he meant by that term in a speech that he delivered on May 14, 1920:

"America's present need is not heroics, but healing; not nostrums, but normalcy; not revolution, but restoration; not agitation, but adjustment; not surgery, but serenity; not the dramatic, but the dispassionate; not experiment, but equipoise; not submergence in internationality, but sustainment in triumphant nationality ..."

"My best judgment of America's needs," he said "is to steady down, to get squarely on our feet, to make sure of the right path. Let's get out of the fevered delirium of war, with the hallucination that all the money in the world is to be made in the madness and the wildness of its aftermath. Let us stop to consider that tranquility at home is more precious than peace abroad, and that both our good fortune and our eminence are dependent on the normal forward stride of all the American people ..."

The voters in that year's election, which for the first time included women, must have been in complete agreement with Harding's message. He and his running mate Calvin Coolidge defeated Ohio Democratic Governor James M. Cox and his running mate Franklin D. Roosevelt in a landslide, garnering 404 electoral votes compared to 127 for their opponents.

Although the voters may have bought into Harding's vision of "normalcy," as the decade began to unfold, it soon became clear that what was taking place was anything but getting back to normal. "Normalcy" quickly evolved into the "Roaring Twenties" and everything that Harding outlined as to what was needed such as serenity, dispassion and tranquility was quickly tossed aside in favor of all that he warned against. While Americans may have wanted the comfort that comes with a familiarity with the past, they were quick to exchange it for the benefits of the advances, technological, and social, that were ushered in during the decade.

Virtually every key aspect of life in the country was transformed during the 1920s including transportation, communication, and production technology. The automobile had perhaps the biggest impact on American life in the 1920s. Henry Ford's new assembly line innovation made it possible to build cars faster and to sell them cheaper thus making them available to the average American family.

By the end of the decade most families owned at least one automobile. To support this increase in the number of cars on the road, by mid-decade, government spending on highways and bridges was more than $1 billion. Not only was the automobile industry thriving but so were those businesses that the auto industry depended on such as rubber, glass, and fabric, not to mention the oil business. All these developments created millions of jobs during this time. The economy was booming.

Air travel also emerged as an option in the 1920s. After the effectiveness of flight had been demonstrated during World War I, private companies began to look for opportunities to establish passenger lines and airmail contracts. In 1920, the first transcontinental airmail route was created from New York to San Francisco. Later in the decade, Charles Lindbergh became the first person to fly solo across the Atlantic Ocean, when he piloted his single-engine plane from New York to Paris in 1927. This gave the aviation industry a much-needed boost and made Lindbergh into a legendary hero. So much for Harding's notion that the country did not need "heroics." Lindbergh would not be the only hero the decade produced.

Also key to the transformation experienced in the 1920s was the radio. Guglielmo Marconi invented the wireless telegraph in 1890, but it wasn't until the 1920s that the first commercial radio station went on the air and broadcasted music to initially only a few thousand homes but by the end of the decade there were 800 radio stations in the country broadcasting to over 10 million radios. In 1924 the first radio network, the National Broadcasting Corporation (NBC) was created. It was followed by the Columbia Broadcasting System (CBS), three years later. NBC and CBS provided networks of radio stations which made it possible for people across the country, for the first time, to listen to broadcasts of news, entertainment, and sporting events.

In 1926, Ford also instituted a 40-hour work week for the employees in their plant which resulted in higher productivity. The workers would now be working eight-hour days, five days a week. Soon other companies followed Ford's lead and so it was that people in the 1920s found themselves with more time, more disposable income, more freedom, and more mobility. By the decade's end most homes had electricity and for the first time more people lived in urban centers than in country towns. In the 1920s the number of millionaires increased by 400 percent over the previous decade.

With the thriving economy and more free time, Americans began to look for sources of entertainment. Although there always was a general interest in sports in the country, the hysteria created in the 1920s was such as to name the decade the "Golden Age of Sports," and to transform American sports in such a way as to have a lasting impact felt to modern times.

"Three forces created the sports hysteria of the 1920s. The American public enjoyed unprecedented prosperity during the period. With more leisure time and disposable income, people turned to sports for fun and entertainment. Second, through serendipity and lucky parenting, a colorful athlete in each sport came along at the right time to focus the fan's interest. Last, the emerging art of promotion exploded into a cultural and economic whirlwind called 'ballyhoo'. The strongest winds blew from exuberant sports journalism, with some sports writers approaching the celebrity status of the star athletes they covered."[1]

Although baseball and college football were the most popular sports at this time, the popularity of all sports was beginning to grow, and in each, at least one star emerged to help drive that popularity. Baseball had the likes of Babe Ruth and Ty Cobb, boxing had Jack Dempsey, football had Red Grange, and golf had Bobby Jones.

There were five Olympic Games during the decade, starting with the Summer Games in 1920, the first since the end of World War I. The first ever Winter Games were held in Chamonix, France in 1924, where over 200 athletes from 16 countries competed. This was followed by the 1924 Summer Games in Paris, the 1928 Winter Games in St. Moritz, Switzerland and 1928 Summer Games in Amsterdam. Each was wildly popular and captured the attention of the world. The big American star to emerge from the Paris Olympics in 1924 was swimmer Johnny Weissmuller, who took home three gold medals in swimming and one bronze for water polo.

Finally on September 17, 1920, a group of businessmen, who were owners of professional football teams gathered in the showroom of a car dealership in Canton, Ohio, owned by Ralph Hay. Hay, the owner of the Canton Bulldogs, invited other teams from the Ohio league to join what was called the American Professional Football Association. Fourteen teams joined the league for its inaugural season. Although it would be decades before professional football would challenge baseball as the country's national pastime, this largely overlooked meeting gave rise to the National Football League.

As sports became more popular in the decade, newspapers assigned it more coverage and the sports pages were no longer manned by "over the hill hacks and cub reporters."[2] For most newspapers during this decade, sports coverage soon accounted for 15 percent of its reporting and the "hacks" and "cub reporters" were replaced by the likes of Grantland Rice, Ring Larder, Damon Runyan, and Westwood Pegler. There was an art to their writing not seen before or since. Mythical terms were used to describe the athletes and their exploits and each of the stars were given a "catchy nickname."[3] Babe Ruth was the "Sultan of Swat," Ty Cobb "The Georgia Peach," Jack Dempsey was "The Manassa Mauler," Red Grange "The Galloping Ghost," and Notre Dame's 1924 backfield, thanks to Grantland Rice, became the "Four Horsemen."

In his reporting on the Notre Dame vs. Army football game in 1924, Grantland Rice penned the perfect example of "ballyhoo" when he wrote: "Outlined against a blue gray October sky the Four Horsemen rode again. In dramatic lore they are known as famine, pestilence, destruction, and death. These are only aliases. Their real names are: Stuhldreher, Miller, Crowley and Layden. They formed the crest of the South Bend cyclone before which another fighting Army team was swept over the precipice at the Polo Grounds this afternoon as 55,000 spectators peered down upon the bewildering panorama spread out on the green plain below."[4] From the moment Rice's words made their way to print, the 1924 Notre Dame football team would be forever referred to as the "Four Horsemen" team.

In addition to the boost given by newspapers, radio also contributed to the growth of sports in the 1920s. It was able to give the fans immediate results and eventually play-by-play broadcasts. The first World Series to be broadcast over the radio was the 1922 series between the Giants and the Yankees. An estimated 5 million people in the New York area tuned into the broadcast. The game in 1921 between Texas and Texas A&M was the first play-by-play broadcast of a college football game.

During the decade an amazing number of new venues were built to accommodate the swelling crowds that were anxious to see sporting events in person. Franklin Field in Philadelphia was built in 1922 and expanded in 1925 to seat 65,000. The Horseshoe at Ohio State was built in 1922 to hold 66,000. The Rose Bowl was also built in 1922 to accommodate 57,000. In 1927 the University of Michigan built its stadium to hold 72,000 fans. Yankee Stadium was built in 1924 to hold 56,000. Illinois, California, and Stanford Universities all also built new stadiums over the course of the decade.

When Walter French left his Moorestown family and friends after his junior year at Moorestown High School in 1917, the start of the "Golden Age of Sports" was still a few years away. It would have been impossible for anyone to predict what the 1920s would have in store given that just a few months before the end of the school year, America had entered World War I.

CHAPTER 2

Football Education, Rutgers Days, Paul Robeson, March Madness, 1917–1920

Walter French was born on July 12, 1899, in Moorestown, NJ, which is located about 15 miles from Philadelphia. He was a direct descendant of one of the town's earliest settlers. Thomas French, and his wife Jane Aitkins French, arrived in the area from England in 1680. The French family settled in a section of West New Jersey which would become Chester Township. Thomas was one of the original proprietors of the region along with men like Edward Byllynge, Thomas Olive, and William Penn.

Chester was bordered on the north by the Rancocas Creek, to the south by the Pennsauken Creek and to the west by the Delaware River. Thomas French made two land purchases, one in 1684 on the north side of the Rancocas Creek, and one in 1689 along the Pennsauken Creek. French was one of the signers of the "Concessions and Agreements" establishing the town, was very active in community affairs, and was an influential member of the Society of Friends which was the dominant religious denomination in the area at the time.

In 1694, Thomas deeded over 300 acres of his land to his son Thomas French, Jr. on very favorable terms "in consideration of natural affection, goodwill and kindness which he hath and beareth to his beloved son."[1] Thomas French, Jr. built a house on the Camden Pike in 1695 which remained in the French family for 150 years. The original French homestead still stands on what is now called Camden Ave.

Eventually the different communities that made up Chester Township began to break off and set up their own towns, which left the 15 square miles that made up the Moorestown section of Chester on its own.

The French family tree, which developed over the next 200 years before Walter's birth, was extensive and its influence was felt throughout New Jersey and Pennsylvania. The French family were major landowners and they were active in a wide variety of businesses.

Walter was the fourth child of Walter S. and Belzora Baker French. He had two older brothers, Joseph, born in 1891, and William, born in 1896. One of his siblings, George Baker French, passed away just shy of his third birthday, two years before Walter was born. He also had a younger sister, Esther, who was born in 1901, and a brother, Cooper, born in 1906.

Walter's father ran a successful construction business in Moorestown and the surrounding communities. The firm's logo, a piece of iron in the shape of a masonry trowel, can still be found embedded in some of the town's oldest sidewalks. His firm also worked on projects in the Philadelphia area as well as in Delaware. He was the first contractor in the country to use the advanced road materials being developed by DuPont at that time, which he tested out by resurfacing the roads in New Castle, DE.

As was the case with their ancestors, and the other original founders of Moorestown, the French family were members of the Religious Society of Friends, also known as Quakers. They brought their children up as Quakers and they attended the same meeting that produced famed suffragette Alice Paul. Quakers believe that Jesus's teachings came in the form of an "inward light." Quakers would gather together in silence in what were called "Meetings" and in those meetings they could be directly influenced by God.

By the early 20th century the Quakers had given up some of the practices such as their plain dress and speech patterns, that set them apart from the other religious denominations, that by that time had outnumbered them in places like Moorestown. It was around this time that Quakers began to intermarry with those from other faiths. The bedrocks of their beliefs, non-violence and equality between men and women were still stressed and would have been taught to Walter and his siblings.

There were a number of French ancestors however, who despite being Quakers, had embarked on military careers, and their exploits would have undoubtedly been discussed with Walter and his siblings. The two that would likely have captured the imagination of an impressionable youngster were Samuel Gibbs French and James Hansell French.

Samuel Gibbs French was appointed to the United States Military Academy in 1839 and was a classmate of Ulysses S. Grant and like Grant he rose to the rank of General in the U.S. Army. He saw a great deal of action in the Mexican American War which was fought between the years of 1846 and 1848 fighting under General Zachery Taylor in the Battle of Buena Vista in 1847, a battle in which he was wounded. After his military career was over, he was elected to the New Jersey legislature. In 1856 he moved to Mississippi to manage a plantation that he inherited, through marriage. When the Civil War began, he sided with the south and served in the Army of the Confederacy.

James Hansell French received his commission to the United States Military Academy in 1869. Graduating with honors in 1874 he entered the cavalry service as a second lieutenant in the Ninth Regiment and was stationed in Texas. Later he served in Arizona and in 1880 was leading a company in pursuit of a group of Native Americans from the Apache tribe led by the famous warrior chief Victorio. It was during this action in the San Mateo Mountains of New Mexico that he was killed. He was 28 years old.

Walter's parents too, were not so rigid in their adherence to the principles of their faith as to feel compelled to send their children to the Moorestown Friends School which was established in 1785. Instead they chose to send him to Moorestown High School, the new public high school which was only 10 years old when Walter followed in his older brother William's footsteps and entered as a freshman in 1914.

While his two older brothers, Joseph and William, were being groomed for the world of business, Walter was free to pursue other interests and for him that meant sports. Although as a boy he showed promise in all sports it was football to which he was most drawn.

Next to the French home on Main Street was a vacant lot owned by Walter's father. As a boy Walter would invite his friends there to play football. To present himself with the biggest possible challenge and to work on his skills, he would arrange for his team to be manned with at least one fewer player than the opposition, and before he let everyone go home, he would challenge all present to stop him from taking the ball the length of the field.

At Moorestown High School he quickly became a star player in football, baseball, basketball, and track. In addition to competing for his high school team, Walter also joined his older brother William as a member of the Moorestown Collegians. The Collegians were a football team made up of local boys who had "performed in their own little way with school and town teams mingled with those were receiving the benefit of college coaching."[2] The Collegians played annual games against similarly constituted teams from the surrounding towns and teams comprised of soldiers from Camp Dix located a few miles to the north of Moorestown. The tradition continued for six years. The teams coached themselves and devised their own plays. Despite being only a high school freshman, Walter was recognized as one of the stars of the Moorestown team. The team did not lose a game over the six-year period and only gave up one touchdown.

Walter transferred after his junior year to The Pennington Seminary (now known as The Pennington School) located in Pennington, NJ. The Pennington Seminary was founded in 1838 by the Methodist Church. Initially established as a boy-only school, the first women were admitted in 1853, but in 1910 the school reverted to a single-sex institution. Women would not be admitted again until the 1970s.

When Walter arrived at Pennington in the fall of 1917, America was four months into its involvement in World War I and he found that compulsory military training was part of the school's curriculum. Students were required to wear military uniforms and began each day with reveille and ended each day with taps. They went on long hikes, constructed trenches, drilled, and practiced marksmanship. Although this type of military training was against the Quaker non-violent principles the fact was that a very small percentage of claims for exemption from military service were granted, and most Quaker men, who were drafted, including Walter's two brothers, served in combat positions in World War I.

All of this seemed to suit him just fine. *Pennington Life*, which was the yearbook for the class of 1918, listed his activities at the school as "Member of Theta Phi Fraternity; Varsity Football; Varsity Basketball; Varsity Baseball; Track Team; First Sergeant Company B; Dramatic Club; member of the Rifle Team."[3] Walter was getting a well-rounded education with little free time.

He also found a school with a long football tradition. Football had been played at Pennington for 38 years when Walter arrived in 1917, making its program one of the longest running in the nation. Despite all he may have learned at Moorestown High School, or by competing against older boys on the Collegians, he would later describe his experience at Pennington as his first real football education. However, any concern as to how he might fit in at the school, with respect to the sports teams, was quickly dispelled at the first football practice. In short order he was named the starting quarterback and led the team to a 5–1 record outscoring their opponents 194 to 32. Their only loss was to Trenton High School.

At the season's end, the Newark, New Jersey based *Sunday Call* newspaper named Walter the second team All-State quarterback. *The Trenton Times*, however, took issue with the selections made by the Newark *Call* writing "we cannot even figure a single player from the eleven that is entitled to a place on the All-State Team."[4] The *Times* then published their own All-State team which listed three players from the Trenton High School team as first team All-State, along with Walter French of Pennington as the first team All-State quarterback.

Walter was also one of the leaders on Pennington's basketball team, which had a 6–3 record in the 1917–18 season. Two of the losses again were to the Trenton High School team, which finished the season undefeated. *Pennington Life* summarized the season stating that "our team was a new team, only one man, Captain Blackwell, having played before on our floor. French and Gray, new men, were remarkably strong men and contributed materially to the good standing."[5]

In baseball, he was also one of the stars of the team playing an excellent shortstop and he was a key member of the Track team. In its year end summary, Theta Phi Fraternity summarized its contributions to the school's athletic program and credited French for his work with the football, baseball, basketball, and track teams.

After graduating from Pennington, Walter entered Rutgers University located in New Brunswick, NJ in 1918, as a member of the class of 1922. As with Pennington, Rutgers had a long football tradition. Rutgers played in the first ever college football game when it went up against in-state rival Princeton in 1869. Rutgers also had a successful track record when it came to recruiting athletes from New Jersey. In the years leading up to Walter's admission to the school, Rutgers sports legends such as Harry Rockafeller, Homer Hazel, and Robert Nash, either came from New Jersey or had attended private school in the state.

He also came to the school at a time of great upheaval for the nation and the school. World War I still would be ongoing for his first 10 weeks at Rutgers. With many students leaving school to serve overseas, the student body at Rutgers during Walter's freshman school year of 1918–19 had dropped to 286 students down from 513 in the previous year. On October 1, 1918, Rutgers, like most colleges and universities became part of the Student Army Training Corps (SATC), a United States War Department program which made it possible for men to prepare for military service while receiving a college education. Much like his life at Pennington, Walter's daily routine at Rutgers included military training and drills in addition to his class work. There was some speculation that the rigorous schedule placed on students in the SATC would keep them from athletic competition but one week before the program was formally instituted, Lt. James C. Torpey, the commanding officer of the Rutgers SATC announced that the men would be allowed to play football and other sports if it did not interfere with their military responsibilities.

The second major challenge facing the incoming Freshman class of 1918 was the outbreak of the Spanish flu which took the lives of an estimated 50 million people worldwide. The pandemic hit New Jersey quickly in the fall of 1918. Experts attributed its quick spread to the number of troops that were in close contact with one another at this time. Camp Dix located near Trenton, New Jersey was a perfect example as was Camp Merritt, in Dumont, New Jersey where close to 600 enlisted men died from the flu. Statewide there were 4,010 deaths reported in September of 1918, with 222 caused by influenza, but in just one month the death toll rose to 17,260 deaths in the state with just under 8,500 attributed to the pandemic. At Rutgers 75 students contracted the flu and four died as a result.

The pandemic caused an upheaval with the college football season. Some games were postponed indefinitely, while others were rescheduled or cancelled altogether. On October 9, 1918, the Big Ten Conference announced that it was dropping all their games scheduled for that month. "The season will open on November 2 and close on November 30, the Saturday following Thanksgiving, instead of the preceding Saturday as has been the conference rule"[6] read the announcement.

The pandemic affected the Rutgers football schedule in 1918 as well. Games scheduled with schools hit particularly hard, Lafayette, Colgate, Fordham, and West Virginia were all cancelled. The game against Lehigh, on October 26, was moved to New Brunswick after a major flu outbreak hit Bethlehem, PA. In the end the Rutgers Queensmen, as they were known at the time, played a seven-game schedule, which included games against Ursinus, the Pelham Bay Naval Station, Lehigh, the Hoboken Naval Station, Penn State, the Great Lakes Naval Base, and Syracuse.

Despite these challenges Walter found college life very much to his liking. He was very popular with his classmates. He was admitted into the Kappa Sigma fraternity and was even elected president of the Freshman class.

The 1917 football season had been a very successful one for Rutgers. They finished the season with a record of 7–1–1. The only blemishes on their record were a loss to Syracuse and a 7-all tie with West Virginia. Georgia Tech, coached by John

Heisman, for whom the Heisman Trophy is named, finished the season with a 9–0 record and was named the national champion. Walter Camp, widely acknowledged as the nation's foremost expert on college football, who selected the All-American team each year, said that, despite their undefeated season, he could not predict who would have won a head-to-head match between Georgia Tech and Rutgers.

George Foster Sanford was beginning his fifth year as the Rutgers head football coach when Walter French arrived on campus in 1918. After a successful career as a player at Yale, Sanford took the job as head coach at Columbia University, giving up a law career to do so. After leaving Columbia he coached Virginia for one season before leaving coaching to start up an insurance business in Manhattan. Rutgers lured him back into coaching for the 1913 season. He continued to live in Manhattan and work in his business and in turn took no salary from the school.

After what amounted to a breakthrough season for Rutgers in 1917, expectations were high for the 1918 season. Freshman Walter French was facing the daunting task of trying to crack a lineup which was returning almost all of its star players. It was here that Walter would encounter the first in what would be a long line of iconic American figures, that he would play with, for, or against for the next 20 years of his life.

Before becoming a world-renowned singer, stage actor, film star, and social activist, Paul Robeson was an All-American football player at Rutgers, earning those honors in 1917 and 1918, becoming the first Black man to be named All-American twice and joining Fritz Pollard of Brown University as the only Black All-Americans to that point.

Paul Leroy Robeson was born in Princeton, NJ in 1898, the youngest child in a family of seven. His father, Drew, a formerly enslaved man, was a minister in the Presbyterian Church. Paul was only six years old, in January of 1904, when his mother died in a terrible accident. Attempting to lift the stove so she could pull the carpet from beneath it, her dress caught fire when the door to it opened and hot coals spilled out.

In 1907, the Robesons moved from Princeton when Paul's father switched to the African Methodist Episcopal Zion denomination and took an assignment in Westfield, New Jersey. Since Westfield had too few Black children to support segregated schools, as had been the case in Princeton, Paul attended Westfield's integrated elementary school. He would later recall "I realize now that my easy movement between the two racial communities was rather exceptional. For one thing, I was the respected preacher's son, and then too, I was popular with the other boys and girls because of my skill at sports and studies."[7] His skill at sports was considerable, excelling in football, baseball, basketball, and track. While only a junior high school student, he was the starting shortstop on the high school varsity baseball team.

In 1910, his father was reassigned to the A.M.E. Zion Church in Somerville, New Jersey, which was located just a few miles from the Rutgers campus. Again, he was only one of a dozen Black students in a student body of 200. The school's principal, Dr. Ackerman, was consistently hostile to Paul. When he joined the glee club, the music teacher had to stand up to Ackerman when he objected to her having selected Paul to be a soloist. Besides being a gifted athlete, Paul's singing voice, which ultimately would be his ticket to stardom later in life, was extraordinary and despite the harsh treatment that he received from the school's principal, his teachers saw something special in him and provided him with much needed encouragement. In his autobiography Robeson wrote: "Miss Vossler, the music teacher who directed our glee club took a special interest in training my voice. Anna Milner the English teacher, paid close attention to my development as a speaker and debater; and it was she who first introduced me to Shakespeare's works."[8]

When Paul entered Rutgers in the fall of 1915, he became only the third Black student to attend the school in its history which dated back to 1766. Foster Sanford, who had seen Paul play football for Somerville High School, was anxious to have the six-foot-two, 200-pound teenager come out for the football team. The veteran players on the team had different ideas however and rebelled against having a Black player on their team. Some of the white players on the team did everything they could during the pre-season tryouts to get him to quit. During scrimmages they would gang up on him, intentionally miss blocks when he was running with the ball, punch, and elbow him in pileups. It got so bad that Paul told his father that he was planning on quitting. Drew Robeson listened to his son and then looked him in the eye and simply reminded him of where his family's journey had started. There would be no quitting.

Finally, at one session, after making a tackle, Paul was just about to start getting to his feet when a halfback named Frank Kelly deliberately stomped on his hand as he was walking back to the huddle. On the next play, with Kelly carrying the ball, Robeson shed multiple blockers, wrapped his arms around Kelly and lifted him over his head. Coach Sanford, witnessing the scene and thinking that Kelly might actually be killed, yelled "Robeson! Put him down! You made the team! You're on the varsity!"[9] Paul proceeded to drop Kelly to the field and walked off holding his injured fingers.

"With growing respect, his white teammates gradually accepted him. They nicknamed him 'Robey' and even protected him from attempted fouls by opponents who were especially hostile to the first black player they had ever faced."[10]

Paul played in four of Rutgers' eight games in 1915. He was thought to be a very promising player, and Coach Sanford took a special interest in him. He taught Paul the nuances of the game emphasizing the importance of playing a smart game rather than simply an emotional and physical one.

In 1916, when faced with an extremely tough schedule and a team with little experience, Coach Sanford began to build his team around Paul Robeson, making full use of his ability to play several positions. However, it was in 1917 when he burst onto the national scene and became a household name throughout the country.

In the lead up to the showdown with the powerhouse West Virginia team, their coach Earl Neale, appropriately nicknamed "Greasy," reached out to Coach Sanford suggesting that it might be best for him to bench Paul for this game. Members of the West Virginia team objected to playing against a team with a Black player, and Neale said he was concerned that Robeson might be badly hurt. Coach Sanford assured him that Paul would be able to take care of himself. West Virginia played the game hard but clean and showed their respect for him by lining up to shake his hand at the conclusion of the 7–7 tie.

At the end of the season Robeson was named by every major All-American selector, including Walter Camp, who referred to him as a "veritable superman." In evaluating Walter Camp's selections for the 1918 All-American Football Team, the *New York Herald* stated that "Now to study the team in detail shows this there was never a more serviceable end, both in attack and defense, than Robeson, the two-hundred-pound giant at Rutgers."[11]

Expectations were high for the Rutgers football team entering the 1918 season. The team's first practice was held on September 18. "The Rutgers football squad held its first practice yesterday afternoon under the direction of Foster Sanford with twenty candidates"[12] the *Trenton Evening Times* reported. "Rutgers will have practically a

The 1918 Rutgers Football Team. Walter French is standing, second from the left. Paul Robeson is seated, second from left. *(1919 Rutgers University Yearbook,* courtesy of Rutgers University Library)

veteran eleven, with the following members of last year's winning team still eligible: Captain Feitner, tackle; Neuschaefer and Rollins guards; Francke, Conner, Breckley, and Robeson, ends; Gardner and Kelly, halfbacks; and Baker, quarterback."[13]

Restrictions imposed by the pandemic protocols limited the amount of time that the team was able to practice. This was evident in a sloppy performance against their first opponent Ursinus on September 28, although one could not tell by the game's final score which was a 66–0 Rutgers victory. Coach Sanford, recovering from the Spanish flu, had to watch the game far from the action. Team trainer Jack "Doc" Besas, put in charge of the team in Sanford's absence, began making substitutions in the third quarter. Walter French, sent in to relieve Cliff Baker at quarterback, saw his first action as a college football player on that day. The *New Brunswick Sunday Times* noted that "French showed up as a snappy little quarterback. His passing to the runners was all right. He uncovered plenty of speed when he caught a kick from the tightly pressed invaders from Collegetown."[14]

The following week was a different story as Rutgers had all they could handle with the team from the Pelham Bay Naval Station. In this hard-fought game, Rutgers quarterback Cliff Baker suffered a neck injury in the first quarter and Walter was sent in to replace him, and although he could not lead the team to any scores it was noted that "French played a good game for two quarters. The youngster will develop into a great little quarterback. He is rapidly becoming experienced in varsity football and has a great deal of speed."[15] Baker badgered Doc Besas to put him back into the game in the fourth quarter and he scored the game's only touchdown, running the ball into the end zone in the final minutes of the game.

Next on the schedule was the game against Lehigh, which had to be moved from Bethlehem, PA to New Brunswick due to concerns related to a spike in the Spanish flu in the Lehigh Valley of Pennsylvania. Rutgers rolled to their third straight victory by shutting out Lehigh 39–0. Inserted into the game late in the second quarter, Walter brought the crowd at Neilson Field, including 700 soldiers from Camp Raritan to their feet when he caught a punt and returned it 66 yards, setting up a Rutgers touchdown. Paul Robeson scored two touchdowns in the game as did Frank Kelly. The headline in the *New Brunswick Sunday Times* blared "Lehigh Failed to Score in Gridiron Battle with Rutgers in which Kelly Starred; Robeson and French Thrill Crowd." It had to be encouraging for Walter to be included along with the recognized stars of the team in the write ups of the game.

Their next opponent was the team from the Hoboken Naval Transport Service on November 2. Rutgers won easily by a score of 40–0. The star of the game was halfback Turk Gardner who scored four touchdowns. Walter entered the game at quarterback to spell Cliff Baker, who had been limited in practice in the week preceding the game due to an injury. He had success running back kicks, completed a 24-yard pass to Robeson, and capped off the day by scoring his first touchdown as a collegian.

After a lopsided win over Penn State by a score of 26–3 on November 9, expectations were sky high for the Rutgers team who had played five games and had outscored their opponents 178–3, coming into their next game against the Great Lakes Naval Training Center at Ebbets Field in Brooklyn. The meeting was only finalized five days earlier, which was November 11, 1918, Armistice Day, which marked the end of World War I.

The Naval team had several All-Americans now stationed there who were part of their team. Their line was anchored by former Notre Dame stars Charlie Bachman, Emmett Keefe, and Jerry Jones. Starting at quarterback and halfback was former Northwestern standout Paddy Driscoll who would later play in the NFL for the Chicago Cardinals and Chicago Bears. Also lining up for Great Lakes Naval was an end from the University of Illinois by the name of George Halas. When the Great War broke out before his senior year, Halas joined the Navy and was stationed at the Great Lakes Center and assigned the task of organizing the football team. Over time he would be known as the founder, owner, and longtime coach of the Chicago Bears and one of the most influential individuals in the history of the National Football League.

Rutgers got off to a good start scoring the game's first two touchdowns, but the Great Lakes team, which played 30 different players through the course of the game, an unusually high number for that time where teams fielded only one unit which played both offense and defense, soon began to wear them down. When Cliff Baker went down with a hip injury, Walter French was inserted into the game to replace him at quarterback. He gave a good account of himself, completing passes and returning kicks. On two occasions he returned kicks over 50 yards, but it was all to no avail as the final score was a disastrous 54–14 drubbing.

Hopes were high for the last game of the 1918 season against Syracuse at the Polo Grounds in New York on November 30. The game was played in front of a small crowd of just over 4,000, one of whom was Walter Camp, certainly in attendance to put the final touches on his All-American choices. Coach Sanford told the sportswriters that he expected his team to bounce back from the game against the Great Lakes Naval Center. It was not to be however, as Syracuse took advantage of three critical Rutgers mistakes to win the game 21–0. It marked the first time all year that Rutgers failed to score. Two blocked kicks in the first half resulted in the Orangemen's first two touchdowns. Once again Walter French entered the game when Baker was injured. "Baker, the Rutgers plucky little field general, was again forced to go to the sidelines in the last half on account of injuries" the *Central New Jersey Home News* reported "French took his place and ran the team exceptionally well."[16] Late in the game however, Walter would contribute to his team's woes when he fumbled the ball during a kick return and Lou Usher, Syracuse's consensus All-American guard, scooped up the ball and ran it in for a touchdown, that apart from the extra point, which was executed successfully for the third time, ended the game's scoring.

The Syracuse game was Paul Robeson's last football game at Rutgers. Summing up the season in an article he wrote for the *Scarlet Letter*, the school's yearbook, teammate Cliff Baker wrote "It is greatly to be regretted that Paul Leroy Robeson should end his football career with two of the worst defeats that Rutgers has ever experienced. 'Roby' is recognized by close critics of the game as the greatest and most versatile player of all time."[17] Despite the way his brilliant career ended Paul was named first team All-American once again.

Due to the disruption caused by the Spanish flu and World War I, it was determined that no team would be named National Champion for 1918.

Walter French and Paul Robeson would still be teammates for the remainder of the school year, as both were members of the basketball and baseball teams. At the beginning of the 1918–19 basketball season six lettermen returned to the team, but when the team lost its starting guard from the previous season Robeson later recalled that "Coach Hill, undaunted, looked over the Freshman material for a real fast man and he found him in French."[18] Like with football, however, the star of the Rutgers basketball team was Paul Robeson, in fact there was a sizeable number of observers that felt he was even better at basketball than he was at football.

The 1918–19 basketball season for Rutgers brought out some "fine prospects for another year," Robeson observed "French should become a valuable man as should the rest of the Freshman combination."[19]

In June of 1919, Robeson graduated Phi Beta Kappa from the school and as class valedictorian.

The school year which began in the fall of 1919 saw a return to normal campus life at Rutgers and other schools throughout the country. The signing of the Armistice ending World War I in November of 1918, made the Student Army Training Corps no longer necessary and it was disbanded in December of that year. Also, the Spanish flu pandemic seemed to subside over the summer although it happened without scientists ever really understanding the cause of the deadly disease and there continued to be periodic spikes in cases until 1920. In the end, the only case of the flu on the Rutgers football team was that of Coach Sanford. The football schedule was also more normal. Games against Naval Air Stations were no longer on the schedule and were replaced with the likes of North Carolina, Boston College, and Northwestern.

The season opened on September 27, 1919, as it did the previous year with a matchup with Ursinus at Rutgers' Neilson Field. As was the case in 1918, Rutgers easily won the game by a score of 34–0. Walter French, now one of the team's starting halfbacks, scored two touchdowns. The newspaper accounts of the game were critical of the effort put forth by Rutgers however, because it did not inflict a worse beating on the inferior opponent. But unlike the previous year's game with Ursinus, the 1919 game was only 36 minutes long compared to the more typical 60-minute contest. Playing games where the time of the periods were less than the typical 15 minutes, was not unheard of at that time. The rulebook spelled out the circumstances where a game could be played in less than 60 minutes, and still be considered an official game.

Spalding's Official Football Guide was the rule book published annually by the National Collegiate Athletic Association (NCAA). The rules committee was made up of representatives from all the top college programs including such football royalty as Amos Alonzo Stagg from the University of Chicago and Walter Camp from Yale. Stagg had built Chicago into a national power, and introduced a new concept which he referred to as "student service payments" to recruit the best players to the school, which was the precursor to what we today call "athletic scholarships." Walter Camp was universally considered the nation's foremost expert on the game.

"Section 1, Rule IV, Length of Game" in the Spalding rule book read "The length of the game shall be 60 minutes, divided into four periods of 15 minutes each, exclusive of time taken out, although it may be of a shorter duration by mutual agreement between representatives of the contesting teams. In case no such agreement has been reached 10 minutes after the time scheduled for beginning the game, the Referee shall order the game to proceed and the full time shall be played." Section 2 of the same rule added a caveat for darkness. "Whenever the commencement of a game is so late that, in the opinion of the Referee, there is any likelihood of the game being interfered with by darkness, he shall, before play begins, arbitrarily shorten the four periods to such a length as shall insure four equal periods being completed and shall notify both captains of the exact time thus set." The penalty for failing to abide by the opinion of the referee was forfeiture of the game.

Whether it was the threat of darkness or some other reason, the next week's much anticipated meeting with North Carolina was played in four 10-minute periods before a crowd of over 3,000 at Rutgers' Neilson Field. Although North Carolina's season would ultimately turn out to be a disappointing one, at this early stage of the season they were considered to be tough opponents. Writing in the *New Brunswick Sunday Times*, sportswriter Harold O'Neill wrote that in North Carolina, Rutgers was facing an "eleven which for years has been 'ding-donging' for the championship of the south."[20]

Rutgers totally dominated North Carolina, allowing only two first downs in the entire game, and defeating them 19–0. Walter French was far and away the star of the game for the home team, rattling off one long run after another and scoring all three of Rutgers touchdowns.

"This French," O'Neill reported "who specializes in the open field, is weirdly fast, and possesses a slithering, squirmy quality which makes him almost untackable."[21]

The first quarter of the game was played even, with both teams feeling each other out. Near the end of the period Rutgers put together a sustained drive, highlighted by a brilliant 12-yard run by French which brought the ball deep into North Carolina's end of the field. Two plays later he ran behind the left tackle for the game's first score, a nine-yard touchdown run. In the second quarter he pulled off a fake punt and ran the ball back 30 yards and a few plays later plunged into the end zone on a short run. Just before the end of the first half, Walter brought the crowd to its feet with his best play of the game. Taking a pitch from quarterback Cliff Baker at the Rutgers 45-yard line, he ran around the end for 55 yards for his third touchdown.

In the second half of the game North Carolina "resorted to an aerial display and failed again. Not because of wildness of throws or any lack of execution, but because of the agility of Storck, Gardner, Baker, and French at breaking up the forwards when they were not intercepted."[22]

The headline in the sports section of the next day's *New Brunswick Sunday Times* read "French and Gardner are Dazzling Brilliant in Rutgers 19–0 Victory over University of North Carolina." The season was off to a great start for Walter French. He was emerging as the team's star player and had stepped into the gap left by the graduation of Robeson and the other seniors from the 1918 team. He had scored five touchdowns in the first two games of the season. Looking ahead to the remainder of the season Harold O'Neill spoke for everyone at the game when he wrote "Rutgers had a man yesterday that accomplished so much individually and who will continue to do so as the season progresses."[23] However, the season was not going to progress for Walter French as he had hoped.

The next opponent on the schedule was Lehigh. The Rutgers team travelled to Bethlehem, PA for the game on October 11 at Taylor Stadium in front of a crowd of 6,000 fans. The Rutgers team must have been feeling pretty good about their chances. They were coming off an important win over North Carolina and they had beaten Lehigh 39–0 in 1918.

Playing quarterback for Lehigh was Arthur "Buzz" Herrington. Herrington was a mirror image of Walter French. Like Walter he was a sophomore, and the two were similar in terms of their build. Also like Walter, Herrington was fast and tough to stop in the open field.

The game started off as a defensive battle with neither team scoring in the first quarter. About midway through the second quarter, Walter French, who had been playing a solid game to that point, took the ball around the end for a gain of 30 yards. As he was slowed, about to go out of bounds "Buzz" Herrington caught up to him and grabbed him around the shoulders and slammed him to the turf. His head violently hit the ground and a hush came over the crowd. The crowd's reaction was the type that occurs when it is obvious that a player, friend, or foe, has been badly injured. He lay motionless on the field, out cold. Rutgers put up a good fight but without their star running back they were unable to push the ball into the end zone, despite being in the shadow of the goal posts four times in the second half. Lehigh won the game by a score of 19–0.

Although newspaper accounts differed in their reporting of how long Walter remained unconscious, one thing was for certain, he was still out when he was taken from the field and rushed to the city hospital in Bethlehem. When the team left to return to New Brunswick he remained behind. "Rutgers left behind here tonight one of her sterling players—Walter French," Harold O'Neill wrote "After being injured in the second quarter, after a great 30-yard run around end, he was taken to the city hospital. It is feared that he sustained a concussion of the brain, though the seriousness of his injuries will not be known until tomorrow."[24] When the Rutgers team returned to New Brunswick, trainer "Doc" Besas and a few other players stayed behind with Walter.

The *Trenton Times* described the mood on the Rutgers campus after the Lehigh game: "A disconsolate Rutgers eleven was back in college today—disconsolate in a measure over the unexpected trouncing suffered at the hands of Lehigh on Saturday, but the reason for most of the gloom the boys brought back from South Bethlehem was easily traceable to the accident which removed the fleet French from the game and perhaps from the Rutgers lineup for the remainder of the season … it was at first thought that he was suffering from a concussion of the brain. After the Rutgers back regained consciousness, however, it was determined that he was suffering from a sprained neck. Until his accident French had been the Rutgers star and his loss would be a severe blow to the hopes of the local eleven."[25]

The reporting on his injury status kept up for weeks, and although the stories differed in a number of details, the reports all insisted that he had some type of neck injury and had not sustained a concussion. The "College Gridiron Gossip" section of the October 14 edition of the *Trenton Evening Times* reported "Walter French, the Rutgers halfback, who was injured in the Lehigh game and was unconscious for 22 hours, yesterday was found to have suffered only a sprained neck and not as was feared, concussion of the brain. He will be out of the game two weeks."[26] However, in two weeks he was a long way from being back "in the game." On October 30, the "Gridiron Gossip" reported he had been transferred to a hospital in New York, more specialized in treating his type of injury, still not being described as a concussion.

Although there is a heightened awareness in the game today, "concussions are not a recent discovery in football."[27] Years before Walter's injury there was "ample evidence that concussions occurred frequently and ample reason to believe that concussions could have long-term pathogenic consequences."[28] Newspapers and medical professionals had been discussing concussions for "more than 20 years as the cause of death and hospitalization."[29] A study done in 1906 found that concussions were happening in "nearly every game." In 1910, 14 football deaths were recorded with concussions of the brain as the leading cause.

Despite all the awareness of concussions around this time, it was not unusual for medical professionals to arrive at some other diagnosis for an injury that was, in fact, a concussion, or accompanied by a concussion. In Walter's case he may have had a neck injury, as reported, but it was in addition to a very serious concussion. The length of time he spent unconscious indicates that he had sustained a severe type of traumatic brain injury. After regaining consciousness he would have experienced amnesia, nausea, and a constant ringing in his ears.

The reason that concussions were often not listed as the official injury was not the "result of carelessness" but rather the emerging demand, at this time, for "experimentally supported, evidence-based diagnosis and therapies. Physicians were increasingly expected to rely on technical diagnostics, visualization technologies that would give proof of the presence of a pathology."[30] This was a standard that was very hard to reach when dealing with concussions at that time. "Physicians were all too aware of their inability to produce visual evidence. Injury, they conceded could occur in the brain without visible damage to the head. For injury hidden beneath skin and bone and inches of seemingly unaffected brain tissue, there was no easy means of detection … as there was for fractures of the skull and visible tearing of the brain."[31] The X-ray technology of the time could not detect trauma to brain tissue.

Despite the considerable amount of knowledge the NCAA had regarding the frequency and dangers of concussions it was not until 1933 that the organization published a medical handbook for its member schools. It warned that concussions were being treated too lightly and laid out recommendations to be followed regarding treatment and a timeline to return to play.

The injuries he sustained in the Lehigh game were serious enough to make him miss almost an entire month of the season. Without Walter the team defeated the New York Aggies from the New York School of Applied Agriculture (today SUNY Farmingdale) 14–0 but lost to Syracuse at the Polo Grounds for the second year in a row, this time 14–0.

Walter did not return to action until the third quarter of the game played on November 8, when over 15,000 fans packed Fenway Park in Boston to witness the game between Boston College and Rutgers, almost all of whom were there to support the hometown school. The game looked to be a challenging one for Rutgers, given that BC had beaten perennial eastern power Yale earlier in the season.

Walter French, back with the team was on the bench in the game's first half. In the first quarter Rutgers blocked a punt and recovered the ball at the Boston College 35-yard line. A few plays later they pushed the ball across the goal line for the game's first score. Their lead stayed at 6–0 after they missed the extra point. Boston College scored a touchdown in the second quarter and converted the extra point to take the lead.

In his recap of the game, Harold O'Neill described what happened next. "French, Rutgers star halfback was injected into the melee in the third quarter, returning to the game after a four-week absence, and he at once became the star in Rutgers' firmament. On his first play back, he caught a pass out of the backfield for a twenty-yard gain, and on the very next play he picked up thirty more yards on an end run. Boston had seldom been treated to such spectacular running … All during the second half French made many spectacular end runs" and eventually Rutgers pushed the ball across the goal line, this time making the extra point to give them the 13–7 lead that would hold up as the final score. "All Rutgers men came out of it in good shape," O'Neill reported, "including French who played the last two periods."[32]

The following Saturday Rutgers hosted West Virginia. Led by their superstar back, Ira "Buck" Rodgers, the Mountaineers came into the game hot off an impressive 25–0 win over Princeton. Although it was customary for the quarterback to do most of the passing in those days, it was not unusual for teams, with backfield players with the requisite skills, to design plays that would call for the fullbacks and halfbacks to pass the ball. Rodgers, in addition to being a powerful runner, also had one of the strongest throwing arms in the nation. Playing from the fullback position he threw for 162 yards in the win over Princeton. By the end of that 1919 season he had scored 147 points, from 19 touchdowns and 33 extra points and he was the first consensus All-American in the school's history. His 313-career point total remained the school record for 60 years. In 1969, during the NCAA 100-year celebration, a team of the century was selected and it included the likes of Bronko Nagurski, Jim Thorpe, Sammy Baugh, Red Grange, and West Virginia's Buck Rogers.

All of the seats in Neilson Field were full at the start of the game and thousands more stood around the field of play. "On all streets and avenues automobiles were parked, many of the visitors motoring to this center for the engagement."[33] Although the first quarter ended in a scoreless tie, Walter French and Buck Rodgers were both chewing up yards in big chunks for their teams. As was customary at this time both men played both offense and defense, and their tackling abilities, in addition to their work on offense, which were on full display, were responsible for keeping each other from the end zone.

Near the end of the first quarter, West Virginia, starting on their own 20-yard-line, embarked on a successful drive that ended when Rodgers failed to make a first down at the Rutgers 32-yard-line. Rutgers had the ball to start the second quarter and were making some progress moving the ball when the Mountaineers halfback Clay Hite intercepted a pass. But the Rutgers defense held firm and forced a punt. From the Rutgers 45-yard line Walter French took the ball, and as he had been doing throughout the game broke into the clear, only this time he successfully eluded Rodgers and crossed the goal line 55 yards later for the games first score. The hometown crowd went wild.

After more heroics by the teams' respective stars the first half ended with Rutgers clinging to a 7–0 lead.

In the third quarter the momentum in the game swung, as is often the case, on a turnover. With Rutgers on offense in the shadow of their own goal line a high snap from center rolled into the end zone where Turk Gardner fell on the ball and was immediately downed by one of the Mountaineers for a safety. Taking possession after the safety West Virginia immediately went to the passing game and moved the ball deep into Rutgers territory. After Rodgers completed a pass to Clay Hite at the

Rutgers one-yard-line, Rogers ran the ball for a touchdown which, with the extra point, gave West Virginia a 9–7 lead. Later in the same quarter Rodgers hurled a long pass to Bill Neale who had gotten behind the defense. He took the pass in stride and crossed the goal line with the team's second touchdown of the game. As the third quarter came to an end Rutgers found itself down by a score of 16–7. West Virginia kept up the pressure in the fourth quarter as Rodgers continued to put on an aerial display. He hit Neale for another touchdown in the period and turned the trick again with a touchdown pass to Hite to end the scoring. West Virginia had come away with a convincing 30–7 win.

Despite the outcome of the game, and despite this being only his second game back from a very serious injury, Walter French played one of his best games as a collegian. In addition to his long touchdown run, he had a run of 30 yards and another of 20. He finished the game with 162 yards rushing, on 19 carries, several tackles, and a pass interception. The newspaper report of the game concluded that for Rutgers "French was the most conspicuous man on the offense."[34]

The final game of the 1919 season was a match up with Northwestern. In his recap of the game, Harold O'Neill indicated that coming into the game Northwestern was "ruled the favorite before the hostilities began." However, Northwestern was finishing a dismal season when they traveled to New Jersey to play Rutgers. They were 1–4 in the Big Ten, with their only win coming against Indiana, the final score of which was 3–2. Despite coming into the game with a losing record, a team from the Big Ten would always draw a big crowd when they played on the east coast, and this was no exception as over 15,000 fans turned out for the game.

Northwestern won the toss and was first to go on offense. Walter French intercepted a pass at midfield and ran it back to the Northwestern 25-yard line. A few plays later Bill Gardner, team captain, ran the ball into the end zone and kicked the extra point giving Rutgers a 7–0 lead, only 74 seconds into the game. Gardner added another touchdown in the second quarter giving Rutgers a 14–0 lead.

In the third quarter Walter French "shoved himself into the football limelight," according to Harold O'Neill, "when on an off tackle play he dashed eighty yards for a touchdown, the most spectacular effort of the matinee."[35] In the third quarter French caught a pass from Cliff Baker and brought the ball to the Northwestern five-yard-line. On the next play he crashed through the line for his second touchdown.

As the clock ran down on the game and the 1919 Rutgers football season, the scoreboard read 28–0 in favor of the home team. The headline in the *Sunday Times* sports section, ignoring Northwestern's poor record, read "Rutgers Gives Her Greatest Exhibition of Football Power in Crushing Strong Northwestern Eleven, 28 to 0, Before Assemblage of 15,000; Westerner's Defense Spreads Before French's Speed and Gardiner's Power."

With the football season at an end, Walter turned his attention to basketball. Coaching Rutgers during Walter's time there, was Frank Hill. Hill had started coaching at Rutgers in 1915 and held that position until 1943. In a situation that would be unheard of today, Hill also coached Seton Hall's basketball team from 1911 to 1930, so for the years 1915–30 he was the head basketball coach at both schools. He was also the head basketball coach at St. Benedict's prep school, in Newark, NJ during some of those years as well.

For scoring coach Hill relied on forwards Leland Taliaferro and Ed Benzoni who were the team's leading scorers. He also got good offensive production from senior captain Calvin Meury, who played opposite Walter French at guard, and Art Hall a junior who played center. As a basketball player the strength of Walter French's game were his ball handling skills and his ability to play defense. In a piece in the *Central New Jersey Home News*, it was observed that "French, the Rutgers basketball guard is a defensive player of the highest caliber. Some days ago, we took occasion to remark that he was not much of a shot, which was not any harsh criticism, for it has been his duty to play defensive ball, and in such work, has made but a few attempts at field goals. On learning through the columns of a newspaper that he was not a field goal shooter, we can imagine French saying to himself 'I'll show those newspaper guys where they can get off in the next game.'"[36] The next game was against Carnegie Tech and Walter scored five baskets which was second only to Muery's seven.

Rutgers went on to defeat Carnegie by a score of 46 to 26 and it would be one of 11 wins against four defeats that they would have during the regular season. Other wins came against Pittsburgh, West Virginia, Syracuse, Temple, and Swarthmore. The biggest win in the regular season came against Princeton, which marked not only the first time Rutgers had ever beaten their in-state rival in basketball, but it was also the first time that Rutgers had beaten Princeton in any sport since their win over them in the first college football game ever played in 1869.

As they began to rack up impressive wins against some top opponents, excitement about the team was building on the Rutgers campus. The team was given more support from the student body than any team before had received. Attendance at all home games exceeded previous seasons so much that the seating capacity of the gymnasium needed to be expanded to accommodate all the students who wanted to attend the games.

Although there were teams in the country with a better record than Rutgers, there was no denying that the quality of their schedule was one of the toughest. In the 1919–20 season, Rutgers opponents ended up winning over 70 percent of their games and so at the conclusion of the regular season Rutgers was invited to play in the National Amateur Athletic Union basketball tournament in Atlanta. As the only national postseason tournament, the winner of the AAU tournament was widely acknowledged to be that season's national champion. Although most of the participants in the tournament were college teams, other high caliber amateur teams were selected in 1920 as had been the case in previous years. Sixteen teams were invited to Atlanta in March to play a single elimination format. To advance to the final a team would have to win games on three consecutive days, with the fourth day for the final game.

Coach Hill was unable to make the trip with the team to Atlanta due to a business commitment and so Doc Besas accompanied them on the trip not as the coach but as more of a chaperone. As if having to play without a coach wasn't bad enough Rutgers only sent the five starters to Atlanta. If Rutgers was going to win, it would mean that each man on the team would have to play every minute of every game and essentially coach themselves. A few days before the team was to leave for Atlanta the *Central New Jersey Home News*, published out of New Brunswick, ran a piece under the headline "Here Are Rutgers Players Who Will Contest for National Title" which pictured each of the five players. "On next Monday," the piece explained, "the Rutgers basketball five, which had a wonderful season, will embark for Atlanta, GA., where, challenging the best amateur clubs and college teams in the country they will contest for the national basketball title. It is the first time that a Rutgers team has ever engaged in such a series and the invitation came as a result of the Scarlet's feat of winning from such teams as Princeton, Syracuse, Pittsburgh, Swarthmore, West Virginia, and others. The players who will make the trip will be Taliaffero and Benzoni, forwards; Hall, center; Meury and French, guards. During the progress of the championship series, which will consume about a week the collegians will remain in Atlanta, GA."[37]

Their first-round opponent was the heavily favored University of Georgia and Rutgers won a close game. On the next two nights Rutgers defeated the University of Utah and the Young Men's Organization of Detroit to advance to the final. Waiting for them was one of their biggest rivals, NYU. The two teams had met during the regular season with NYU coming away with the victory.

With only one player over 20 years old, the Rutgers team was the youngest in the tournament. Meanwhile, NYU was led by its star player Howard Cann, who was considered one of the best, if not the best, basketball player in the country. He started his college career playing for Dartmouth as a freshman and later transferred to NYU. His career was also interrupted by his two years of military service in World War I. Later he would be named All-American and the Helms Foundation Player of the Year for 1920. In 1968, Cann was inducted into the Basketball Hall of Fame in Springfield, MA. Rutgers played hard but they were no match for Cann and the more seasoned NYU team and they came out on the losing side by a score of 49–24.

In the early morning hours of the following day, the team boarded a train back to New Brunswick. Despite losing in the final, the effort put forth by the five Rutgers players, without a coach, was the talk of the tournament and a real shot in the arm for the Rutgers basketball program. The closeness of the game with Georgia, for example, was the impetus for discussions exploring scheduling the two teams in the next year's regular season.

Doc Besas issued a statement to the Atlanta Constitution thanking the people of Atlanta and the Atlanta Athletic Club, who managed the tournament saying, "We certainly do appreciate the treatment we received in your city, and we only desire that, at some point ... we will have the opportunity to reciprocate."

The tournament was a big hit with the people of Atlanta too. There had been some speculation with games being scheduled on four consecutive nights that the city's interest might wane, however as the Constitution reported that "the fact that Atlanta really and truly enjoyed the tournament is proved conclusively by the fact that the semi-finals and finals were well attended."

While the team was traveling back to New Brunswick the AAU announced its All-Tournament team. Walter French and Ed Benzoni were selected as first team guard and forward respectively, making Rutgers the only team to place two players on the All-Tournament team.

Before the book was closed on the 1919–20 basketball season the team played one more game against the Rutgers Alumni team, which included their former teammate, Paul Robeson. The 1920 team won by a score of 33–12.

After Coach Hill left Rutgers in 1943, the *Central New Jersey Home News*, reflecting on his 28-year career, wrote that "Perhaps Hill's greatest team was in 1919–1920, when Art Hall of Woodridge played at center. Walter French, later a West Point star and outfielder on the Philadelphia Athletics, also played, along with Taliaferro, Meury and Edward Benzoni, undoubtedly the greatest of all Rutgers court aces." In 2019, the five-man team was inducted into the Rutgers Athletic Hall of Fame.

One notable event took place at the end of the baseball season and the school year in 1920. The University of California baseball team was on a national tour playing 22 games against some of the best teams in the country. It was the first time that a baseball team from a Pacific coast school had traveled east. In addition to playing Rutgers the Golden Bears had games scheduled with Penn State and Carnegie Tech, in the mid-Atlantic swing of their tour, to be followed up with two games against Michigan.

The game with Rutgers was set for June 14 which also happened to be commencement day at the school. Rutgers clung to a two-run lead in the top half of the sixth inning when California took advantage of sudden wildness on the part of Rutgers pitcher Luke Waterfield to plate four runs. They would go on to win 6–4. The newspaper accounts of the game singled out Walter French for his "hitting and daring base running." He finished the game with two triples and two walks in four plate appearances. He scored three runs, knocked one run in and just for good measure threw in one stolen base.

After the game with California, Walter French, like the other students, was ready to head to his home in Moorestown for the summer. It had been quite a school year. His versatility and success in the school's three major sports made him the most valuable athlete at the school. Although his football season was limited by his injury

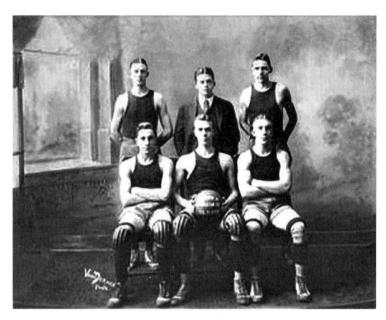

The 1919–1920 Rutgers Basketball Team. "Perhaps Hill's greatest team was in 1919–1920, when Art Hall of Woodridge played at center. Walter French (seated on the right), later a West Point star and outfielder on the Philadelphia Athletics, also played, along with Taliaferro, Meury and Edward Benzoni, undoubtedly the greatest of all Rutgers court aces." In 2019, the five-man team was inducted into the Rutgers Athletic Hall of Fame. (*1920 Rutgers University Yearbook,* courtesy of Rutgers University Library)

in the game against Lehigh, he had scored eight touchdowns in what amounted to, for him, an abbreviated, four- and one-half game campaign. He then helped lead the school's basketball team to within one win of the national championship and was one of the baseball team's star players.

Before they were dismissed Coach Sanford gathered the players expected to be part of the 1920 Rutgers football team. He told them what he expected of them over the summer and that they were to be back on campus on September 7 to start practice for the new season. Sanford was expecting French to be his bright star in 1920 but it was not to be.

CHAPTER 3

The Big Game: Army vs. Notre Dame, Knute Rockne, and George Gipp, 1920

When the new Superintendent of the United States Military Academy at West Point assumed command in June of 1919, he found a campus in chaos with morale at an all-time low. In response to World War I, and the need to supply officers to the Western Front, Congress had reduced the school's curriculum from four years to two and in the process eliminated a variety of programs and training. "Not only was the war time disruption a critical problem, but the academy itself, the curriculum, environment, the austere discipline, and the entrenched traditions had caused the school to develop a paternalistic and monastic regimen that caused it to fall behind other institutions of higher learning. In other words, West Point was mired in the past. The disorder caused by the World War and the stagnation needed a major reform, resuscitation, to breathe life and hope back into the academy and resurrect the poor morale of all assigned. This mission would require a special leader, a West Pointer with the vision and clarity to reform, instill a positive spirit and to lead entrenched department heads who were ensconced in their scholarly chairs for decades to a new culture."[1]

The choice to replace 70-year-old Samuel Tillman as Superintendent of West Point was 39-year-old General Douglas MacArthur, the youngest general officer in the Army and the most decorated soldier of World War I. He was the second youngest Superintendent ever appointed and several professors and department heads, who made up the all-powerful Academic Board resented having to deal with the younger man as a peer. They also resented his casual manner. Despite being the most decorated soldier to emerge from the war, he was never seen with any of his medals or ribbons. "He dressed in a short overcoat and faded puttees that were lashed to his skinny shanks by curling, war-weary leather straps. He carried a riding crop, and when cadets saluted him, with the usual solemnity of cadets, he replied with a nonchalant elevation of the riding crop to the peak of his shapeless, grommetless cap."[2]

He immediately embarked on a mission to reform what he referred to as the "Monastery on the Hudson." His first action was to change the curriculum back to a four-year program. He sought to have the academy accredited to present a formal Bachelor of Science degree and added courses in history, economics, and government.

MacArthur loved sports, especially football. As a cadet he played on the West Point baseball team but was too skinny for football. So, desperate to be around the sport, he took the position as team manager.

While serving in the Great War, MacArthur observed that many of the American soldiers appeared not to be in the best of shape, so he also instituted a rigorous physical training regimen for the cadets. He even went as far as to require every cadet to participate in sports. His "Every Cadet an Athlete" program is credited with starting the first intramural sports program at West Point and with his arrival intercollegiate sports had greater emphasis than ever before. Under his command the number of varsity sports at West Point doubled in the years immediately following World War I.

The recruitment of athletes to West Point dates back to 1890 when the first Army football team was established. Like their contemporaries at the other schools, the coaches at West Point pushed hard to recruit the best players possible, which included recruiting athletes that had had successful careers and had earned varsity letters at other top colleges.

This was one practice that MacArthur had no intention of reforming. Recruiting players who had established themselves as stars at other schools was not prohibited at the time although most schools frowned upon it. The practice drew the ire of all of Army's rivals, especially the Naval Academy, which observed a three-year eligibility rule. Things got so tense over the issue that the 1928 and 1929 Army/Navy football games were cancelled due to a "dispute of player eligibility." Army did not adopt the three-year eligibility rule until the 1930s and a review of the minutes for the Army Athletic Association board reveals that adjustments to it were still being wrestled with as late as 1941.

The poster child for the practice was Elmer Oliphant. Born in Bloomfield, Indiana in 1892, Oliphant moved with his family to Washington, Indiana when he was eight years old, eventually settling in the coal mining town of Linton. In high school he was the star of the football, baseball, basketball, and track teams. He was such a dominant athlete in High School that legends were created around his prowess. One story told was that while playing centerfield on the Linton baseball team, he called time out. He jogged over to the track where a meet was taking place. He proceeded to run in, and win, the 100-yard dash, and then jogged back to the baseball field, once again took up his position, and the game proceeded. The track and football field complex at Linton High School was named Oliphant Field until 1980, in his honor.

Oliphant entered Purdue University in 1910. While at Purdue he lettered in football, basketball, baseball, and track, making him the first athlete at the school to letter in four major sports. He was named first-team All-Big Ten in 1912 and again in 1913. In a game against Rose-Poly in 1912 he scored five touchdowns and kicked 13 extra points to set the school's single-game scoring record, which still stands.

In 1914 he graduated from Purdue with a degree in Mechanical Engineering, and upon graduation he was accepted as a cadet at West Point, where he again played multiple sports for the next four years, with similar results. He became one of the most decorated athletes in the history of Army sports. He lettered in all the major sports, he also boxed, was a member of the swim team and held the world record for the 220-yard low hurdles. He was named All-American in football in 1915, 1916, and 1917 and he is in the Hall of Fame at both Purdue and West Point. In 1955 he was named to the College Football Hall of Fame. While he was playing football at West Point the team's record was 21–4–1.

There were other examples of Army's practice of recruiting players from other schools. Chris Cagle, who had played football for four years at what is today called the University of Louisiana at Lafayette from 1922 to 1925, earning All-American honors in three of those seasons. He attended West Point from 1926 to 1929 serving as team captain during his senior year. For two years Cagle shared the backfield with another All-American named "Lighthorse Harry" Wilson who attended West Point after a three-year stint with Penn State where he earned All-American honors.

The details of Army's seduction of Walter French are unknown but the news of his departure from Rutgers, which was not announced until a few weeks before the football players were to report for pre-season workouts was met with disbelief and rage at the school. The headlines in the *New Brunswick Daily Home News*, on the day the story broke, screamed: "West Point's Round-UP of College Football Players includes Walter French, Rutgers Star Halfback." Don Storck, the team's talented end, was also moving to West Point, to make matters worse. The moves were criticized by the New Jersey press covering Rutgers' football. "In the gush preceding the approaching dawn of another football season, the outlook at Rutgers has been obscured and the large amount of optimism which prevailed at the conclusion of the 1919 season has evaporated due to the usual eleventh-hour circumstances which habitually emerge about this time every year. The main reason for this feeling is due to the departure from Rutgers to West Point of Donald Storck and Walter French two of the ranking members of last season's somewhat erratic combination"[3] the *Daily Home News* reported.

The news regarding Storck was expected. He had left Rutgers after the 1919 football season, when his appointment to West Point was confirmed. "But the removal of French," the *Daily Home News* reported "under circumstances not usually prevalent in these days of sportsmanship came as a shock to the football regime, inasmuch as this individual, the bright scarlet star, was being relied on to be an important cog in this season's formidable gridiron machine." The papers covering Rutgers' football weren't the only ones weighing in on the subject. Lawrence Perry of the *New York Evening Post* wrote "there are indications that persons interested in the football prestige of the

United States Military Academy are embarked on a recruiting campaign that is far reaching and systematic." Athletic departments at other schools put out statements condemning Army. Rutgers announced that they would not play Army again in any sport until the practice of recruiting players from other schools was stopped. (With respect to football it was not that big a threat as Army and Rutgers hadn't met since 1914 and they did not play each other again until 1965.)

For the Rutgers faithful, Army became the bad guys and Navy the good guys. The sports pages of the newspapers in New Jersey were making the case that grabbing Walter French and Don Storck was the only way that Army could compete with Navy, which contrary to Army was building their team the "right" way. "New men and good ones will be needed in the molding of the 1920 machine, for several veterans have been lost to the team for one reason or another. Storck and French are at West Point along with a number of other college stars marshalled together in a daring effort to overthrow the Middies in late November."[4] This, of course overlooked the fact that from 1913 to 1916 Army had defeated Navy each year by a combined score of 71–16. World War I cancelled the games in 1917 and 1918, and Navy won the 1919 game by a score of 7–0.

Looking for someone to blame, the Rutgers community, including the local media, at first suspected that those officers running Rutgers ROTC program may have had a hand in convincing Walter to make the jump to West Point, but that theory was quickly debunked, "it is understood that the military authorities at Rutgers had nothing whatever to do with the transfer of either Storck or French to West Point. The Army captain who succeeded in interesting both these men in military life, was not in any way connected with Rutgers."[5] While speculation as to how this could have happened was running rampant, the explanation was no more complicated than the fact that the West Point coaches and athletic department had their eye on Walter and reached out to him when he was there to play baseball for Rutgers against Army in the spring of 1920. Much in the same way as would happen today, before returning to Rutgers Walter was taken to New York City and wined and dined by an Army captain to influence him to join the Academy.

As the 1920 season neared however, the New Jersey newspapers would not let go of the French transfer story, even speculating that he had somehow been coerced into jumping teams. They even went so far as to suggest that he was not happy with the move, and they floated conspiracy theories that claimed that he was being held at West Point against his will. "On reaching West Point after accepting the appointment under influence, he made an effort to resign, but the authorities refused to accept it and put him in the Army hospital for a time."[6] Even weirder was the story of the wife of a mystery captain who reportedly went to his College Ave. fraternity house in New Brunswick and packed up his belongings and took them to West Point.

It all seemed farfetched because as we shall see going forward the military life seemed to suit Walter French very well. It is always possible that he gave out mixed signals to his former coaches and teammates in an effort to let them down easily. It is also possible that he did have second thoughts after arriving at the school and if so, he wouldn't be the first cadet to experience that feeling, but to suggest that there was some confrontation that ended up with him being admitted to the hospital simply strains credulity.

There is one oddity regarding his appointment to West Point in 1920 that does call into question the extent that Army went through to bring Walter French to the academy.

In 1843, with the support of then President John Tyler, the Congress increased the class size at West Point to 223 which just so happened to match the size of the U.S. House of Representatives at that time. Tyler assigned the job of selecting the new cadets to his Secretary of War, who in turn asked the congressmen for nominations. This was the start of the system that exists today which requires that a service academy candidate, except for those to the Coast Guard, be recommended by a member of Congress. Typically, that recommendation would come from a member of the Congressional delegation from the candidate's home state. However, Walter's recommendation did not come from any of New Jersey's members of Congress. Walter's recommendation came from Congressman Christopher "Christy" Sullivan, who represented New York's 13th Congressional District, which was made up primarily of Manhattan.

After serving four terms as a New York State Senator, Christy Sullivan ran for and was elected to Congress in 1918 and he would remain in that position until 1941. In the 24 years he served in Congress, Sullivan never made one speech. His attendance record was abysmal, and he was more likely to be spotted at any number of Maryland's horseracing tracks than in the halls of Congress. His power came from his position as one of the last bosses of Tammany Hall. Tammany's political power was derived from favoritism and patronage and if Superintendent MacArthur was inclined to put the arm on a congressman for a favor, Christy would be a likely target. Was it that all of the New Jersey members of Congress had already made their recommendations on behalf of other constituents that required the congressman from New York City to step in, or is it possible that those congressmen from New Jersey were reluctant to incur the wrath of the boosters of their state university's football program?

It is more likely that, with MacArthur's emphasis on intercollegiate athletics, Walter was offered admittance to the Academy, and once he accepted, the nomination process was put in motion with Sullivan on his behalf.

In any event, the recommendation of a New York congressman for a candidate from New Jersey must have raised some eyebrows and fed into the hysteria at Rutgers over the departure of its star player.

It might have been different if Walter had arrived at the Academy prior to MacArthur's arrival, but he had been on the job for over a year, and most of his reforms were in place. His reforms were enormously popular among the cadets with the exception of his restrictions on hazing but given that the victims of hazing were the fourth-year men or plebes, as they were called, Walter could not have had a problem with that change. Some of the other reforms instituted under his superintendentship meant that "Cadets could afford ice cream now, because one of MacArthur's first innovations had been to allow each of them five dollars a month spending money. On weekends they were now granted six-hour passes and, in the summer months, two-day leaves. They could travel as far as New York City on their own. During the football season they were allowed to follow their team Black Knights to Harvard, Yale, and Notre Dame. Their mail was no longer censored."[7]

And then there was MacArthur's love of sports, especially baseball and football. He showed up at almost every practice for both sports and was even known to give the players a pointer or two and throughout his tenure had been known to let transgressions slide when a key athlete was involved.

But even though he never played the game while at West Point, it was football for which he had the most passion because football he believed made men better soldiers. "Over there," he said to a colleague, "I became convinced that the men who had taken part in organized sports made the best soldiers. They were the most dependable, hardy, courageous officers I had. Men who had contended physically against other human beings under rules of a game were the readiest to accept and enforce discipline. They were outstanding. I propose, therefore, to obtain for the Academy athletes, those who have had bodily contact, especially football."[8] He encouraged congressmen like Christy Sullivan to appoint gifted athletes to West Point and gave special privileges to members of the football team in the fall. He also proposed the construction of a 50,000-seat stadium for football.

The fact of the matter was that Walter French could not have entered West Point at a better time, and any reticence he may have felt on his first day, was no more or less than what any fourth-year man from a small town in New Jersey would have felt. Which is not to say that he would not have found the Academy life challenging even with the MacArthur reforms in place. The West Point curriculum for fourth year men in 1920 included Mathematics, English, French, Surveying, and Gymnastics. In addition, cadets also had to deal with room and uniform inspections and the obsession with physical fitness and punctuality.

Coaching the Army football team when Walter arrived at his first practice was Charlie Daly. Born in Roxbury, Massachusetts in 1880, as a player Daly was a first team All-American four times in his five seasons as a college quarterback. He played for Harvard from 1898 to 1900 and was first team All-American all three of his years playing for Harvard. Then, in the Army tradition he received an appointment to West Point from Massachusetts Congressman John H. Fitzgerald and played quarterback for Army in 1901 and 1902, earning first team All-American in 1901 and third team honors in 1902. After working in business and serving in the military for a few years he was named the assistant football coach at Army in 1907. He later served as the Fire Commissioner for the city of Boston from 1910 to 1912 until he was given the opportunity to be the head football coach at West Point. He served as the coach from 1913 to 1916 compiling a record of 31–4–1. He left the post to serve in the military in 1917 and 1918 during World War I and returned to his coaching position in 1919 and compiled a record of 6–3 in that season.

West Point's practice of recruiting players who had played for years in other programs really did make it hard for them to schedule games with the top schools. The schedule Walter had to face in 1920 had only two top caliber opponents, Notre Dame and Navy. The rest of the schedule included Union, Middlebury, Springfield College, Tufts, Lebanon Valley, and Bowdoin. Had he stayed at Rutgers, by contrast, he would have gone up against the likes of Maryland, Nebraska, Virginia Tech, West Virginia, and Cornell.

Army's first opponent in 1920 was Union College. Over, almost before it started, Army dispatched with the Dutchmen without breaking a sweat, by a score of 35–0. They followed that up with another easy win against Middlebury, by a score of 26–7. Coach Daly went easy on them in practice leading up to their third game of the season against Springfield College. The Springfield game, like the ones before it, was played at West Point. Newspaper accounts after the first two games of the season singled out French's play as being key to the team's early success writing that "The work of French, Army's speedy back is pleasing his mentors. The former Rutgers star is one of the shiftiest backs in the game and bound to be heard of frequently during the season."[9]

Coach Daly was so confident that his team could easily handle their next opponent Tufts, that he sent the starting 11 to the Princeton–Navy game to scout out the midshipmen. The entire West Point varsity team went to Princeton to see the Tigers take on Navy, leaving the second team behind to defeat Tufts 28–6. The Cadets made the trip in autos. During the return trip French, Don Storck and the others stopped at the Hotel Pines in New Brunswick for a bite to eat. While passing George and Albany Streets, French inquired of the traffic officer on duty there as to the outcome of the Rutgers–Virginia game. Still smarting from the Army's recruitment of French, the *New Brunswick News* reported that "if that same French had been in the Rutgers lineup Saturday, they would be celebrating a victory instead of bemoaning a defeat. For the speed that only French can supply was all that was needed to put the local collegians on the winning side. The Rutgers backfield has no fast back to cover long distances at a clip such as French used to do."[10]

So, the stage was set for one of the biggest college football games to be played at that juncture of the season and the seventh meeting between Army and Notre Dame on October 29, 1920. Prior to the construction of Michie Stadium in 1924, Army played their home games on a 40-acre piece of land on the campus that was known as "The Plain." The Plain was used primarily as a marching ground and the site for the summer camp outs for the cadets. Temporary stands were set up to seat about 10,000 fans before each game.

Both teams came into the game undefeated although no one could argue that Notre Dame with opponents like Nebraska, Syracuse, and Boston College had played the tougher schedule to that point of the season and thus was a heavy favorite.

Although it is hard to picture today, historically the rivalry between the two teams was fierce. Legendary Notre Dame coach Frank Leahy later said of the rivalry that "for 34 years the Army game was the high-water mark on the Notre Dame schedule." Adam Walsh, a member of the 1924 national champion Notre Dame team and later head coach at Bowdoin College described the battles between the two teams this way: "If we weighed 180 pounds, we'd always hit with 200 pounds of power against Army and the Cadets would meet us in the same manner." Walter's teammate on the Army Baseball team, Earl "Red" Blaik, who later became the Athletic Director at Army speaking in 1948 described the Army-Notre Dame rivalry as "one of the greatest in all of sports."

Writing in his syndicated column in 1943, Grantland Rice recalled that "the Army-Notre Dame contest was always Knute Rockne's favorite game." "It is usually the toughest game we play," Rockne told Rice, "But it is the type of game I like to play, hard and tough, but clean. Always full of action. Always full of color. We've won some close ones that we might have just as well lost. I know that, but it was the game that helped lift Notre Dame in football and it was the game that gave us our first and biggest eastern break. Even when we had the better team, I was never sure of this Army contest for those Cadets always gave us at least 100 percent of all they had and often just a little more. I can't remember an Army-Notre Dame game that was not interesting."[11]

The rivalry between Notre Dame and Army began with the first game played between the two teams in 1913. Leading into the 1913 season the *Spalding Record Book* had Notre Dame rated on a par with the reigning Big-10 champion Wisconsin and so the feeling was that many of the midwestern coaches were reluctant to play Notre Dame, afraid that their reputations would have little to gain from a victory and a lot to lose with a defeat. Prejudice against the Catholic institution also contributed to this reluctance. This required that Notre Dame be open to the idea of traveling far to fill out its schedule for 1913 if they wanted to break into the national limelight.

In the summer of 1912, Bill Cotter who was the student manager of the Notre Dame team and Knute Rockne, at that time the team's top end and one of its star players, were working together as lifeguards at a resort in Ohio named Cedar Point, which was located on the shores of Lake Erie. It was there that they first discussed the idea of scheduling games with the cadets. What better way to enhance the school's reputation than playing an east coast power like Army? The following January the first communication between the two schools took place regarding, not football, but baseball. An agreement was reached which would have the Notre Dame baseball team play Army during a swing through the eastern part of the country in May. On May 24, 1913, Notre Dame defeated Army 3–0, in the first ever sports contest between Army and Notre Dame.

At about this time Army found itself in a similar predicament with respect to their football schedule for 1913. The Cadet football manager, a student named Harold Loomis, was informed that the 1912 game between Army and Yale would be the last of that series. Both teams apparently agreed with the decision. Earnest "Pot" Graves who was the Army coach and Lt. Dan Sultan, the Army Athletic Association representative and the coaches from Yale felt that the game took too much out of their players each year. So, Loomis found himself in a bind as he tried to fill an open spot in the Army schedule in the late October early November time frame. He first wrote to all the eastern schools but each one replied that their schedules were all full. Desperate he started writing to every school in the country but as of spring 1913 he still had no game scheduled. Finally he got a response from newly hired Notre Dame coach Jesse Harper. Harper played under Amos Alonzo Stagg at the University of Chicago from 1902 to 1906. He became the coach at Alma College in Michigan and later coached Wabash before coming to Notre Dame in 1913.

Harper was not ready to commit to the game but wanted more information including how much money could be guaranteed to the Ramblers for making the trip (Notre Dame would not officially adopt the Fighting Irish nickname until 1927). If those types of requests were not unheard of in those days, it was, at least, an out of the ordinary request in Army's view. Well-heeled schools like Yale always paid their own way, but Notre Dame, in 1913, was not well heeled.

Army initially offered Notre Dame $600 to cover their expenses but Harper replied that to bring his full team would cost $1,000 and he couldn't justify bringing them for a penny less. Eventually Army agreed to meet Harper's demand and the game was set and the teams squared off on November 1, 1913. Notre Dame won the game by a score of 35–14 and they would finish Coach Harper's first season undefeated. In addition to being the start of a great rivalry, however, the game was destined to be remembered as one of the turning points in the evolution of the game of football.

In 1906 John Heisman convinced the football rules committee to legalize the forward pass. He believed, correctly, that opening up the game would save it from dangerous tactics like the Flying Wedge and plays of similar mayhem. Heisman had the backing of then President Theodore Roosevelt who had expressed his concern about the number of fatalities that occurred in the previous two seasons. In addition to the legalization of the forward pass, the rules committee, in a move to open up the game, also approved the creation of the neutral zone along the line of scrimmage between the offensive and defensive lines and the doubling of the distance required for the offense to obtain a new set of downs to 10 yards.

Initially the rules regarding the forward pass had several restrictions which kept it from becoming popular with the top teams in the country. These included limiting pass plays to 20 yards, the assessment of a 15-yard penalty for an incomplete pass and a requirement that the ball go over to the defense if an untouched pass fell to the ground.

The restrictive rules did not stop the team from the Pennsylvania Carlisle Indian Industrial School from being the first team to widely use the forward pass, along with a few other trick plays in 1907. Coached by "Pop" Warner and led on the field by Jim Thorpe, Carlisle used a wide-open style of play to compensate for a lack of size and finished the season with a record of 10–1 and outscoring their opponents by 200 points.

Finally in 1912 the NCAA Rules Committee did away with many of the restrictions that had been imposed on the passing game. They also approved new specifications for the football making it longer, slimmer, and much easier to throw.

However, most of the nation's coaches still considered the play a risky gimmick and the forward pass was not widely used until the Notre Dame vs. Army game in 1913.

Also joining Bill Cotter and Knute Rockne on the staff of that Ohio resort was Notre Dame quarterback Gus Dorias and he and Rockne spent much of their free time working on the passing game, and on November 1, 1913, they rolled it out against a shocked Army team. What Rockne and Dorias worked on was a departure from the normal way the passing game was executed in those days. Rather than the receiver running out for a pass and stopping in an open spot as was customary at the time, the two teammates worked on pass patterns which called upon the quarterback to deliver the ball not to where the receiver settled down in the coverage, but to anticipate where the receiver was going to be and complete the pass while the receiver was on the run. Dorias completed 14 of 17 passes for 243 yards, mostly to Rockne. With its size advantage neutralized, Army was helpless to stop the Notre Dame attack. The game put Notre Dame on the national football map to stay, and established the forward pass as a weapon that every team would have to have as part of their playbook. One newspaper account summed up the game this way "the westerners played the fastest game of football seen on the gridiron in years. Their open field running, brilliant forward passing, and sure handling of the ball was pretty to watch but was a source of much discomfort for the cadets, who seemingly never had a chance."[12] The origin of the way football is played in the modern era can be traced to this game and it also opened the door for players with the size and skill set of Walter French to find a place in it.

By the time the 1920 Army vs. Notre Dame game came around, the Ramblers had won four of the six previous contests, winning in 1915, 1917, and 1919 in addition to the win in the inaugural 1913 game. Army was victorious in 1914 and 1916. There was no game in 1918. Knute Rockne had also succeeded his mentor Jesse Harper as the head coach of Notre Dame when he retired after the 1917 season. After going 3–1–2 in 1918, the Ramblers finished the 1919 season with a perfect 9–0 record.

At the heart of the Notre Dame team at that time was George Gipp. Gipp, the son of a minister, was born in 1895 in the town of Laurium located on Michigan's upper peninsula. After dropping out of high school, according to Gipp biographer George Gekas he "spent much time at Jimmy O'Brien's Pool Room, which was three blocks from his house on Hecla Street in Laurium ... For money Gipp would drive cabs on the weekends, ferry copper miners to and from the bars and local houses of prostitution."[13] He also played semi-professional baseball at this time. A friend by the name of Wilbur "Dolly" Gray, who had been an outstanding catcher for Notre Dame's baseball team convinced Gipp and Coach Harper to have him enroll at the school through a baseball scholarship. Because he had not completed high school he was admitted as a conditional Freshman, with the plan being for him to make up his credits during summer school. In his book *Shake Down the Thunder: The Creation of Notre Dame Football*, author Murray Sperber wrote that "The twenty-one-year-old Gipp arrived at Notre Dame in September of 1916 and discovered that his job as a waiter in Brownson Hall covered only his room and board bills; he would have to pay out-of-pocket for his books, supplies, fees, and other expenses. Gipp immediately embarked on what fellow students called 'his own private job plan'—earning money by playing pool and cards in downtown South Bend. He was so skillful a gambler that he quit his job waiting tables after one semester and eventually moved out of the dormitories, living the rest of his Notre Dame years in the luxurious Oliver Hotel in South Bend, home to various affluent citizens, commercial travelers, and high-stakes billiard, pool, and poker games."[14]

Although Gipp went to Notre Dame to play baseball he also played on the Freshman football team in 1916. It was as a member of that team that his football potential first came to Rockne's attention. In a game on October 16, 1916, against Western State Normal of Michigan, Gipp kicked a 62-yard field goal. Soon he was playing multiple positions on the team and regularly going up against the varsity team in practice. He joined the varsity team for good in 1917 and led the team in rushing, passing, and kicking for the next three years. Legendary sportswriter Ring Lardner reflecting on Gipp's years at Notre Dame stated that "Notre Dame had one formation and one signal ... have teams line up, pass the ball to Gipp, and let him use his own judgement."[15]

While his football, poker, and pool skills were first rate, Gipp's academic performance left a lot to be desired. He rarely went to class and never completed many of his courses. On March 8, 1920, Notre Dame attempted to expel him but "immediately there were at least six major universities in contact with George trying to lure him to their schools in spite of his scholastic predicaments"[16] including the athletic department at West Point, no doubt with the encouragement of Superintendent Douglas MacArthur. A telegram was sent to Gipp from Captain Philip Hayes, from the Army Athletic Association on July 27, 1920, telling him that "You have been recommended for appointment to the United States Military Academy ... please write me collect whether or not you will consider acceptance."[17] And so it was that his expulsion was brief, all was forgiven, and a few weeks later he was back living at the Oliver Hotel, playing cards and semi-pro baseball.

As the 1920 season began to unfold, Walter French was emerging as Army's star player. His break away running style was reminiscent of the style of play that made Elmer Oliphant a star, and Army coach Charley Daly found in French a more than suitable replacement for Oliphant.

At the time Army played a single wingback system, which usually called for big bruising style runner as opposed to French's game which was based on his ability, not to run over defenders but to elude them. The single wing, however, also presented a player with Walter's skills with the ability to disguise whether he intended to run or pass when he had the ball, at which he was equally good. Writing in *The Big Game: Army vs. Notre Dame 1913–1947*, Jim Beach and Daniel Moore described French's play this way "He slithered through slight openings and was gone before the defense knew what had happened. He was small of physique and shifty with the agility usually characteristic of a scat-back. He was also tough and could stand up under the battering a little man has to take in football."

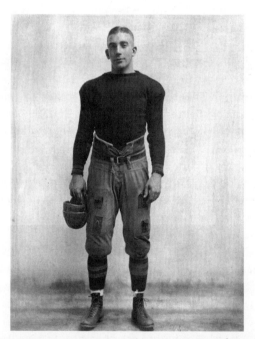

Walter French was the star of Army's football team and named All-American in 1920. "He slithered through slight openings and was gone before the defense knew what had happened. He was small of physique and shifty with the agility usually characteristic of a scat-back. He was also tough and could stand up under the battering a little man has to take in football." (Courtesy of French Family)

So, the stage was set for one of the most anticipated showdowns of the college football season. In their advance stories, the sportswriters were playing up the head-to-head meeting between George Gipp and Walter French.[18]

The weather in the West Point area in the week before the game was dreadful. The *New York Times* reported that the Cadets "drilled in the rain" in the days leading up to the game.

After a 22-hour train ride, the Notre Dame team comprised of 23 players arrived on the West Point campus in the late morning of October 29, 1920, in what the *New York Times* described as a "driving rainstorm." Experts were predicting that the field would be sloppy with a slower than normal track. After arriving on campus, the Notre Dame team held a light workout in the rain.

It was not uncommon in those days for teams to wager on their own games, with each team collecting cash from the players and throwing it into a winner take all pot. Gipp's best friend on the team and fellow Upper Michigander, Hunk Anderson collected the Notre Dame share and met with the Army team manager to arrange for a wager to be placed on the game. Each team put in around $2,000 into the pot for a purse that would equal about $55,000 in today's currency.

The temporary stands on The Plains were filled to their 10,000-seat capacity, with a sizeable contingent of Notre Dame fans on hand. Also in attendance were all the top sportswriters of the day including Grantland Rice of the *Herald Tribune* and Ring Lardner of the *Chicago Tribune*. Years later, Rice would recall that "Ring Lardner, a keen Notre Dame and Midwestern rooter, went with me on that trip to the Point in the fall of 1920. We ran into John J. McEwen, the big Army assistant coach. John J. was loaded with confidence. One of Army's all-time centers, John coached the Cadet line. Army's strong squad was headed by the flying Walter French, who earned his spurs—and an appointment to West Point at Rutgers."[19]

The weather had cleared, and the windy conditions helped to dry out the field, so it was a little faster than what had been anticipated earlier in the week but was still soggy. Kickoff was scheduled for 2:30pm and the referees concerned that darkness might fall before the conclusion of the game used their authority to declare that the time of the periods for this game would be 12 minutes rather than the more typical 15-minute quarters. So, one of the greatest college football games to that point in time would only be 48 minutes long.

At the conclusion of the warm-ups and just before the start of the game Gipp walked out to the 50-yard line with four footballs. Without giving any indication that what he was about to attempt was anything special or out of the ordinary, he proceeded to dropkick two balls through the uprights in one direction and then turned around and kicked the other two balls through the goal posts at the other end of the field.

Notre Dame received the opening kickoff and immediately started moving the ball downfield, moving into Army territory in just four plays. On the next play Notre

Dame center Ojay Larson snapped the ball from Army's 38-yard line directly to fullback Chet Wynne. Wynne, known as the Kansas Cyclone, ran into the line for three yards, where he was met by three Army tacklers, and fumbled. George Gipp and Army's Don Storck both went for the loose ball and a struggle ensued. After he arrived on the scene the referee pointed to the Notre Dame end of the field. Storck had recovered for Army.

Glenn "Willie" Willhide was Army's quarterback and on Army's very first offensive play he handed the ball to running back Charlie Lawrence who slammed into the line and promptly fumbled the ball, but he was able to recover his own fumble and Army retained possession. On the next play Willhide handed the ball to Walter French who ran the ball into the line behind the right tackle. Once free of the initial Notre Dame defenders he eluded Chet Wynne and burst into the open field with only the safety between himself and the goal line. The safety made a touchdown saving, shoestring tackle pulling down French but not before he had advanced the ball 40 yards to the Notre Dame 23 yard-line. On the next play Willhide went back to Charlie Lawrence who plowed through the left side of the line, and after being initially stopped at the five-yard-line, powered his way into the end zone. After Fritz Breidster's extra point kick was good, Army took the early lead 7–0.

The ensuing kickoff was a low, bouncing ball that Gipp fielded at his own 10-yard-line and ran back 28 yards to the Notre Dame 38-yard line. Chet Wynne took the ball on the next play up the middle to his own 44-yard line. Gipp carried the ball on the next play to midfield where he was tackled by a host of Army defenders and buried in a big pile up. Gipp, feeling that the Army defenders had gotten away with unnecessary roughness, jumped up and started to confront the entire Army team. Gipp ripped off his helmet and a fight broke out between the two teams. Gipp began mixing it up with two of the Cadets until the officials were able to restore order and march off a penalty against Notre Dame, which wiped out their gains of the last few plays.

Furious with what he felt was an unfair call, on the next play Gipp took the ball around the right end and dashed through the open field. Walter French, playing the safety position, moved up to the Army 40-yard-line and made a flying tackle to bring Gipp down. After a few short gains the Notre Dame quarterback fumbled the ball, but this time Gipp was there to recover it and maintain possession for Notre Dame. Gipp then completed two forward passes, the second to end Roger Kiley who brought the ball to the Army five-yard-line. From there, halfback Johnny Mohardt finished the drive when he plunged into the end zone. Gipp kicked the extra point and the game was tied 7–7 as the first quarter came to an end.

On their first possession of the second quarter Army went three and out and were forced to punt from their own five-yard-line. Walter French was standing just in front of the back line of the end zone, with very little room to maneuver, set to punt the ball. In what must have been one of the best punts of his life he sent the ball some 60 yards in the air as it crossed the 50-yard line on the fly and forced Gipp to retreat to his own 35-yard line to retrieve the ball and start to head up field. Gipp, taking advantage of Army defenders who had overrun the play, was able to return the ball into Army territory before being tackled from behind as he attempted to reverse field. After a couple of running plays, Gipp threw a pass to Roger Kiley, who had made it seem like his role on the play was simply that of a blocker and then broke wide open, catching Gipp's pass and running into the end zone. The extra point gave Notre Dame a 14–7 lead.

After the teams exchanged punts on the next few possessions Notre Dame found itself with the ball on their own 25-yard line. An errant snap from center got away from Chet Wynne and he was forced to fall on the ball at his own 10-yard-line, requiring Gipp to punt the ball from behind his own goal line. The punt, a low driving kick that cut through the wind sailed over the head of Walter French, who was back to receive the punt. Walter quickly ran back and picked up the ball at his own 40-yard-line and began to run diagonally to the sideline. Suddenly he changed direction, running past would-be tacklers. With the help of a few blocks from his Army teammates, he continued to weave his way through a wave of Notre Dame defenders. At some point he outran his own blockers and with one last change of direction he crossed the goal line for a touchdown which, after the extra point, tied the game at 14–14.

As the first half was coming to an end Johnny Mohardt took the kickoff and was swarmed under by an Army team now pumped-up by Walter's heroics. After going three and out, George Gipp was forced to punt from the shadow of his own goal line. Army applied a big rush and, in his haste to get the kick off quickly, the ball went off the side of his foot and out of bounds at the Notre Dame 15-yard-line. After three running plays failed to produce any favorable results for Army, they called on Walter French to kick a field goal from 21 yards out. His kick was good and Army, to everyone's surprise, took a 17–14 lead.

With time running out in the first half, Notre Dame had the ball inside its own 10-yard line. On fourth down Gipp got ready to punt the ball. Before the snap he pulled end Roger Kiley aside and instructed him to "tear down the left side," where Gipp's plan was to catch Army by surprise by foregoing the punt, in favor of a long pass. Gipp took the snap from center, dropped back, and launched a pass 45 yards down field to a streaking, wide open, Kiley. The throw was right on target, but uncharacteristically Kiley dropped the ball. Luckily for Notre Dame, Army was unable to capitalize on the excellent field position which resulted and as time ran out Army took a 17–14 lead into halftime.

In the locker room at halftime, Rockne was angry about Gipp's gamble near the end of the first half, and generally not pleased with the situation in which Notre Dame found itself. It was in times like this that he would single out players that he thought had not played up to their potential. Eddie Anderson, who played end was one of Rockne's targets on this day. "Anderson," he barked "where were you on French's runs?" As Anderson tried to explain, the coach shot back "don't you talk back to me." Then he turned his attention to Gipp. "And you there Gipp," he said in voice dripping with sarcasm. "I guess you don't have any interest in this game." "Look, Rock, I've got four hundred bucks bet on this game and I am not about to blow it," Gipp replied, evoking laughter from his teammates and even a grin from Rockne.[20]

"Before the third quarter the reporters in the press box wired their papers for extra space when they sensed that they were covering one of the great football games of all time. Never had they seen such a duel as that in progress between Gipp and French—and what might happen next was anybody's guess."[21]

Walter French kicked off for Army to start the third quarter. The kick coverage was excellent and pinned Notre Dame at its own seven-yard line. On the first play from scrimmage Gipp broke free on an end run and took the ball to the Army 45-yard line. Mohardt took the ball on the next play and advanced it 10 yards to the Army 35. The Army defense stiffened and Gipp missed a field goal from the 43-yard line.

Army was able to move the ball in their next possession but eventually the drive stalled, and Walter French was forced to punt. On its next drive Notre Dame went to the passing game. Gipp threw consecutive completions first to Mohardt and then to Kiley. Despite being set back twice by penalties Notre Dame would not be stopped. Chet Wynne carried the ball on two successive runs followed by Gipp who brought the ball to the Army 10-yard-line as the third quarter came to an end.

The fourth quarter began with consecutive runs by Gipp. It appeared that it would be three in a row when he faked a run, then pulled the ball back and sent a pass to Mohardt who easily took it into the end zone. After the extra point, Notre Dame jumped into the lead by a score of 21–17.

Army was unable to make any progress on its first drive of the fourth quarter and Walter French was forced to punt the ball away to Gipp who fielded the ball and ran it back 50 yards. On the next play Gipp connected with Roger Kiley on a pass play that brought the ball to the Army 20-yard-line. Notre Dame then ran a misdirection play with two running backs heading out to the flanks, and once the defense reacted, the ball was handed to Chet Wynne who took it up the middle for a touchdown. The extra point was missed, and the score stood at 27–17, which is how the game would end.

As the clock ran down and darkness fell at West Point, Gipp was removed from the game, having more than done his job. Gipp biographer Pat Chelland summarized his effort this way: "With his brother Alexander in the stands cheering him on, George Gipp had put on one of the greatest performances of his career. Gipp's statistics were as follows: 150 yards rushing in twenty carries; 123 yards picked up as a result of five completed passes out of nine attempts; an additional 112 yards gained in running back punts and kick-offs. All of this against one of the greatest teams of the era."[22] It should also be noted that he generated those statistics in a game that was only 48-minutes long. In its coverage of the game the *New York Times* said "A lithe limbed Hoosier football player named George Gipp galloped wild through the Army on the Plains here this afternoon giving a performance which was more like an antelope than a human being. Gipp's sensational dashes through the Cadets and his marvelously tossed forward passes enabled Notre Dame to beat Army by a score of 27–17."[23]

After showering and dressing, Hunk Anderson made a quick trip to the Highland Falls businessman who had been holding the $4,200 that had been wagered on the game by the two teams. Gipp's share of the winnings was $800 which would be the equivalent of about $10,000 in 2021.

Army center Frank Greene recalled how surprised he was to see Gipp after the game. After just completing a performance for the ages, Gipp looked emaciated and "literally down to skin and bones" when Greene saw him coming out of the shower room. As we shall see and sports fans everywhere would soon learn, that Frank's concern for Gipp's health would be a prescient one.

Today the 1920 game between Notre Dame and Army, simply referred to as "Gipp's Greatest Game," is listed by Notre Dame's athletic department as one of the greatest moments in the school's long and fabled football history. For Walter French, his heroic effort was overshadowed by Gipp. The headline in the *New York Times* the following day read, "Gipp Plays Brilliantly … French Also Shines."[24]

Over the next few weeks Army played games against Lebanon Valley and Bowdoin, winning both by a combined score of 143 to 0. In the Bowdoin game, Walter French scored touch downs on runs of 40, 80, and two of 65 yards. This brought their record to 6–1 coming into the game against the 5–2 team from Navy, on November 27, 1920.

Army and Navy began playing football games against each other in 1890. Navy won that first game played at West Point 24–0 and between that first game and the one in 1920, the games were played each year with only three breaks. No games were played from 1894 to 1898. The series resumed in 1899 and continued until 1909 when the Army football program was disbanded after the death of a Cadet who was fatally injured in a game against Harvard. The series resumed in 1910 and the teams met annually until 1917. No games were played in 1917 and 1918 due to World War I.

Of the first four Army–Navy games, two were played at West Point and two at Annapolis. From 1899 to 1912 inclusive, all but one of the games was played at Franklin Field in Philadelphia. In 1913, 1915, 1916, and 1919 the games were played at the Polo Grounds in New York, which would be the case for the showdown in 1920. The two teams came into the game with similar records and the series, to that point, was essentially in a deadlock. Of the 22 Army–Navy games played prior to 1920, Army had won 11 and Navy had won 10 and the game played in 1905 ended in a 6–6 tie.

Like the years before and since, the 1920 Army–Navy game was among the year's great sporting spectacles. Tickets for the game were in such high demand that the schools had to send out a warning to their supporters indicating that the sale of tickets to "speculators" would be frowned upon. The *New York Times* reported that "Major Philip Hayes, in a statement issued tonight, says that if members of the Army Athletic Association should be discovered putting their tickets up for sale, and should the responsibility for such unauthorized use of tickets be fixed, the responsible parties will be dropped from the rolls of the association and tickets in the future will not be sent to them."[25]

In the lead up to this game the sportswriters focused on the matchup between Walter French and Navy captain Eddie Ewen. Newspapers featured a picture of the two, in a three-point stance, facing each other head-to-head on the front page of their sports sections. The caption read "When Army faces Navy there is always a display of artillery. While Uncle Sam's military maneuvers are more or less secret, the dope is out that the elevens are mighty evenly matched for the annual game, which will be played at the Polo Grounds on November 27. French the speedy fullback will lead the Army boys in the attack against Captain Ewen, star end, of the Middies."

Writing in the *New York Herald* on the Wednesday before the game, sportswriter William Hanna predicted that "Army's fleet back, Walter French will be watched zealously by the midshipmen and isn't going to have it any easier for having been heralded as one of the backs of the year. Right often in such cases the man thus exploited, and this sort of advance notice business is really unfair to him if he doesn't come up to expectations."[26] The *Herald* article would turn out to be prophetic.

Over 48,000 fans were at the Polo Grounds under a gray sky and soggy conditions on the field. The *New York Times* described the scene this way: "There are football crowds and Harvard-Yale-Princeton crowds, and there is also the Army-Navy game crowd. It is composed quite largely of people, but, oh, what people! Of course, a lot of them are only human, but they seem rather more. What with the Generals and Admirals and thence downward; and what with the epaulets and gold and silver laces, the thousands upon thousands of uniforms and shoulder and sleeve straps, the average commonplace onlooker comes away feeling as if he himself were at least a diplomat."[27]

The game kicked off at 2:12pm. Navy won the coin flip and elected to defend the west goal. Navy took the opening kickoff, running it back to the 20-yard line but after three running plays failed to pick up a first down, they were immediately forced to punt the ball back to Army. Walter French returned the kick 15 yards, but Army also failed to advance the ball and Walter had to punt the ball back to Navy. The punt came down near the Navy goal line and Navy quarterback Vic Noyes fielded it and was immediately dropped in his tracks by Army end Don Storck. Again, Navy was unable to advance the ball against the Army defense and had to punt from their own end zone. Walter French fielded the punt at the Navy 45-yard line and returned it 10 yards. After one running play and two pass attempts were unsuccessful, Walter French attempted a field goal from the 35-yard line. The kick was low and Navy took possession of the ball at their own 20-yard line.

After Navy made two first downs the Army defense stiffened and forced another punt. This time as Walter was waiting for the punt to come down, he was bowled over by the Navy ends covering the play before he had a chance to catch the ball. The play resulted in a 15-yard penalty and placed the ball at midfield but again they were forced to punt to Navy. Back and forth it went, with neither team able to sustain any drives.

The game's first turnover occurred in the second quarter when Navy fumbled, and Army recovered the ball on Navy's 25-yard line. After three running plays did not result in any progress, Walter attempted another field goal, and once again his kick sailed off target. Navy took over on their own 20-yard-line and began what looked to be a promising drive but that was cut short when Army intercepted a pass at its own 37-yard-line. Once again Army was unable to advance the ball and Walter tried his third field goal and this time from around midfield, and once again the kick came up short. The first half ended scoreless.

For the third quarter and most of the fourth, not much changed. The game was primarily played between the 40-yard-lines, with both teams unable to generate much in the way of offense. Navy's focus on stopping Walter French was keeping him bottled up, holding him to less than 100 yards of total offense.

It looked like the game was going to end as a scoreless tie when late in the fourth quarter Army decided to punt one more time. Walter's kicking woes continued with a bad kick that netted only 20 yards in field position. The ball glanced off the side of his foot and went out of bounds on the Army 47-yard-line. Navy backs Vic Noyes and Ben Koehler began banging away at the Army defense, which appeared to be tiring. A pass completion to Eddie Ewen brought the ball to the Army 27-yard-line and on the second of two dazzling runs by Koehler, Navy broke the deadlock with a touchdown. The extra point kick was good and the Midshipmen took the lead 7–0. Navy went on another drive just before the end of the game and brought the ball to the Army 14-yard-line but Noyes fumbled the ball and Army recovered as the game came to an end. The Navy win tied the series at 11 wins for each team, with one tie.

Newspaper accounts of Walter's performance in the game were mixed. The *New York Times*, justifiably called him out for his poor kicking reading "French's weak effort puts Navy in a position to start drive for Touchdown." In its coverage of the game however, the *New York Times* also wrote "French, the Army fullback, of whom much had been expected, sometime showed flashes of real power in carrying the ball. However, he suffered in marked degree from the unstable footing, for the soil had not dried out from the recent rains."[28]

The Army football team returned to the West Point campus at noon the next day, where they were met in the mess hall by the entire Corps of Cadets, who gave them a rousing cheer. "Full credit is given to Navy for its effectiveness in stopping French," one paper reported, "something no other team has been able to do this season."[29]

Army finished the season with a respectable 6–2 record, and with all of the team's starters expected back for the 1921 season, prospects for the team's future appeared bright. However, one person was not so sure. The team's performance was disappointing to the Superintendent. MacArthur was miffed that, at least in his mind, Army could handle the inferior teams like Bowdoin and Lebanon Valley, but in the two most important games of the season against Notre Dame and Navy they came up short. A seed of doubt was planted in his head regarding whether Coach Daly was the man for the job.

The last bit of business was the naming of the year's All-American team. As the 1920 season came to an end many newspapers and football experts were publishing their All-American teams. There were primarily four All-American selectors recognized by the NCAA at that time. *Colliers Weekly Magazine*, *Football World Magazine*, the International News Service, and the man considered the foremost expert on college football at the time, Walter Camp. In addition, sportswriters like Walter Eckersall of the *Chicago Tribune* and Lawrence Perry of the Consolidated Press also published their own selections as did the *New York Times* and the United Press International. Walter French was named to a number of the All-American Teams. He was selected as the first team fullback by the *New York Times* and *Football World Magazine*. Lawrence Perry named him to his second team as did UPI and the most respected of the selectors, Walter Camp.

As with virtually every selector, Camp's first team fullback selection was George Gipp, making him Notre Dame's first All-American. (Gipp was named to the *New York Times* first team as a halfback.) The teams were announced on December 15, 1920, but sadly Gipp would never know of his selection. Hospitalized in South Bend with a streptococcal infection, Gipp died from the ailment on December 14, 1920, the day before Camp's and the other selectors' picks were announced, and only six weeks after his greatest game. As the funeral cortege bearing Gipp's body completed its over 500-mile trip from South Bend and pulled into his hometown of Laurium, MI, the entire town turned out to pay their respects to their favorite son. In the 100 plus years since his final game, only nine Notre Dame running backs have managed to amass more career rushing yards than the great George Gipp.

For Walter French the end of the football season meant that he was moving on to another sport at West Point and without much of a break. Of all Army athletes earning varsity letters in those years, Walter was one of only two to have done so in three sports, football, baseball, and basketball. At some point something had to give, and there were indications in early 1921 that for Walter, what was to give, were his grades. He ranked near the bottom of his 572-member class in almost every subject and he especially struggled in Math and English.

Coach Joseph O'Shea was in his second year as head coach of the Army basketball team. O'Shea was originally hired away from St. John's prior to the 1919–20 season. The 1920–21 season got underway in early December of 1920 with a victory over St. John's by a score of 55–14. Walter was a starting forward on the team which would compile an 18–5 record on the season. Wins came against teams like St. Joseph's of Philadelphia, Villanova, University of North Carolina, Williams, and Brown while losses came at the hands of Columbia, New York University, Swarthmore, Pittsburgh, and worst of all Navy. The loss to Navy was particularly troublesome for coach O'Shea whose contract called for him to be paid $2,500 per season, unless his team lost to Navy, in which case his salary was reduced to $1,500.

A summation of the basketball season published in the *Howitzer* the West Point yearbook concluded that "Army's 1921 basketball team attempted an extremely difficult schedule with a great deal of success, discounting that fact that Navy's victory of February 26th, was, from a West Point outlook, a disastrous culmination to an otherwise very successful season." For his part Walter was once again an important contributor to the Army cause. The *Howitzer* described his play this way: "Vichules and French teamed up well at forward and played brilliant games through the entire year … French was the fastest floor man on the team. He dribbled with great speed, followed the ball closely and was a good shot from the middle of the court."[30]

CHAPTER 4

Hans Lobert and Army Baseball, 1921–1922

After a 14-year major league career, John "Hans" Lobert, based on a recommendation from legendary major league manager of the New York Giants, John McGraw, was hired to be Army's baseball coach in 1918. Lobert was a colorful character that was one of the game's stars during the dead ball era. He began his career after Barney Dreyfuss, owner of the Pittsburgh Pirates, saw him playing for a semi-professional team in the Pittsburgh area in 1903. Dreyfuss invited him to try out with the Pirates. On his first day with the team he made the acquaintance of his boyhood idol, the great Pirate shortstop Honus Wagner. As Lobert would recall "it was like looking into a mirror" as both men bore an amazing resemblance to one another. They also shared their first names, which is how Lobert would eventually be known as "Hans." Wagner's real first name was "Johannes" as was the case with Lobert, and the players referred to him as "Hans." Given the resemblance and to the fact that Lobert was about 20 pounds lighter than Wagner, he became known as "Hans Number Two," a nickname that Wagner would use for him for the next 50 years of their friendship.

Coach Lobert took a particular interest in Army's new center fielder Walter French. This was undoubtedly because he saw a lot of himself in Walter, especially his speed. Lobert was considered the fastest man in baseball throughout his 14-year major league career, which included seasons with the Pittsburgh Pirates, Chicago Cubs, Cincinnati Reds, Philadelphia Phillies, and the New York Giants. When he retired, he had a lifetime batting average of .274 and had stolen 300 bases. He was an excellent bunter, and it was a rare occurrence for him to strike out. He held the record of 13.8 seconds for the time it took to round the bases. This record that stood for many years. In 1910, he raced and defeated the great Olympian Jim Thorpe in the hundred-yard dash. In 1913, as a member of a barnstorming all-star team managed by John McGraw, Lobert raced a horse around the bases as a stunt to appease the cowboys in attendance at a game in Oxnard, California. Hans was leading as they rounded second but was bumped by the horse between second and third, which allowed the horse to cross home first. He also had the distinction of being the first batter to face Babe Ruth when Ruth broke into the major leagues as a pitcher for the Boston Red Sox in 1914. After grounding out to shortstop, Lobert recalled commenting to a friend who was a teammate of Ruth's, "boy that kid has some stuff" to which the friend replied: "wait until you see him hit."

Seeing in Walter the makings of a star player Lobert took him under his wing. He served as his personal tutor, drilling him in fielding and hitting, and he quickly developed into the team's best player.

Lobert's coaching paid off as Walter's season got off to a torrid start. In the team's first five games, all Army victories, he had 15 hits in 24 at bats, reaching base 19 times in that span. In addition to 10 singles, his hits included two doubles, two triples, and a home run for a .625 batting average. He scored 10 runs, had six runs batted in, five stolen bases and a perfect fielding percentage as well.

The first loss of the season for Army came at the hands of Lafayette University by a score of 9–5 on April 20. Their next game with Lehigh was cancelled due to rain. A week later they went up against Syracuse University. Trailing by a score of 3–2 in the bottom of the seventh inning Walter was part of an Army rally that plated four runs leading to a 6–3 win for the Cadets. Over the next few weeks Army went 3–4 winning games against West Virginia, Colgate, and Fordham, while losing to Swarthmore, Catholic University, Columbia University and Brown. All was set for the Navy game on May 28, 1921.

Navy came into the game with a powerhouse squad that most objective observers gave a big advantage over the Army team, of which, according to the school yearbook, little was expected. An overflow crowd of 12,000 fans jammed the Army baseball field. A virtual fleet of destroyers, submarines, and other Navy craft were anchored in the Hudson River after having transported a large Navy crowd of officers and men to the game. On the Army side high-ranking officers traveled from far-off posts to be on hand.

Army took an early 1–0 lead after scoring a run in the bottom of the first inning. Taking advantage of two walks and a hit batsman, Navy pushed across three runs in their half of the second inning. The Army pitcher's continued wildness and some sloppy defense in the third inning plated three more runs for Navy giving them a 6–1 lead. In the bottom half of the third inning Walter French hit a single and stole second base, which was as far as he got before Navy retired the side without giving up any runs.

After holding Navy scoreless in the top of the fourth inning however, Army seemed to come to life. Taking advantage of consecutive walks by the Navy pitcher, Army pushed across two runs to make the score 6–3. Then with two men on base and after Walter French made the second out with a deep fly that was caught, Army infielder Glenn Willhide, with a count of two balls and two strikes, smashed the next pitch deep into the crowd in left field for a home run. The game was tied.

After Navy failed to score in their half of the fifth inning, Don Storck hit a leadoff home run in the bottom of the fifth to give Army a one-run lead. Navy in turn tied the game in the sixth inning. There was no scoring by either team in the seventh or eighth innings. In the top of the ninth Navy squandered a leadoff single, when an attempt to sacrifice the runner to second was snuffed out by the Army pitcher and a long fly ball was run down by Walter French.

In the bottom of the ninth inning Army outfielder George Smythe hit a ball to deep shortstop and made it to second when the throw from the Navy shortstop went wild. Smythe then advanced to third on a single by Don Storck. The next batter for Army was outfielder Charles "Steve" Stevenson, who laid down a perfect squeeze bunt which found its way past the pitcher and left the Navy infielders sprawling for the ball as the winning run crossed the plate.

The reaction on the West Point campus to the unexpected win over the powerful Navy team was ecstasy.

"After the Army baseball team pulled an unexpected upset of a powerful Navy team, the Cadets paraded around the Plain at midnight in their pajamas. Half a dozen or so were beating drums. The cadets bawled West Point fight songs, yelled their class yells, and built a huge bonfire on the edge of the Plain. The TACS were noticeable by their absence. The next morning a grim-faced MacArthur summoned Commandant Robert Danford to his office 'Well that was quite a party last night' MacArthur said. Danford replied 'Yes sir, quite a party'. After thinking about it for a moment MacArthur asked how many of the cadets had Danford punished. Danford, no longer able to contain himself replied 'Not a damn one!' MacArthur reacted by pounding his hand on his desk and responded 'Good! You know I could hardly resist the impulse to get out there with them.'"[1]

In late summer months Coach Daley had given the members of Army's football team "their preliminary work. Then most of the men got into boxing, wrestling, swimming, etc. and football as such was given a rest. September 1921, then brought the future stars together, and from then on, they thought, ate, talked, and played football" according to the *Howitzer*.

The season got underway on October 1, 1921, with two games scheduled. The varsity took on Springfield College and came away with an easy 28–6 victory, while the second team lost a close game, 10–7 to New Hampshire State College. The following Saturday another doubleheader was scheduled and this time both Army teams came away with wins. The varsity defeated Middlebury by a score of 19–0 and the second team took down Lebanon Valley 33–0.

In the game against Middlebury, Walter French sustained an injury to his knee which would cut into his playing time for the next few weeks. He sat out the game on October 15, 1921, against Wabash, and was initially on the bench for the game at Yale the following week, but when he eventually got into the game, he turned in one of his greatest performances although limited by his injury.

The Yale Bowl in New Haven, Connecticut was the site of the much-anticipated game between Yale and Army. The 1921 game between the two schools represented a resumption of a rivalry which had been dormant since the last time the two teams met at West Point in 1912, when Yale won 6–0.

In what was one of the largest crowds ever to see a game at the Yale Bowl, 75,000 spectators were on hand to watch the two teams square off. This marked the first time that Army had ever played a game away from West Point, except for the Army–Navy game.

The Army team and corps of cadets traveled from West Point to New Haven on a special train the morning of the day of the game. At 1:45pm, with the stands full, the cadets marched onto the field and gave their exhibition drill. Shortly after the cadets made their way to their seats the two teams ran out onto the field ... first Yale and then Army.

Army won the toss and elected to defend the south goal in order to gain an advantage given that the wind was blowing from that direction. To say that the first quarter was a defensive struggle would be to put it mildly. Yale managed only two first downs in the period while Army was unable to move the chains even once.

The second quarter of the game was more of the same and at halftime the game was a scoreless tie. To this point in the game, Coach Daley, careful not to make Walter's knee injury any worse, kept him on the sidelines.

Initially, the third quarter picked right up where the first half had ended, as both teams were still unable to mount any offense and both teams were forced to punt on their first possession of the second half. After the exchange of kicks, Yale took the ball at midfield. Having failed to score with their straight-ahead running attack, Yale halfback Mac Aldrich, a consensus All-American and Yale captain, threw a pass to George Becket the team's quarterback which was completed for a 30-yard touchdown, and the game's first score.

As the game reached the halfway point of the third quarter, Daley decided to see what Walter could do despite playing with a bad knee. Army had the ball at midfield. The first time he touched the ball he peeled off a dandy 30-yard run to the Yale 20-yard-line. On the next play he attempted a pass into the end zone, however Yale's Aldrich beat the Army receiver to the ball, intercepted the pass, and ran it back 80 yards before being dragged down at the Army 15-yard-line. Army was penalized for being offside on the next two plays which led to another Yale touchdown giving them a 14–0 lead early in the fourth quarter.

At this point Walter began to put the Army team on his back and attempted to lead them on a furious comeback. In its coverage of the game the *Philadelphia Inquirer* noted that after Yale kicked off after their second score that "French started his offense single-handed."[2] In the account of the game printed in the 1922 edition of the *Howitzer* it was noted that "French was dodging, running, and passing in an almost uncanny way. He was winning against the whole Yale team, but fortune was against him and with the knee that refused to function any longer ... he hurled a long pass to Johnson for Army's touchdown."[3] As time was running out in the game,

Walter kept up his one-man assault on the Yale defense. As the game clock ran down to zero, he had Army on the Yale five-yard-line and had made the fourth quarter what the *Philadelphia Inquirer* described as a "nightmare for the Yale supporters."[4]

The *Philadelphia Inquirer* went on to say this about Walter's performance, "French of West Point ... went into the game late in the third period, proved a veritable whirlwind and gave a good indication of how the affair might have ended had he been able to play the entire game. He alone represented about ninety percent of the visitor's offense, and in fact, until he came in, they had none at all. His brilliant end runs, and off tackle dashes accounted for the only first downs the cadets could make by rushing the ball while his long pass to Johnson in the middle of the last quarter accounted for the visitor's only score."[5]

His valiant effort in a losing cause at Yale exacerbated his knee injury and as a result he needed to be kept out of the next two games. The first of the two, against Susquehanna, was an easy 28–0 Army win. The next week, however, was the annual match up with Notre Dame. The 1921 edition of the "Big Game" did not have the big buildup of the 1920 game and there would be no repeat of the classic battle fans witnessed between French and Gipp. Without Walter French, Army was no match for Notre Dame who won the game easily 28–0.

The last game on the schedule before the season finale with Navy was against Villanova. Walter also sat out that game but the same can be said of the entire first team. The Army second team easily won the game 49–0.

As the 1921 Army–Navy game approached, the sportswriters of the day had installed Navy as a heavy favorite in the game. Navy came into the game undefeated and had only allowed one touchdown all season. Coach Daley and his staff made the determination that the only chance they had to win the game would be to make some changes to their attack in the hopes of catching Navy by surprise. The number of practices increased in the two weeks leading up to the game and in addition, the practices were held in secret.

The game also marked the first time that players for the service academies wore numbers on their uniforms. Army wore the even numbers and Navy the odd. Walter was assigned number "20."

The game was being played at the Polo Grounds in New York on November 26, 1921, and a large crowd including Vice President Calvin Coolidge and his wife, and a large contingent from official Washington, D.C., were traveling to the game. The *New York Times* reported on the day before the game that "reservations on the night trains for New York are at a premium early today, when the onward rush for the Army-Navy football game began, to continue through the early hours of tomorrow."[6] In addition to the Vice-President, the Secretary of War, the Secretary of the Navy, the Secretary of Labor, many officers from both branches, and Cornelius and Mrs. Vanderbilt were also on hand for the game. Socialites of all types were throwing parties at venues like the Ritz-Carlton. The *New York Times*, almost as a passing thought and most likely overlooked by most readers, also reported that a Mrs. Cromwell Brooks would be "entertaining a party on the Army side of the field"[7] in the box of Army Superintendent General Douglas MacArthur. Brooks was a recently divorced, wealthy socialite who had made the acquaintance of MacArthur at a party at Tuxedo Park, a resort just south of West Point. The entry of Henrietta Cromwell, or Louise as she preferred to be called, into MacArthur's life, as we shall learn later, will have an impact on Walter French.

As the Army team worked overtime to practice their new formations and plays, they were forced to do so in wretched conditions. The *New York Times* reported on Tuesday of game week that the team's practice had been hampered by a "steady fall of sleet and hail, which made a heavy wet ball and a treacherous turf. Gathering darkness necessitate the use of artificial lights."[8] In all the coverage of the team's practices, Walter French's name was always included with that of the first unit as expected but, in an article, published in the *New York Times* on the Thursday before the game it was reported that "an announcement was made by Charles Daley of the probable line-up of the soldiers eleven … the surprising feature of this announcement was the fact that it did not contain the name of Walter French, Army's great backfield player. Daley did not say that French would not play, but he did not include him among those that would face the Navy. A reservation that the line-up was subject to change at the last-minute was made with the announcement. It is therefore expected by close followers of the Army team that French will get into the game at some stage. Army adherents believe that with French in the game the soldiers will give a good account of themselves, but without going to the extent to predict victory. However, if the West Point star does not start, the odds prevailing, which are understood here to be 2 to1 on the Navy to win, are considered perfectly justified."[9]

The Army faithful breathed a sigh of relief when they saw that Walter was part of the starting unit after all. Army won the toss and chose to defend the east end of the field. Navy kicked off and Walter made a modest gain with his return. Army started to move the ball downfield, making short gains but moving steadily largely on the strength of Walter's running. The drive stalled on the Navy 30-yard-line and an Army field goal attempt missed its mark. From there Navy was held without any gain and the teams exchanged punts. Near the end of the first quarter Navy back Steve Barchett broke through the Army line and was brought down by a touchdown saving tackle by French at around the Army 20-yard-line. On the first three plays of the series Navy was only able to advance the ball five yards. Navy decided to go for the touchdown on fourth down and Army stopped them. In the second quarter the teams continued to exchange punts.

Near the end of the first half, Navy's star running back Stephen Barchett made another long run around the Army end and again Walter French made another touchdown saving tackle deep in Army territory. As the first half was coming to an end, Navy, with the ball sitting on Army's two-yard-line, pushed the ball across the goal line for what would be the game's only score.

As the second half got underway the field conditions deteriorated considerably. The rain that had been falling throughout the first half intensified in the second half, weighing down the ball and making the field a slippery, muddy mess. But in a scene reminiscent of the Yale game, Army came out fighting in the second half, and led by the great play of Walter French outplayed the midshipmen throughout the rest of the game. Army would advance the ball but ultimately be forced to punt the ball back to Navy, and the same was true for the other side.

Late in the fourth quarter, Army's George Smythe caught a pass that resulted in a 35-yard gain and took the ball to the Navy 28-yard line. Three running plays by French and Smythe advanced the ball 13 more yards. With their fans in a frenzy, Army attempted a pass into the end zone where Navy's Hamilton jumped in front of the Army receiver and intercepted the ball, bringing an end to the Army threat. Navy, clinging to the ball for all they were worth, was able to run out the clock and walk away with a hard fought 7–0 win, and with the added bonus of now leading Army in the series 12–11.

In their write-ups after the game, the newspapers all singled out the brilliant play of Walter French in a losing cause. "The condition of the playing field," the *New York Times* acknowledged "doubtless proved a greater handicap to the Army than it did to the Navy. The Army plan of attack was built around French to no small measure, and he more than justified the confidence imposed in him."[10] This description in the *Times* does a good job of capturing how this defensive battle went for Army "The Navy more than once advanced toward the Army's goal, but on the majority of occasions the cadet line braced and forded a kick, and after French had launched his attack Smythe would lift one of his long spirals, putting the ball back in the Navy territory, and the possession would then take up where it had left off."[11]

In December when the All-American selections were announced, the time he missed due to injury kept Walter off most of the lists that he had been included on the year before. The one exception to that was the one list that mattered more than any of the others, the selections of Walter Camp. When Walter Camp's All-American selections for 1921 were published, Walter French was listed as the third team selection at halfback.

Writing in the *Howitzer* yearbook, Coach Daly summed up the 1921 football season this way: "Our football record since the war is far from satisfactory. We have lost practically all of our major contests, including our Navy games. The fact that two of these past three seasons were played with cadets of but two years academic experience is possibly a mitigating circumstance, but not one from which we take much satisfaction. However, it is well to note that during this period our defeats (except for the final Notre Dame game) have been accomplished only after hard and bitter fighting, and then with close scores. We have never been outclassed and practically all of our junior institutions have been easily vanquished. With this background we can look ahead with decided hope, as we can all see, going on about us, the great increase in cadet athletic strength, due to the four-year course."[12]

One person who must have wholly concurred with Daly's assessment was General MacArthur. He would certainly agree with the coach on the impact that his reintroduction of the four-year program at West Point had on all aspects of cadet life including "athletic strength." He would also heartily agree with the fact that the football team's performance since the end of World War I to be "far from satisfactory." It rankled him that once again the cadets were unable to defeat their principal rivals, especially Navy, so much so that he was contemplating replacing Daly at the end of the 1921 season and had even toyed with the idea of trying to recruit Knute Rockne away from Notre Dame, but Daly would survive and be at the helm of Army football for the 1922 season.

One issue that Walter French had hanging over his head continued to be his poor academic performance. In the major courses of study at the Academy he was still near the very bottom of his class in each and his particular struggles in Math and English continued. When asked about this later in life he would acknowledge that he had been protected by MacArthur and his interest in "building up the sports program" at West Point. The fact was that Walter French was the best football and baseball player that Army had and one of the best basketball players as well. If the Superintendent was going to keep the Academic Board at bay for any athlete, it would be Walter.

However, if he was looking for some free time to catch up on his studies and improve his grades that was a luxury he would not be afforded. Unlike the modern collegiate athletes who are aided by special tutors when they need help, that was not available to the student athletes in 1921 and for Walter there was no rest after the end of a grueling football season. Immediately following the Navy football game, he was working out and practicing with the basketball team for their 1921–22 season. In fact, the first basketball game on Army's schedule against St. John's College was played on December 3, 1921, only one week, to the day, from the football team's loss to Navy. So while most of the Army football team now had a sizeable break from athletics to focus on studies, Walter's break lasted only seven days.

Adding to Walter's academic woes was the method of teaching used at the United States Military Academy, known as the Thayer Method. Named for Col. Sylvanus Thayer, who was the Superintendent at West Point from 1817 to 1833, the Thayer Method relied on the Cadets to be responsible for their own learning. Under this system the student was expected to study the course material on their own, prior to the class, and then have their learning supported through an in-class question and answer period followed by group learning and exercises. It is not hard to imagine the problems such a system presented to Walter, a self-described poor student, who was earning three varsity letters. Not to mention the fact that as now a third-year cadet, the subjects of history, technical drawing, military tactics, and practical military engineering were added to math, English, and French.

The 1921–22 Army basketball season was, to that point in time, the most successful in the school's history. The team posted a record of 17–2 with wins over teams like Columbia, NYU and Harvard in addition to a win over Navy in the final game of the season on February 25, 1922. The following season the team went 17–0 and when combined with the fact that Army had won their last 13 games of that 1921–22 season, represented a 30-game winning streak. It would take until the Bobby Knight coached teams of the late 1960s for Army basketball to have that type of success in consecutive seasons.

While the basketball season was winding down in the month of February, the baseball team was beginning their indoor workouts. The Army team promised to be a good one in 1922 as all but one of the previous year's starters were returning. As the weather cooperated in early March the team was able to begin practicing outside.

The early scouting report on the Army team was that they looked to be a hard-hitting team with solid, although not above average pitching. If there was any glaring weakness it was in the overall team defense which was rated as mediocre at best.

It was anticipated that Walter French and Don Storck would be the team's best hitters based on their performance in the previous season. Walter's first home run came in the second game of the season, an 11–2 victory over City College of New York, and a game in which he also ran wild on the bases.

The next game on the West Point schedule was the annual exhibition game against the New York Giants, who happened to be the defending World Series champions. Although the game did not count against the cadet's record, and although the Giants won the game easily, Walter had to feel pretty good about his performance against the major leaguers as he hit two doubles. The next game was an easy win over NYU and the *Howitzer* reported that "French hit savagely in this game." In a win over Williams College Walter led the way with a three-run homer in the eighth inning. On May 6, Walter hit his fifth home run of the season in a 10–4 win over Columbia. On May 17 in a 7–5 win over the University of Delaware, Willhide, Storck, and Walter French pulled a triple steal and "Frenchy hit the ball all over the lot getting two singles, one double and a home run."[13] One week later against Penn State he hit two home runs leading the way to a 4–3 Army win.

On May 29, Army traveled to Annapolis for the season finale with Navy. As with the previous year's game at West Point an overflow crowd was in attendance for the contest. In its summation to the game, the *Howitzer* reported that "French hit hard and often in the game getting a single and a pair of doubles. His scoop of Harris' liner and the throw he made to the plate on the dead run, to catch Barchet, was the feature of the game."[14] Walter's heroics were not enough however, and although the game was in doubt until the final out, Navy held on to win the game 8–6.

Army finished the season with a record of 11–5. For Walter the 1922 baseball season at West Point would rival his 1920 football season for the best of his time at the academy. His .463 batting average far outpaced any other player on the team, including Don Storck, who hit .400. Walter led the team in hits, doubles, and stolen bases. In the 16-game season he hit eight home runs, which also led the team. By comparison George Smythe was second on the team in home runs with three.

Meanwhile change was in the air at West Point. The typical tour of duty for a West Point Superintendent had been four years and it appeared that despite the pushback he was getting from the Academic Board and other members of the old guard at the academy, that MacArthur would remain in his position for at least that long. However, on January 30, 1922, less than three years after being appointed, Army Chief of Staff John Pershing, nicknamed "Black Jack," abruptly announced that MacArthur was being transferred to the Philippines. On the same day, Pershing sent a letter to MacArthur chastising him for ignoring Army protocol, after MacArthur attended a Congressional hearing on the West Point budget, without calling on Pershing while in Washington, D.C. In his letter back to Pershing, MacArthur wrote "I regret exceedingly if this incident may have given any impression of discourtesy …." In his biography of MacArthur, William Manchester wrote: "There is no record that his apology was accepted. MacArthur should not have expected that it would be. Pershing's anger had nothing to do with the superintendent's visit to Washington. Like his posting to the Philippines, it was evidence of a very different affront. Brigadier General MacArthur was guilty of one of the oldest wrongs one man can inflict on another. The four-star general had had his eye on a woman, and the dashing brigadier had heisted her."[15] On January 15, 1922, less than two months after she and her party joined MacArthur in his box at the 1921 Army–Navy football game at the Polo Grounds, Louise Cromwell Brooks and Douglas MacArthur announced their engagement. The following month on Valentine's Day, in an elaborate ceremony and reception at the Palm Beach, Florida home of Louise's mother and stepfather, the two were married.

Before meeting MacArthur, Louise had made the acquaintance of Pershing, a widower, while on an extended stay in Paris. "Back in Washington," according to Manchester, "she became his official hostess, and capital rumor had it that she would become the second Mrs. Pershing."[16] As the New York writers started to put two and two together they descended on West Point and Mrs. MacArthur did not pull any punches when asked for an explanation of her husband's sudden transfer. "To one newsman she said 'Jack wanted me to marry him … I wouldn't do that—so here I am, packing my trunks'. She told another that Pershing was 'exiling' her and her new husband to the Philippines and that the Chief of Staff had warned her that 'if I married MacArthur, he would send him to the islands and there was a terrible climate there and I wouldn't like it. A letter critical of MacArthur's transfer from the Point appeared in the *New York Times*. Shortly thereafter the paper carried a page-three story headed 'Pershing Denies Exile Order'."[17]

On June 30, 1922, MacArthur turned over the reins of the United States Military Academy at West Point to Brigadier General Fred W. Sladen. Sladen had graduated from West Point in 1890, 13 years before his predecessor. While many of MacArthur's reforms succeeded his tenure, there were those that were reversed, and certainly any influence he may have exerted on behalf of Walter French with the Academic Board ended with his departure. On July 6, 1922, just one week after MacArthur's departure, the Academic Board "turned back" Walter French from the class of 1924 to the class of 1925 for failing English and Mathematics. His one chance to avoid dismissal was to pass exams in both of those subjects. When that failed, he was discharged from the academy on September 13, 1922.

The communication from the Academic Board informing a cadet of their discharge in 1922 was short and to the point. "Cadet Walter Edward French, 3rd class, USMA," it read, "is upon recommendation of the Academic Board, discharged from the service of the United States on account of deficiency in studies … By order of the Secretary of War." The letter was accompanied by an affidavit that the discharged cadet must complete in his own handwriting stating if he suffers from any lingering injuries from his time at West Point and confirming that he was not subject to any hazing or harassment of any type while a cadet. Walter appears to have taken this news without complaint and there is a tone of resignation to his responses. He answered the injury question by indicating that he had injured his knee while a cadet, a reference to the injury he sustained in the football game against Middlebury in 1921, but that it did not bother him any longer and he simply answered "no" to the question about hazing.

And with that, for the time being, his career at West Point was over. "I really wasn't much of a student; not like I should have been" he told Jim Bailey of the *Arkansas Democrat Gazette* in a 1979 interview, "When General MacArthur left, the professors got me."[18]

CHAPTER 5

Connie Mack and the Philadelphia Athletics, 1923–1925

Although his dismissal from the United States Military Academy did not create the furor that resulted when Notre Dame temporarily expelled George Gipp, there was a great deal of interest expressed in Walter French. Shortly after his dismissal he was approached by former Rutgers football star Howard Parker Talman who was the athletic director at the University of Chattanooga. Talman had been an All-American football player for Rutgers in 1915 and 1916, once scoring six touchdowns in a game against RPI. Talman pushed hard to have Walter enroll at Chattanooga where he knew he would make an immediate impact on the school's athletic program. So certain were the sportswriters that Walter would be accepting the offer that reports began to surface that he had made a final decision to attend Chattanooga as early as September 20, just one week from the date of his dismissal from West Point. However, Walter was also considering another option, enlisting in the Army. If he could not become an Army officer by graduating from West Point, then perhaps he could achieve this goal of becoming a second lieutenant by passing the civilian exam which was next scheduled to be administered on October 23.

The following week Walter joined a number of his former teammates at Rutgers when they gathered to help their old football coach Foster Sanford get his team ready for the upcoming season. Joining Walter for what the reporters were calling "alumni" day, was Frank Kelly, Mike Whitehall, and Paul Robeson. Robeson, who at the time was studying at Columbia Law School, was also signed to play for the Milwaukee Badgers in the new National Football League.

The reporters covering the event pressed Walter on his plans and he took the opportunity to announce that reports that he had decided to attend the University of Chattanooga were premature. Walter informed the assembled media covering the Rutgers practice that he, in fact, intended to take the civilian officers exam, and that he would not be attending Chattanooga as had been widely reported.

There were, however, a few hurdles that he would have to get past to make that dream a reality, not the least of which was the fact that the examinations for civilian officer candidates were extremely rigorous at that time and included sections on math and grammar, the very subjects he struggled with mightily and which led to his dismissal from West Point. In addition, given the fact that if he was able to pass the exam he would outrank his former West Point classmates, the members of the West Point graduating classes of 1924 and 1925 would have to waive their right to force him to wait until they had graduated before he could be commissioned as an officer. Finally his old nemesis, the West Point Academic Board, would also have to give their blessing to his plan. In the end it was the Academic Board that frustrated Walter's ambition. While his fellow classmates waived their right to graduate before he could be commissioned, the Academic Board refused to allow him to take the examination.

While considering what his next career move should be in the fall of 1922, Walter was signed to play for the Washington Football Club, an independent professional team based in the Washington, D.C. area. On October 15 the team went up against the Akron Pros of the NFL at American League Park in the nation's capital. Although Washington went down to defeat by a score of 7–0, Walter French, who was responsible for all the team's offense, was the star of the game for Washington. His nifty 50-yard run was the game's lone highlight.

His performance for Washington only added to the speculation on the part of the press as to what Walter French's next move would be. One week after the game against Akron, a *Baltimore Sun* report predicted that French would be the Army's secret weapon in the much-anticipated football showdown between the Army Third Corps team and that of the Marines stationed at Quantico, VA set for December 2. "Reports to the effect that Walter E. French, the former great halfback at Rutgers and West Point will be among those present in the game against the Marines persists," wrote sportswriter Don Riley.[1] If Walter decided to continue to pursue a military career it was almost certain that he would be assigned to the Third Corps making him available for the game.

The first real indication that Walter initially had decided to pursue a military career came in early November, when for the first time his name appeared on the Third Army Corps football team's roster, when they squared off against the University of Pennsylvania Junior Varsity team in Philadelphia. The Army won the game by a score of 19–0 with Walter scoring his team's third and final touchdown. A few days later all of the newspapers were reporting that he had officially enlisted in the regular Army as a private and that he would be in the lineup in the game against the Marines.

The game between the Third Army Corps and the Marines from Quantico in 1922 was the second meeting between the two teams. The Marines had won the 1921 game, played at Johns Hopkins University by a score of 20–0. The 1922 game was played at the brand-new Municipal Stadium on 33rd Street in Baltimore. A crowd of over 43,000 people were on hand. It was the largest crowd at that point to ever witness a sporting event in the city's history. There were over 100 congressmen in attendance and reporters came from all over the country to cover the game. Tickets were sold out a week prior to the game.

In addition to Walter French, the Army team was led by former West Point star Gene Vidal. Vidal, in addition to being a star football player, was a member of the 1920 US Olympic Team where he competed in the Decathlon.

The team captain for the Marines was Frank Goettge who was a World War I veteran who had played semi-professional football in Ohio. He turned down a contract with the New York Giants to stay with the Marines.

The Army took an early 6–0 lead on field goals by Gene Vidal but the Marines on the strength of two touchdowns by Frank Goettge, who the *Baltimore Sun* described as an "embodied tornado" came back to win the game by a score of 13–12. In their wrap up of the game the *Pittsburgh Press* noted that "Gene Vidal, Walter French, Johnny Greene and Van De Graff, all former West Point stars graced the lineup of the area corps with all of their brilliancy."[2]

Just a few days after the game between the Army and the Marines, on December 6, the Rutgers football team held its end of the year banquet. Over the last few weeks the rift that had developed due to Walter's departure from Rutgers for West Point was beginning to be smoothed over as a result of the assistance that Walter had given coach Sanford with the team back in the fall. However, in making his remarks that night, Coach Sanford sought to dispense with any animosity that might remain at Rutgers on the subject of Walter French. Sanford told the 200 people in attendance that although there was no changing the fact that Walter had abandoned the school at which he first became a star in favor of West Point, that recent events had proven that he did it with "an honest purpose." Sanford went on to explain that Walter "wanted to be an officer and although he has flunked out at West Point, he has enlisted as a buck private, and many of us must change our estimation of him."[3]

On December 11 the newspapers reported that Walter French had been hired to coach the Young Men's Hebrew Association's basketball team, which played in an amateur league in the Baltimore area. Although it was his first attempt at coaching, the *Washington Times* praised the hire writing "The YMHA authorities made a ten-strike when they secured the services of French. No better man could have been selected for the position."[4] The Baltimore area was a hotbed of basketball both amateur and professional. Everyone that coached the sport in the region was compared to Bill Schuerholz who was recognized as one of the best coaches in the country. He coached both the Baltimore Orioles of the professional American Basketball League, and Loyola High School, the most dominant secondary school team in the section.

Walter worked the team hard during the month of December and despite a tough schedule that called for them to play mostly college teams they were undefeated going into early March. Pressure was building for a match between the YMHA team and the professional Baltimore Orioles prior to the YMHA team's run at the annual Amateur Athletic Union tournament. Believing that a game against a professional team, while not something that the AAU encouraged, would not mean automatic sanctions, the managers of the YMHA informed Walter that they had agreed to play a three-game series with the professional team. However, after the first game, which was won easily by the Orioles, the local governing board of the AAU ruled that the YMHA team had violated the spirit of amateurism and they were banned from the AAU tournament that was scheduled to begin in the next few days. So ended Walter's basketball coaching career.

Beginning as early as September of 1922, reports were circulating that Walter French was in discussions with the Philadelphia Athletics. Connie Mack's chief scout Mike Drennan, who was instrumental in bringing such stars as Jimmy Dykes and future Hall of Famers Al Simmons and Jimmie Foxx to the A's, had seen Walter play during his remarkable 1922 Army baseball season. The two first made each other's acquaintance on the train ride back from that year's Army–Navy baseball game. Drennan offered Walter a contract for the 1923 season making $500 per month. In an interview with sportswriter Frank Graham years later he recalled "I was so happy about it I didn't even ask for a big bonus for signing ... I discovered later I could have got as much for signing as I got for a whole year's pay, but I was dumb then." He went on to explain to Graham that he was not worried about his commitment to the Army. "I wasn't worried about that. They had a rule that if you could show them you had a job waiting for you, you could be discharged. So, I knew that all I had to do was to prove that Connie had sent me a contract."[5]

Walter was given furlough from the Army so that he could attend spring training with the Athletics in Montgomery, AL but in early April of 1923 it all became official when Walter received written confirmation that he had been given an honorable discharge from the U.S. Army.

When American League President Ban Johnson set out to have his league challenge the monopoly of the National League in 1901, he knew that to be successful he needed to establish teams in some of the same cities that already had National League franchises such as St. Louis, Chicago, and Philadelphia. Charles Somers, a Cleveland business executive who had made his fortune in the coal business, agreed to finance franchises in four cities including the one in Philadelphia which was nicknamed the Athletics after a team which played there in the late 1800s.

Before the first season was over however, Philadelphia businessman Ben Shibe put together a group that included A's manager Connie Mack and two local sportswriters, Butch Jones, and Frank Huff, and bought out Charles Somers. Under the arrangement Shibe would own 50 percent of the team, Connie Mack would own 25 percent of the team, and the last 25 percent would go to Jones and Huff.

Connie Mack, whose real name was Cornelius McGillicuddy, was born in 1862 in East Brookfield, Massachusetts. He was the son of Irish immigrants Michael and Mary McKillop McGillicuddy. His father fought with the 51st Massachusetts infantry in the Civil War.

Mack got his first job in baseball in 1884 as a catcher for a professional team in Meriden, Connecticut. After a few stops with teams in the American Association he was eventually sold to the Washington Senators, then a team in the National League, in 1886. In his autobiography *My 66 Years in the Big Leagues* he wrote that "I was one of the first players to go south on a Spring Training trip in 1888. The manager in Washington was Old Ted Sullivan, and he conceived the idea that if he could get the jump on the other clubs by putting them in spring training, it would enhance his chances of winning the pennant. So, he took all of his players to Florida, a practice followed today."[6]

After an ankle injury ended his playing career, Connie Mack caught on as the manager of a team in Milwaukee, where he met Ban Johnson who hired him to manage the American League franchise he was putting into Philadelphia to challenge the National League Phillies team.

When he arrived in Philadelphia, Mack had no team and no place to play. They finally settled on a plot of land located at Twenty-Ninth and Oxford Streets and broke ground on what was called Columbia Park. He then set about to build his team and the first place he looked was the rival Phillies and began negotiations with four of their players the crown jewel of which was future Hall of Famer Napoleon Lajoie. The signing of Lajoie eventually ended up in a court case that made its way up to the Pennsylvania Supreme Court, which ruled that Lajoie could no longer play for the A's. In order to keep the star player in the American League, Mack traded him to Cleveland.

Eventually Mack made the decision to start looking for prospects among college players. He found Chief Bender at Carlisle, Jack Coombs at Colby, Eddie Collins at Columbia, Jack Barry at Holy Cross, Mickey Cochrane at Boston University and now Walter French at Army. In speaking with *Baltimore Sun* reporter Don Riley, Connie Mack predicted that after a year or two of seasoning in the minor leagues, that Walter French would be a successful major league player. "He is very fast," Mack told Riley "and his speed is a great asset. He has looked better at bat than in fielding, but he ought to improve, and I think he will."[7]

Walter's initial stay with the A's in Montgomery was cut short when he received a telegram on March 20 from his family back in Moorestown with the sad news that his father, Walter S. French had died somewhat unexpectedly at the age of 57. Newspapers reported that "Walter Edward French, star athlete for West Point, and one of the most promising recruits in the Philadelphia spring training quarters at Montgomery, was called to his home at Moorestown, N.J. last night by the death of his father, Walter S. French."[8]

After his father's funeral, he returned to Montgomery and resumed his spring training. It was during that same time that he met his future wife, Elizabeth Bazemore.

She was four years his junior and like his own mother, a native of Alabama. Elizabeth, or Beth as she was called, had grown up in Montgomery and attended Sydney Lanier High School, where she was a classmate of her first cousin Zelda Sayre, the future American novelist and wife of writer F. Scott Fitzgerald.

Elizabeth had traveled from her home in Birmingham to stay with her sister who at the time was dating a member of the A's front office staff and he brought Walter along on a visit to keep his girlfriend's sister company. One newspaper described Beth as one of the most beautiful girls in all of Alabama. Their attraction to each other was immediate and the two began a long-distance courtship during which Walter wrote to her every day.

At the conclusion of the 1923 spring training, Walter was assigned to the Williamsport Billies of the newly created New York–Pennsylvania league. Mack believed that Walter would benefit most by being placed with a club where he had the best chance to play every day.

In its inaugural season the New York–Penn League consisted of six teams. In addition to Williamsport there were teams in York, Scranton, and Wilkes-Barre in Pennsylvania, and Binghamton and Elmira in New York. Walter quickly established

Walter French met his future wife Elizabeth Bazemore during Spring Training in Montgomery, Alabama. (Courtesy of French Family)

himself as one of the A's top prospects during his season with the Billies, who won the league championship by nine games over the second place York White Roses. He played in 112 of the teams 124 games and finished the season with 167 hits and a league high .360 batting average. He also recorded 43 stolen bases which was also tops in the league. He finished the season with a league best 13 triples and he hit 9 home runs.

His success with the Williamsport club earned him a call up to the Athletics in September. He appeared in 16 games with the big-league team, starting in 10 of them and playing the outfield. In addition to the starts, he made five appearances as a pinch hitter and one as a pinch runner. His first major league start came on September 15 when he started both games of a doubleheader against the St. Louis Browns. He started in centerfield and batted leadoff in both games. In the first game he had two hits in four at-bats, scored two runs and recorded his first RBI. He followed that up by going two for four in the second game. He played in five games of the team's next series with the Detroit Tigers and while his hitting cooled off, he still managed to get four hits in the five games.

He made his first big splash in a game against the Chicago White Sox on September 20 in a 5 to 3 A's victory. "The first local tally" the newspaper's account of the game reported "was due to the hitting ability of Walter French, the new Mackian outfielder, whose single sent Dykes over the rubber in the third stanza. French had a fine day in the field and proved that he is right in line for a regular berth on the local nine for his work in center."[9] The writers also made mention of the comparison that fans were making between Walter and Maurice Archdeacon of the White Sox.

Like Walter, Archdeacon was a rookie and a late season call up from Rochester of the International League. Both men played centerfield, both batted left-handed, they were almost identical to one another in terms of their weight and height, and they both possessed blazing speed. The writers commented that "an interesting comparison was made by the fans in the speed of French, the local lad, and Archdeacon of the White Sox, who is reputed to be the fastest man to break into big league baseball this year. The visiting star was a sensation in the International League, and yesterday he showed flashes of his real speed by twice beating out bunts and once reaching first on a fielder's choice when it seemed certain a double play would result. Even with his great speed Archdeacon did not look any better than French, and the fans were still divided in their opinions when they went out of the park discussing the latest victory of the awakened Mackmen."[10]

One person who wasn't divided about which man was faster was Athletics' coach Danny Murphy. "That's the fastest bird in the business" Murphy observed about Walter French, adding "Give that boy a couple of weeks more to get into condition and I'll pick him to beat anybody in either league getting down to first base. He's the fastest man on that stretch that I ever saw, and I've been looking them over for a quarter of a century."[11] The Athletics' 1923 season mercifully ended with a 9–7 victory over the New York Yankees on October 7. The A's finished the season in sixth place, with a record of 69–81–01.

A few days later Walter signed on to play football for the first of three different professional teams for whom he would compete in 1923. At this point the National Football League was still in its infancy and most of the professional teams existed independent of the new league. Without a single authority to govern their actions, players would move from team to team, offering their services to the highest bidder, and Walter was no different.

On Sunday, October 14, Walter appeared in a game for the independent Wilkes-Barre (PA) Panthers against the Tacony Athletic Club. The Panthers won easily by a score of 21–0. Walter scored one touchdown and kicked two extra points. A few days later it was announced that he had also signed with the Frankford Yellow Jackets. The 1923 season would be the Yellow Jackets' final one as an independent team. They would join the National Football League in 1924. Walter's first game with the Yellow Jackets was against the New Haven Independents, the team billed as the New England Champions. In this game, won by the Yellowjackets by a score of 25–0, Walter scored two touchdowns and kicked two extra points. Teaming up with Walter on the Yellow Jackets were the Stein brothers Herb and Russ. Russ Stein had played his college football at Washington and Jefferson University in Pennsylvania, and Herb played for "Pop" Warner at the University of Pittsburgh. In 1921 the Steins became the first brothers to be named by Walter Camp as first team All-Americans.

A week later he appeared once again for the Yellow Jackets in a game that finished in a scoreless tie against the Gilberton Catamounts. Like many of the other small towns with professional football teams, Gilberton was located in the coal mining region of Pennsylvania, and was led by Fritz Pollard, who along with Paul Robeson, was one of only two Black men to have been named All-American to that point in time, for his work at Brown University.

On November 11 Walter played quarterback and threw for two touchdowns for Wilkes-Barre in a 26–0 win over Scranton. The next day he went up against Gilberton again, this time for Frankford and kicked the winning 40-yard field goal in a 3–0 victory.

Only six days after defeating Gilberton, he signed on to play for them against the Pottsville Maroons, another coal region team. This turn of events now teamed up Walter French with player-coach Fritz Pollard as the two former All-Americans shared the same backfield. Back in October the Maroons had defeated the Catamounts by a score of 27–0. With Pollard and French leading the way however, the Catamounts turned the tables on the Maroons and came away with a hard fought 16–7 victory. The following week he was back playing quarterback for Wilkes-Barre when they defeated the Avoca Buffaloes on Thanksgiving Day by a score of 20–0. It was while playing in this game for Wilkes-Barre that he first made the acquaintance of Tony Latone.

Born in the coal mining region, Latone left school to work in the coal mines at the age of 11 to support his mother and five siblings, after the death of his father. While working in the mines often destroyed men physically, the opposite seemed to be true for Tony. Years of pushing and pulling heavy coal cars had built him into an imposing physical specimen. In his playing days he was 5'11" tall and weighed 195 pounds and had the build of a quintessential fullback. In the game against Avoca he scored two touchdowns including a 50-yard return of an intercepted pass.

In January of 1924, Walter proposed to Beth and their engagement was announced. The two were married in Birmingham, Alabama on February 28, 1924, at the home of the bride's parents. It was a small service which took place on a weekday afternoon. Only Walter's mother and one of his aunts attended from his side of the family. After a brief honeymoon in Florida they rushed back to Alabama so Walter could join the Athletics at their spring training facility in Montgomery.

After a small wedding at the home of the bride's parents on February 28, 1924, the couple spent a brief honeymoon in Florida before Walter had to rush back to Alabama for Spring Training. (Courtesy of French Family)

Walter played well during spring training and there was some speculation that he might make the major league roster. In December of 1923, Connie Mack had released one of the team's regular outfielders, a player by the name of Clarence "Tilly" Walker, when it became evident that his best days were behind him. Sportswriters covering the A's listed Walter French as a likely addition to the big-league roster if Mack decided to carry an additional outfielder. In the end Mack decided that Walter would benefit more from another season in the minors than by sitting on the bench behind Bill Lamar, Frank Welch, Bing Miller, and future Hall of Famer Al Simmons playing in his first major league season. Therefore, at the conclusion of spring training, Walter was assigned to the Shreveport Gassers of the Texas League, which not coincidentally, was the team that Simmons had played for in 1923.

The promotion of Simmons to the Athletics was a big concern for the Shreveport fans and writers covering the team. According to the *Houston Post* "the big hole in the Gasser line-up will be in left field, the berth left vacant by Al Simmons, the $50,000 beauty, now with the Philadelphia Athletics. It is this loss that the Gassers must strive to overcome and many doubt they can do it. Walter French is being asked to fill that berth and he faces a hard task."[12] Aside from the fact that both men hit with an unorthodox batting style they had very little in common. Simmons was a slugger who specialized in the long ball and driving in runs, while Walter's strength was his speed and his ability to reach base by simply putting the ball in play, stealing bases and scoring, rather than driving in, runs.

Managing the Shreveport club was former A's player and Connie Mack favorite, Ira Thomas. Like his mentor, Thomas not only managed the Gassers but he had an ownership interest in the team as well, so when they started the season with seven straight losses, he was not inclined to show much patience. By the end of April, Thomas was threatening wholesale changes to the team. If things didn't improve quickly, Thomas was planning on bringing up players from the lower minors and demoting some of the team's veteran players. The one exception was Walter French, whose play Thomas felt was getting better each game. By the end of the month of April and with their fortunes not improving many critics were echoing the sentiment expressed by the *Houston Post* writing "the Shreveport club, as it is at present constituted, is a hopeless tailender" adding that the team had a "trio of good outfielders and hitters in Walter French, Donaldson and Sullivan."[13]

In May, instead of the promised shakeup to the team, changes were made to the management. Ira Thomas stepped down as the on the field manager to become the team's president. He was replaced by the team's shortstop Billy Orr. Orr worked the team hard and did everything in his power to reverse the team's fortunes, but they continued to lose.

As happens when teams continue to lose, the players began to get on each other's nerves and disputes between players began to surface. One such incident in July involved Walter French.

In the fifth inning, in a game against the Fort Worth Panthers, with Jack Calvo on second and Art Phelen on first, Panther Ziggy Sears lined a sharp single into right field and assuming that Phelan would stop at third base, Walter threw the ball to second. Phelan did not stop at third base however and came around and scored. When Walter got back to the dugout after the inning ended, he was confronted by Gassers catcher Ray "Peaches" Graham who told Walter to "keep your head up." By his comment did Graham mean for Walter to not think twice about the play and that he would get them the next time or did he mean that Walter had made a poor decision in throwing to second instead of home? Whatever his meaning, Walter did not take the comment well.

He may have reacted differently if Graham had been a seasoned and proven professional ballplayer but he was a journeyman player at best, who had played 41 games over two seasons in the major leagues before joining the Gassers for the 1924 season. He had a lifetime batting average of .188. Words were passed between the two men and as some of their teammates tried to intervene Graham threw a punch at Walter and missed. He would not get a second chance. Walter threw one punch which landed flush on Graham's face and drove his head against a post in the dugout. A cut was opened over Graham's right eye that required stitches to close. Billy Orr, determining that Walter had been the aggressor in the dust up, suspended him indefinitely. However, given the fact that at this point in the season, Walter French was far and away the best player on the Gassers and near the top of the league in batting and base stealing, Orr, despite his displeasure, could not keep him out of the lineup for long and in a few days, he was back playing the outfield and hitting leadoff.

By August 24 Walter's batting average, at .361, was tops in the league and he was the leading base stealer as well. He had received word that he would be joining the Athletics for the last few weeks of the season as he had in 1923 but in his last game with the Gassers before joining the big-league team, he tore a ligament in his leg attempting to steal home. He had to be carried from the field and was forced to use crutches to get around. That would be the end of his baseball season.

Walter had put together another great minor league season in 1924 playing for Shreveport. It was the Gassers last year of existence in the Texas League. The team set a Texas League record for the most losses in one season, finishing with a record of 54 wins and 100 losses. Walter French was the one bright spot on an otherwise disastrous season finishing with 184 hits including 34 doubles and 11 triples.

With his 1924 baseball season over, Walter and Beth decided to move back to Moorestown and take up residence. They were confident that after two very successful minor league seasons that he would be on the Athletics in 1925. He finally had the opportunity to bring his bride home to Moorestown to meet his friends and family. His brothers teased Beth about her southern accent until finally their mother Belzora, reminding them that she too was from Alabama, told them to knock it off.

Although back in the late summer he expressed an interest in playing football once again for Wilkes-Barre in the fall of 1924, that plan had to be abandoned when he was injured at the end of the baseball season. He began looking for employment opportunities near to where he and Beth had settled in Moorestown. On September 3 it was announced that he had been hired by the Riverside Athletic Association, in Riverside New Jersey to be the head coach of the Riverside "Big Green" professional football team. Riverside played in a loosely organized league that was made up of teams from the Southern part of New Jersey. Towns such as Collingswood, Millville, Camden, and Atlantic City, in addition to Riverside, all had entries in the league. They also scheduled games against other professional teams from Pennsylvania, New York, and the northern part of New Jersey. The scheduled for Riverside, according to one newspaper was "no basket of plums" and included games against teams such as the Thomas Athletic Club of Bethlehem, PA and Stapleton, Long Island, New York and "the best teams that can be induced to come to Riverside."[14] A rough and tumble style was played by the teams in the league and the games were usually low scoring. The game between the Riverside and the Thomas A.C. played on October 19, 1924, resulted in a 3–0 win for the "Big Green" with most of the yards gained by the winning team coming as the result of penalties leveled against the Thomas team for unnecessary roughness. One newspaper covering the game reported that the Thomas tactics "were bordering on deliberate attempts to injure the opposing players."[15]

As the season progressed Walter French's team was struggling. Injuries had hit the team hard and he was at a loss as to how to make them improve. He was even thinking about inserting himself into the lineup even though he was still recovering from the leg injury he sustained playing for Shreveport. Such a move would have been very risky for him.

During this period he was also earning a few extra dollars by refereeing high school and college football games in South Jersey and the Philadelphia area. One day, while refereeing a game involving Moorestown High School, for whom his younger brother Cooper was the star, Walter collided with a player and felt some pain in his injured leg. Although it did not result in a setback in his recovery, the close call made him abandon any plans to play football for the remainder of 1924.

Unable to ever get above .500, the season for Riverside mercifully came to an end on Thanksgiving Day with a loss to Collingswood by a score of 23–6.

The Athletics would have a new spring training home in 1925. Although he had been generally happy in Montgomery, Mack was concerned about the lack of major league opponents in the area which made it difficult to schedule practice games. He began looking around for a new location. It was about this time that the business leaders in Fort Myers, located on the west coast of Florida, began looking for a way to elevate the community's profile. Connie Mack biographer Norman L. Macht wrote: "Led by energetic go-getter Richard Q. Richards, owner of the Royal Palm

Pharmacy, the Kiwanis Club set out to put Fort Myers on the tourist map. If they could entice a major league team to train there, the writers' dispatches would give them publicity to draw the sporting crowd."[16]

Richards visited Connie Mack in Philadelphia late in 1923 to make his case. Mack told him that he was bound to Montgomery for one additional season but in January of 1924 he paid an unannounced visit to Fort Myers. After spending a few days in Fort Myers, and happy with what he saw, Mack met with the Kiwanis board of directors. "Mack expressed his pleasure at everything he had seen and set out his terms: a suitable field and grandstand, a cash guarantee for exhibition games, railroad fare for away games. All gate receipts, ads, scorecards would be handled by the city. The Athletics would pay their own hotel expenses."[17] Connie Mack signed a contract which committed the A's to Fort Myers for the next 10 years and on February 22, 1925, Walter French, anxious to get back on the field, reported there for spring training, one week ahead of what was required of him.

As the sportswriters were submitting their annual "outlook" pieces for the 1925 season three teams were rated as the most likely to win the pennant by the prognosticators: the Washington Senators, having added depth to a pitching staff that was good enough in 1924 for them to win the World Series were considered the favorite, the New York Yankees, who also had strengthened their team from the previous season, and the Detroit Tigers who would benefit by having hard throwing pitcher Dutch Leonard as part of their rotation for the entire season. The Athletics were considered at best a "take a chance" bet in the American League.

Connie Mack, however, was more optimistic about his team's chances. The biggest move made by the Athletics during the offseason was the acquisition of a 28-year-old catcher by the name of Mickey Cochrane. The Bridgewater, MA native, and Boston University star was playing for Portland in the Pacific Coast League and had been on Connie Mack's radar for months. Cochrane, who was described as a "star performer in all departments" was both an outstanding hitter and defensive catcher. In exchange for Cochrane, Mack gave up five players and $50,000 in cash.

In addition to Cochrane, Connie Mack also purchased a hard throwing left-handed pitcher from the Baltimore Orioles, then a minor league team, by the name of Robert Moses Grove for $100,600. It was said that the extra $600 was to surpass the price the Yankees paid to the Red Sox for Babe Ruth. Although "Lefty" Grove would have an up and down season in 1925, like Cochrane, he would wind up in the baseball Hall of Fame and be considered one of the best pitchers of all time.

Although he left the door open to other trades and moves before the start of the season, Connie was confident that his team, with the additions of Cochrane and Grove was good enough to make a run at the American League pennant in 1925. Along with Lefty Grove, the pitching staff was anchored by lefthander Rube Walberg and righthander Eddie Rommel. On the infield he had three solid players returning in Max Bishop, Chip Galloway, and Jimmy Dykes. The regular outfielders looked to be Bill Lamar, Al Simmons, and Bing Miller, with Frank Welch, Bill Bagwell, and Walter French in reserve.

After the incident at the Moorestown High School football game, where he nearly re-injured his ailing leg, Walter took great care to "nurse" his injury with an eye toward being ready to compete for a spot on the A's major league roster. The *Philadelphia Inquirer* observed that he "is to be seriously considered. The former all-around athlete of West Point, with enough minor league schooling, is here to make the grade … he looks the well-balanced ball player, fast, clever fielder, and timely hitter." The *Inquirer* went on to compare him to future Hall of Famer Wee Willie Keeler, a comparison that Connie Mack would make from time to time as well. "He never knocked them a mile but he hit them 'where they ain't'. French may not be a Keeler but he has Willie's style somewhat, and he pleases Mack."[18]

The first action the players saw came on March 6 when an intrasquad game pitted the assumed first team against the second team, or the Yanigans as they were called. In the 1920s the term "Yanigans" was used throughout baseball to describe a team's second string and rookies. The exact origin of the term is a matter of conjecture but some baseball historians believe that the name was borrowed from a player by the name of Coy Yanigan, who played first base for teams in the Hartford, CT area in the 1890s. He was an outstanding player even though he played with an artificial leg.

The Athletic "Yanigans" on this day beat the "regulars" by a score of 7 to 6. Cochrane was the big star of the game delivering a clutch triple in the sixth inning. Walter French had one hit and scored one run. Although his team won, Lefty Grove gave up five runs and nine hits in his first action of the season.

The next day the Athletics played a team made up of college players and sponsored by a company known as the Everglades Construction Co. As expected, the A's easily won the game by a score of 36 to 0. The Athletics pounded out 31 hits, including a "flock of doubles and triples" but just one home run which was hit by Walter French.

A few days later the "Yanigans" and the "Regulars" squared off once more with the same result as the second team came away with an 8–2 win. In this game Walter had one hit, a double, in two official at-bats and scored one run. He was also singled out for his fine play in the field as he used his speed on three occasions to rob the first-string players of extra base hits. The *Philadelphia Inquirer* reported that "three times he snipped off varsity bids for base hits with the ease of a champion." Later adding that he had "speed and plenty of it."[19]

On March 30, the first wave of nine players who had made the big league roster arrived at Shibe Park, under the watchful eye of the former Shreveport Gassers manager Ira Thomas, now a coach with the Athletics. By the end of 1925's spring training, Walter had earned a spot on the big-league club and was one of the nine early arrivals. He was paid $3,000 for the season and was on the bench when the Athletics began their annual campaign for the American League pennant.

The Philadelphia Athletics, in 1925, were coming off another of a long line of rough seasons. The team finished the 1924 season with a record of 71–81 which landed them in fifth place some 20 games behind the pennant winning Washington Senators. To make matters worse it was their tenth consecutive losing season. The team's poor performance also placed them at the bottom of the league in terms of attendance as well.

In 1909, the Athletics, having outgrown Columbia Park, moved to a new facility named after the team's owner Ben Shibe. Shibe Park was the first baseball stadium built completely with concrete and steel and was considered the finest in all of baseball. Prior to the 1925 season alterations were made to Shibe Park. In his book *Lost Ballparks*, Lawrence Ritter wrote that the 1925 alterations gave "the stadium the basic appearance that would identify it for the rest of its days ... all singled-decked stands were double-decked and covered, so that the ballpark now consisted of roof double-decked grandstand enclosing the entire playing field except for right field. After the renovations of 1925, the park's dimensions shrank to 334 feet from home plate down the left field line, 468 feet to center field and 331 feet down the right-field line."[20]

The A's opened the 1925 season at home against the Boston Red Sox with a 9–8 victory. Walter was inserted into the game as a pinch hitter and singled in his only at bat. The A's won three of the four games with the Red Sox and split a two-game set with the Washington Senators. By the time he made his second plate appearance, again as a pinch hitter, on May 4, in a win over the New York Yankees, the A's were riding high with a record of 11–4. The team then went on a run that saw them win 10 of their next 11 games. Not wanting to mess with his team during a hot streak, Connie Mack stuck with his set lineup for the next two weeks. Finally on May 21 Walter pinch hit and scored a run in a blowout 20–4 win over the St. Louis Browns. At this point in the season the A's were 22–7 but only in first place by two games over the defending World Series champion Senators. A few days later Walter singled and scored a run in a loss to the Senators. On May 30, he was put into the game as a pinch runner and scored a run.

In the month of June, Walter was sent to the plate as a pinch hitter on eight occasions and he had three hits and came around and scored twice. He also appeared in five games as a pinch runner. One of those games, played on June 15th against the Cleveland Indians, he scored ahead of Al Simmons who had homered to bring the Athletics all the way back from a 15–4 deficit.

By the end of June, the American League pennant race was already down to two teams, the Athletics, and the Senators. The Chicago White Sox were sitting in third place 7.5 games behind the A's, who had dropped back to second after losing three of four games to the Senators. The rest of the American League was playing under .500 as the first half of the season ended on June 30.

It was on this day that Walter French would be introduced to the great Senator pitcher Walter Johnson, when he came to bat against the man Grantland Rice nicknamed "The Big Train."

Walter Johnson's plaque in the Baseball Hall of Fame reads: "Conceded to be the fastest ball pitcher in the history of the game. Won 414 games with a losing team behind him most years. Holder of strikeout and shutout records." His 414 victories is third all-time after Cy Young and Pud Galin and his career earned run average of 2.17 is twelfth all-time. His 3,509 career strikeouts was a record that stood for more than 50 years. Once, on Labor Day weekend in 1908, his second year in the big leagues, Johnson started and completed all three games against the Yankees on consecutive days, shutting them out each time giving up six, four, and two hits respectively. The great Ty Cobb once said about Johnson that his fastball "looked about the size of a watermelon seed and it hissed at you as it passed."

By 1925 Johnson was in his twentieth season with the Senators, but by no means over the hill. He finished the 1924 season with a record of 23–7, an earned run average of 2.72 and led his team to its first World Series title. By the time the 1925 season was complete he would post a record of 20–7 and an earned run average of 3.07.

Walter French came to bat against Johnson in the ninth inning as a pinch hitter. The Senators were winning the game by a score of 6–0. To that point in the game Johnson had only given up one hit. Johnson only had one no-hitter in his illustrious career. Earlier in the game the A's Chip Galloway, got what was initially deemed to be a hit but the official scorer later admitted that upon further reflection he was prepared to change it to an error. Walter French made the scorer's job easier for him when he lined a sharp grounder into the hole between shortstop and third base. Roger Peckinpaugh, the Senators' shortstop went hard to his right but could not make a play on the ball and it scooted into left field for a clean single.

Walter French would come to bat 20 more times against "The Big Train" before Johnson retired at the end of the 1927 season. Most American League hitters were happy to see Johnson retire, but as we shall learn, Walter French was not one of them.

Following the series with the Senators the A's went into a slump and lost six of their next nine games and in the process fell 3.5 games behind their chief rival. However, they followed that up by going 8–2 on a 10-game road trip. Throughout that period Walter French emerged as Connie Mack's most reliable pinch hitter. He had six hits and two sacrifices in 10 pinch hit appearances in the month of July and entered the month of August hitting an even .500. Nationally syndicated sportswriter Billy Evans observed "in the difficult job of pinch-hitting French had a batting streak from June 30 to July 25 that was decidedly out of the ordinary. In that period he was used ten times. He responded with six hits and two sacrifices … thus he delivered the way Connie Mack would have him, with six hits and two sacrifices as per instructions. Average .750."[21]

By August 8 the teams had each played 100 games of the season and still only 1.5 games separated the first place Athletics from the Senators. Still clinging to their slim lead on August 15, the bottom fell out of the A's season when they lost 17 of their next 19 games. Suddenly, after holding on to first place for all but a few days of the summer, they found themselves a full eight games out of first place behind the Senators. Throughout the remainder of August and the first half of September, Walter continued to be used exclusively in the role of a pinch hitter, and although he cooled off from his hottest period he was still coming through on a regular basis and was the league's leading pinch hitter, including two pinch hit plate appearances against Walter Johnson which resulted in a base on balls in a game on September 1 and a single in a game on September 7.

The month of August was special for Walter and his wife as Beth gave birth to their first daughter Mary Francis. To help celebrate, Walter's friends from Moorestown, in attendance at a game at Shibe Park on September 14 against the Yankees, made a presentation before the game. The *New York Times* reported that "New Jersey friends of Walter French, Athletic utility outfielder and one-time West Point football star, presented him with a baby carriage and a chest of silver before the game. The vehicle will be pressed into service at once as conveyance for Walter's month-old child."[22]

The A's fall from contention provided Walter with an opportunity to prove to Connie Mack what he could do if used on a regular basis and so on September 16 he was inserted into the starting lineup in the first game of a double header against the Chicago White Sox. He was playing right field and batting fifth in the lineup behind Al Simmons.

On the mound for the White Sox that day was Ted Lyons. Lyons was a tough right-handed pitcher who had a 21-year major league career, all with the White Sox. He won 20 games on three different occasions. Lyons had come up to the White Sox in 1923 and in his first full season in 1924 he went 12–11. He would finish the 1925 season with a record of 21–11 and an earned run average of 3.26. Walter responded to this opportunity by getting three hits in four at bats in a 4–1 win for the Athletics. Connie Mack kept the same lineup in the second game of the double header and Walter once again responded with one hit in four at bats.

Mack continued to start Walter in right field in every game for the remainder of the season and he hit safely in 14 of the final 16 games of 1925. On September 17 he went one for four with two runs batted in, the following day he went one for three and knocked in two more runs in the first game of a double header. In the second game he went one for three again and knocked in his fifth run in two days. On and on he went. It must have seemed to him like he was back at West Point. He went three for five on September 21 with a run batted in and two runs scored. In the final two games of the season against the Yankees, Walter French collected five hits in seven official at bats and drove in five runs.

The Athletics finished the season in second place in the American League with a record of 88–63 and eight games behind the pennant winning Washington Senators. Although he was disappointed in not winning the pennant, Connie Mack had to be pleased with the fact that even in such an up and down season the Philadelphia fans had come out and supported the team. The Athletics drew over 800,000 fans in 1925 which was tops in the American League.

For Walter French the 1925 season must have seemed like a turning point in his big-league career. His streak at the end of the season raised his batting average to .370 and he was statistically the best pinch hitter in the American League. He was also able to demonstrate to his manager that he could be a major contributor if inserted into the lineup as one of the team's regular outfielders.

Shortly after the season concluded, Billy Evans reported that "Connie Mack in summing up his plans for the coming season, has made a definite announcement that French is his choice for right field."[23]

Walter French in Spring Training with the Philadelphia Athletics. (*ACME Wire Photo*, March 12, 1928, courtesy of National Baseball Hall of Fame and Museum)

CHAPTER 6

The Pottsville Maroons and the Stolen NFL Championship of 1925

As the 1925 baseball season came to an end, Charlie Berry, who was a reserve catcher for the Athletics had signed on to play for the Pottsville Maroons in the fledgling National Football League. Berry had joined the Athletics in June of 1925 and had only played in 10 games over the remainder of the year. He had been a standout end at Lafayette College and was selected by Walter Camp as a first team All-American for the 1924 college football season. Like Walter French, Berry was a native of New Jersey.

There is no way to know for sure, who approached who, but at some point, Walter French had decided that he wanted to join Berry on the Maroons for their 1925 season. There was just one catch, unlike with the sparingly used Berry, the A's manager had just announced that French was going to be the Athletics starting right fielder in 1926. This was a completely different scenario from when he played football after his first minor league season in 1923. This would need to be cleared with Mr. Mack.

Connie Mack initially balked at the idea of allowing his emerging star outfielder to play in the National Football League. Mack had raised French's salary from $3,000 for the 1925 season to $5,000 for 1926 but Walter argued that the money he would make playing for the Maroons was desperately needed now that he was a father. In a 1939 interview with Frank Graham, Walter recalled the exchange with Mack. "I told him that I wanted to play football for Pottsville in the National Football League, he did not like the idea very much at first. Nowadays I don't suppose any baseball manager would let one of his players play football, even if he was just a kid who hadn't yet proved that he was a big leaguer. But I showed Connie where I could make some dough that I really needed now that I had a wife to support, and he gave in after a while."[1]

Pottsville, Pennsylvania is located in Schuylkill County and sits along the west bank of the Schuylkill River. Schuylkill County was home to large anthracite mining operations. Anthracite is also referred to as hard coal and is the highest ranking of coals. Although today anthracite is mined in a number of countries around the world, the first commercial mining in the United States was in Pennsylvania.

Working in the mines was the principal occupation of the people of Pottsville and the surrounding communities in the 1920s. The work was dangerous and backbreaking, and as if their jobs weren't hard enough, the men would play pick up football games when they had a few minutes to themselves. Eventually these games began to draw crowds from the residents of the area, who would come out to cheer for their town's team. Soon people began gambling on the games and eventually a semi-professional football league was formed in 1924. Because it was made up of teams from towns in the anthracite coal mining region the league was known as the Anthracite Association. The team from Pottsville, known as the Maroons, was far and away the best team in the League.

The Maroons' owner was a local surgeon named John G. "Doc" Striegel and after the team dominated the Anthracite league in 1924, going 12–1–1 and easily winning the league championship, he began to set his eyes on the National Football League. Striegel believed, and with good reason, that his team could compete with any of the teams in the NFL. The Maroons were led on the field by Tony Latone, who had been Walter French's teammate when they both played for the Gilberton Catamounts in 1923.

"I can get this team into the National Football League if the patrons so desire it,"[2] Striegel challenged the Maroons' supporters. The key in his quest was the game between the Maroons and the team from Atlantic City, which was being played in Atlantic City on November 9, 1924. If the Maroons' fans could show up in sufficient numbers in Atlantic City, the NFL would be hard pressed to deny a franchise to Pottsville. Striegel was "as confident with the prospect of thousands of his patrons showing their allegiance and admission ticket buying power as he was that the Maroons could win the game." So many fans from Pottsville wanted to attend the game that the "railroads were called on to aid the movement with three extra cars."[3]

The Maroons won the game easily, but the turnout, estimated to be nearly 5,000, was really the big story.

After Olympic legend Jim Thorpe served a short term as league president of the National Football League, the owners appointed Joe Carr, the owner of the Columbus Panhandles, to fill that position. Believing that it needed a set of rules, Carr created the league's first charter and by-laws and he saw to it that they were strictly enforced. In 1922, when the Green Bay Packers were caught using college players, which was a practice forbidden under Carr's rules, he kicked them out of the league. When Curly Lambeau took over the team, he was able to have them reinstated for the 1923 season, but Carr had made his point that teams needed to adhere to his rules, or they would be severely penalized. That was especially true for the small market teams. Carr knew that the future success of the league would depend on its acceptance in large metropolitan areas. The purpose of the small market teams, in his view, was to fill out the schedule, but in the long term he wanted to transition the league away from what he thought of as unsustainable small-town franchises.

Doc's guests on the sideline of the game with Atlantic City were the Stein brothers, Russ and Herb. As with Tony Latone, the Stein brothers had played with Walter French in 1923 on the Frankford Yellow Jackets, Philadelphia's NFL team and they were also on the team in 1924. The Stein brothers were the foundation of the Yellow Jackets' offensive and defensive lines.

Shortly after the game in Atlantic City, Striegel visited the Stein brothers and offered them a contract for the upcoming season. Shep Royle, who was the owner of the Yellow Jackets, was waiting until closer to the opening of the season to offer the Steins a contract for 1925, as was customary in the early days of the NFL. However, Doc's quick action and generous offers convinced the brothers, two of Frankford's best players, to jump to the Maroons.

A short while after landing the Stein brothers, Doc Striegel attended a game at the University of Pennsylvania, which was his alma mater, to scout some players for his team. It was at this game that he saw Charlie Berry for the first time along with quarterback Jack Ernst both of whom were playing for Lafayette. Within a short period of time Berry and the strong-armed Ernst were both signed to the Maroons.

The turnout at the game in Atlantic City along with Joe Carr's belief that the Maroons would be crushed by any NFL team and put an end to any challenge to his league's dominance, opened the door to the Maroons' admittance into the National Football League. Doc Striegel met with Carr and the other owners and paid his $500 for the franchise fee along with a guarantee of $1,200 and they were in.

To coach the Maroons in their inaugural season Doc Striegel selected Harrisburg, PA native Dick Rauch. After graduating from high school in 1910 Rauch went to work in the steel mills near his home for six years. In 1916, he entered Bethlehem Preparatory School and was eventually accepted into Penn State. After playing football on the Freshman team at the school he made the varsity squad in 1917. His college career was interrupted by World War I as Rauch entered the Army, returning in 1919. As his time at Penn State progressed, he became a favorite of the school's legendary coach Hugo Bezdek and when he graduated in 1921, he was given a job as assistant coach. In 1923, he moved on to be the offensive line coach at Colgate.

To say that Dick Rauch was an interesting character would be a major understatement. Besides being a football coach, Rauch was a serious ornithologist and traveled all over North America studying the habits of all species of birds and in his spare time he also wrote poetry.

Clarence Beck, who was the player coach of the Maroons in their last year in the Anthracite league, recommended Rauch to Doc Striegel. Making Rauch an offer would have to wait until he returned from a bird watching expedition in the late summer of 1925 but when they finally were able to meet, Doc made Dick a very attractive offer which he accepted with certain conditions. "The team would practice regularly. Not only would players be expected to live in Pottsville but they would become active members of the community. Rauch knew that the players had their work cut out for them." It turned out that Doc was on the same page as his new coach and agreed with all of the conditions.[4] Doc and Dick also shared a vision for the approach the Maroons would take in terms of the type of game plan they wanted to institute. Both men were keen on installing a style of play more in keeping with that being played at the collegiate level which was considered vastly superior to the professional game.

With the team's core players in place, Doc proceeded to extend himself financially to put together a roster that would challenge the best that the NFL had to offer. To add to the line, he signed former All-Big Ten lineman from the University of Indiana Russ Hathaway, added end Frank Bucher from Detroit-Mercy and the fleet-footed Hoot Flanagan who had played for Pop Warner at the University of Pittsburgh. He also added Penn State fullback Barney Wentz and former coal miner and semi-pro legend Frank Racis who could play any number of positions on the line. Walter French and Charlie Berry would have to wait until the baseball season was over before joining the Maroons.

The Maroons' home field, Minersville Park, was a converted High School Stadium with a capacity of 5,000 which was small for an NFL team even in 1925. Minersville Park was the site of the Maroons' first NFL game against the Buffalo Bisons, on September 27. The Bisons were the worst team in the league at that time. They would finish with a 1–6–2 record and only score three touchdowns all season. The Maroons made short work of the Bisons coming away with an easy 28–0 victory.

Next on the schedule was another home game against the Providence Steam Roller. The first of two games between the teams in the next three weeks. The *Pottsville Republican* reported however that the Maroons were "slightly crippled" coming into the game. "Hoot Flanagan and Harry Dayoff will be lost to the backfield." Flanagan was reported to have an "infection in his arm," and Dayoff "pulled a tendon." The newspaper also reported that "French and Berry were not at practice" which should not have been a surprise because on the day before the Providence game, Walter French was batting in the fifth spot in the Philadelphia A's lineup and getting two hits in three at bats with three RBI.[5]

The weather in Pottsville on the day of the game was terrible with heavy rains pouring down throughout the game. Neither team could mount much of a sustained offense, but the Maroons were clearly getting the best of Providence. They would finish the game with 15–0 advantage in first downs. However, after a scoreless first half, with the Maroons deep in their own territory, substitute center Denny Hughes snapped the ball before the backfield players were set and the loose ball went bounding toward the end zone. Providence player Red Maloney scooped up the ball and ran a few yards into the Maroons' end zone for the game's only score. The Maroons attempted a comeback but frustratingly kept turning the ball over to Providence. As good as the Maroons were, the loss to Providence revealed a weakness in the way the team was constituted. On offense they were too one dimensional and overly reliant on the running of players like Tony Latone, but help was on the way in the persons of Charlie Berry and Walter French. They would give Coach Rauch the opportunity to run the wide open, collegiate style of play he so desired.

Four days after the loss to Providence, a headline in the *Pottsville Republican* predicted "Walter French to Get Going." The article went on to explain that "Fans will more than likely get a slant at Walter French, the former Army star, now with the Pottsville Maroons when the Canton Club lines up against the locals in the next game. French has been drilling with the first squad the past few days and has mastered the signals. Coach Dick Rauch is working him in at a regular halfback job and it is thought that Rauch intends on showing him to the public in the next game."[6]

The Canton Bulldogs came into the game with a record of 2–1. They sustained their first loss of the season at the hands of the Frankford Yellow Jackets, the day before the game with the Maroons. After a scoreless first quarter, Hoot Flanagan, just off the injured list, ran for a five-yard touchdown and Charlie Berry, in his first game of the season, kicked his first of four extra points to give the Maroons a 7–0 lead at halftime. In the third quarter Berry blocked a punt and scooped up the ball and ran it in for a touchdown which with the kick gave the Maroons a 14–0 lead. Later in the third quarter Flanagan ran in his second touchdown of the day and with Berry's kick the Maroons extended their lead to 21–0. Tony Latone finished off the scoring with a one-yard plunge into the end zone in the fourth quarter.

The Maroons' fans were encouraged by the improved play of their team. While Berry played the entire game and was one of the Maroons' heroes, Walter French did not get into the game until the fourth quarter. The Republican explained that "Berry was in the entire game at left end and the former Lafayette star looked mighty good. He has made the grade and will be a permanent fixture on the Maroons." The newspaper's review of the play of Walter was positive as well. "The former West Pointer showed some of his old-time speed when he replaced Wentz in the fourth quarter. He got off one fine end-run displaying to the spectators that he still possesses a lot of speed and cunning that made him famous in college football."[7]

Next on the Maroons' schedule was a rematch with the Providence Steam Roller on October 18 in Providence. In the lead up to the game the Republican assured the Pottsville fans "That the squabble over the club's finances has not affected the morale of the club was evident by the final practice. The boys went through the daily workout with just as much pep and vigor as they did on the eve of many a college in the past."[8]

The newspaper also reported that Coach Rauch had "perfected a fast interference for Walter French and it is believed that he will be used in a greater part of the Providence game than any to date" and adding that "the Maroons' plan of attack will be changed so as to compel the Steam Rollers to change their defense."[9] There would be no repeat of the first game against Providence.

The Maroons left Pottsville on Saturday, October 17, taking the Reading Railroad to New York City. From New York they traveled by boat to Providence, RI. Every member of the 16-man Maroons' squad was healthy and ready for action.

By combining their normal powerful straight ahead running attack with some passing and end runs the Maroons completely overwhelmed the Providence team and exacting what the Republican referred to as "sweet revenge" in the process. The 10,000 fans, including a contingent of Maroons' fans, that packed the Providence Cycledrome witnessed a game that bore no resemblance to the first meeting between the two teams. The *Republican* reported that "from the beginning to end it was a series of gains by Latone, Wentz, and Flanagan, with touchdowns the ultimate result in nearly every case."[10] The Maroons scored three touchdowns in the fourth quarter alone. "French" the *Republican* reported "substituting for Flanagan carried off long distance running honors when he got away in the fourth quarter for a dash of 34 yards. On this play French followed his interference as far as the line of scrimmage then swung across and completed the remainder of his journey unaccompanied and, incidentally, was not tossed until Ogden halted him near the Rollers citadel."[11] The game ended in a 34–0 victory for the Maroons.

At 5'7" and 155 pounds, Walter French was by far the smallest of the Pottsville Maroons. His secret to success in sports throughout his life was his quickness and speed, which he had in abundance. Beginning with his time at Moorestown High School his brilliant speed was his calling card. Ironically, he was not even the fastest runner at Moorestown. His teammate on the school's track team was future Olympic Gold Medal winning sprinter Alfred LeConey. LeConey, like three of the Pottsville Maroons (Berry, Millman, and Ernst) was a star athlete at Lafayette College. In 1922 LeConey won the AAU Championship in the 220-yard race and was known as the "Fastest Man in the East." At the 1924 Summer Olympics in Paris he ran the anchor leg in the 4x100 meter relay which won the gold medal in a world record time of 41.0 seconds. Movie buffs will remember that the 1924 Olympics were featured in the Academy Award-winning film *Chariots of Fire*. Finishing second to LeConey in the relay race was Harold Abrahams, one of the athletes featured in the movie.

Due to his small physical stature, the local sportswriters began referring to French as "Little Walter" and if he ever formally objected to the moniker no record of it exists. At Army he was often referred to as "Fritz," a nickname he used when signing autographs, which he preferred. However, to judge his physical abilities by simply comparing his height and weight to that of his teammates is to ignore the fact that he was built as sturdy as they come. Pictures of him in his playing days reveal someone without as much as one ounce of body fat. He possessed big muscular arms, shoulders, and legs. In a picture of him taken in his Army football uniform one notices that he had hands that were as big as those of someone twice his size but like it or not "Little Walter" would be his nickname on the Maroons.

The next opponent for the Maroons would be a home game against the Columbus Tigers from Columbus, Ohio on November 1. It would be one of two games that Walter found himself in the starting lineup. On the opening play of the game, he took the kickoff back 25 yards. After Berry caught a pass and Latone and Wentz smashed through the Columbus line for nice gains, Walter broke free on a 15-yard run to the Columbus 30-yard-line. There the Maroons drive stalled. Columbus was unable to move the ball against the Maroons' defense and was forced to punt. A slew of Maroons blocked the punt, and the ball traveled a number of yards in the air and eventually Barney Wentz grabbed it and raced with it to the Columbus one-yard-line. The Republican described what happened next: "Little Walter showed his real stuff to the fans next. Something happened. What it was is not exactly known. It looked as if somebody got the signals balled up and when Denny snapped the ball there was nobody there to get it. This happened in the Providence game and Maloney scored on it but not this time."[12] As the ball rolled back to the 20-yard-line Walter bolted back like he had been shot out of a gun, scooped up the ball and began to run to the far side of the field he then cut back and reversed direction, dodging would-be Tiger tacklers until he had the ball back at the Columbus one yard line. It was about as pretty a run as the fans had seen to that point of the season and when it was over Walter again had the ball in position to score. And score they did. On the next play Tony Latone plowed his way into the end zone. Charlie Berry kicked the extra point and the Maroons took a 7–0 lead. After reeling off several long runs in the remainder of the first and second quarter, Walter brought the Maroons' fans to their feet one more time. As the third quarter was winding down, he took a handoff and sped around the right end, following his blockers and eluding tacklers, he sped down the sideline for a 30-yard-touchdown to close out the scoring and give the Maroons a 20–0 victory.

Walter's performance had electrified the Maroons' fans, who, as was customary, had bet heavily on their team. One former player recalled that "after games the miners would be pushing ones and fives at you-passing you a cut of the money they had just won betting on the Maroons." He recalled that "following the Columbus victory on November 1, by the time Walter French made it back to the Maroons, he looked like a scarecrow stuffed with greenbacks."[13]

It is hard to imagine a fan base more rabid than that of the Maroons. The importance of the team to Pottsville was amplified in 1925 by a coal miners' strike, the third in a five-year period, that devastated the region's economy. The miners, represented by the United Mine Workers of America, were seeking an increase in wages and maintenance of the "checkoff system," which increase the power of the union by allowing for closed shops.

As the showdown with their rivals the Frankford Yellow Jackets approached, *The Morning Call*, an Allentown, PA based newspaper wrote that "there may be a coal strike and many anxious faces in the anthracite region around here, but one silver lining in the clouds is the powerful Pottsville Maroons, the classiest collection of football players that has ever represented this section. The one topic of conversation in Pottsville and the surrounding towns this week is 'Will the Maroons beat the Frankford Yellow Jackets on Saturday.'"[14]

After easily defeating the Akron Pros on November 8 by a score of 21–0, the team had finished a four-game stretch in which they did not allow a single point to be scored against them and speculation was that the game against Frankford would go a long way to determining the NFL championship. It was anticipated that over 1,000 of the Pottsville faithful would make the trip to Philadelphia along with a 40-piece band to "back up the prowess of Charlie Berry, Walter French, Jack Ernst, et al. against the powerful Yellow Jackets of Philadelphia." The fans were optimistic because the same Akron team that the Maroons shutout "with French and other stars on the sideline" made a much better game of it against Frankford losing 17–7.[15]

"Walter French, outfielder from the Athletics, and Charlie Berry, the Mack men's rookie catcher, obtained permission to play football this fall" the *Morning Call* reminded its readers, adding that "French received his football training at Moorestown High, Rutgers, and West Point while Berry was an All-American at Lafayette."[16]

After his performance against Columbus, Walter assumed a much higher profile with the sportswriters and the fans. Interviewed for the *Morning Call*, Walter spoke for the entire Maroons' team. "We just have to win for this town" he told the newspaper, "They've backed us to the limit in spite of business troubles and the people have enough civic pride to lay their last dollar on us to win. It will take a better team than ours to beat us. We have a great line with two stars in Hathaway, late of Indiana, and Russ Stein of Pitt, and our backfield featuring Barney Wentz, Latone and Ernst isn't so bad. Charlie Berry, of course, is the best end in professional football. It's going to be a great game and everyone can rest assured the Maroons will do their best … we can do no more. We are not overconfident or boastful. We figure we are in for a hard game."[17]

It is not surprising that Frankford and Pottsville were bitter rivals. Frankford was a small independent borough until it was annexed by Philadelphia in 1854. The team's owner Shep Royle and their fans all looked down their noses at Pottsville as being a mere coal town, while the Pottsville faithful considered the Yellow Jackets and their fans to be snobs. Adding to the natural dislike the two teams had for one another, was the small matter of Doc Striegel signing the Stein brothers away from Frankford at the beginning of the season, a move that the Jackets' owner Shep Royle would never forgive or forget.

The Maroons came into the game with a 5–1 record and having only allowed six points to be scored against them to that point in the season. The Yellow Jackets, on the other hand, had played almost twice as many games and stood at 9–2, and on this day that experience won out. The Maroons took the opening kickoff and began to march the ball 79 yards downfield and all seemed to be right in the world.

However, rather than punching the ball into the end zone, they were stopped when Tony Latone dropped a pass on fourth down. Things for the Maroons went downhill from there. The *Philadelphia Inquirer* summed up the contest writing "Fans saw a Pottsville team completely swept from the field, wilt, and fall before the onslaught of captain Russ Behman's eleven. They saw a relentless Hornet, carry on in such a marvelous fashion that Pottsville never loomed as a winner and in only three instances during the entire fuss even threatened to score."[18] So the Maroons limped back to Pottsville, victims of a 20–0 drubbing, while their bitter rivals had put themselves in a perfect position to make a run at the NFL title.

Any dwelling on the loss to Frankford or time spent licking wounds, would have to wait. The Maroons still had a chance at the title. They had five games remaining to be played in the season starting with one against the Rochester Jeffersons the very next day.

Although the remaining games on the Maroons' schedule included a rematch with Frankford, the Maroons could not look past Rochester given that the Jeffersons had not played in four days and would undoubtedly be fresher than the Maroons. "Walter French ran back a punt for forty yards" and then "broke loose again for fifteen yards"[19] setting up the Maroons' first touchdown by Latone. With the Maroons clinging to a 7–6 lead in the third quarter Ernst and Berry connected on a series of pass plays which took the Maroons the length of the field and into the end zone and with Berry second extra point kick of the game, they took a 14–6 lead. From there they hung tough in the fourth quarter and despite a furious comeback attempt by Rochester, kept them out of the end zone.

In 1925, there were no playoffs in professional football. Post-regular season playoff games would not be introduced to the NFL until 1933. The team with the best regular season record when all the official games were completed would be declared the champions. Prior to 1925 November 30 was the cutoff for games to be completed to count as the "regular season," but at the league meetings at the start of the 1925 season it was moved back to December 20. And so, when word reached Pottsville, as they were preparing to play the defending NFL champions, the Cleveland Bulldogs, that Frankford had lost both games they played over the weekend, the Maroons understood that their fate was back in their own hands. They were now in essentially a five-way tie at the top of the standings with Frankford, the Detroit Panthers, the New York Giants, and the Chicago Cardinals.

With a full week's rest, the game against Cleveland on November 22 was much more of what the Pottsville fans had come to expect from the team. Jack Ernst ran a punt back 55 yards for the games first score. Tony Latone intercepted a pass and ran it back 45 yards for the Maroons' second touchdown. Charlie Berry kicked a 29-yard field goal to move the score to 17–0 and then Walter French scored his second touchdown of the season going around the end for 12 yards to ice the game.

The win over Cleveland left only one more hurdle before the rematch with Frankford and that was a home game against the Green Bay Packers on Thanksgiving Day. The Packers were founded in 1919 by Curly Lambeau, who was still serving as player-coach for the team. For Walter French going up against Curly Lambeau now meant that he had gone head-to-head with two of the NFL's founding fathers, after having played against George Halas, founder of the Chicago Bears, while playing for Rutgers in 1918.

In the game against the Packers, the Maroons' captain Charlie Berry put on a football clinic. The Maroons scored 24 points in the first half of the game and Berry was responsible for all of them. He caught two touchdown passes for a total of 47 yards, scooped up a blocked punt and ran it in for his third touchdown, converted all three of his extra-point kicks and then topped it off with a 28-yard field goal. The final score was 31–0 and the victory marked the sixth time in the season that the Maroons had not allowed an opponent to score a single point. The stage was set for the rematch with Frankford three days later on November 29.

"The Frankford rematch was shaping up to be the biggest sporting event in Pottsville history," wrote Dave Fleming, adding "The Hotel Allen was filled to capacity with sportswriters from all over the East Coast and VIPs like Curly Lambeau and Tim Mara, the owner of the New York Giants. The Reading Railroad company had to add 11 extra cars to a train from Philadelphia. Football fans came from as far west as Cleveland, as far north as Rochester, east from Boston, and south from Washington, D.C." As game time was approaching "more than 11,000 fans had assembled in and around Minersville Park."[20]

As if things were not tense enough Coach Rauch, as part of his pregame speech confirmed that a game was being planned to be played by the eventual NFL champs against the members of the 1924 Notre Dame legendary Four Horsemen team. The 1924 Notre Dame team had turned in an undefeated season, won the national championship and were considered by the experts, and fans alike, to be simply the best football team ever assembled. It is hard to imagine today, but in the early 1920s there was no debate about the fact that, in football, the college game reigned supreme. That was especially true of the 1924 "Four Horsemen" team.

However, it is not difficult to imagine what was going through the minds of the Maroons upon hearing this news. Some may have thought of the glory that a victory in such a game would bring, some may have thought "let's just get through today's game please," but all of them would have no doubt been thinking about the payday that would be in store.

Right from the opening kickoff the Maroons' fans knew this game was going to be a very different affair from the first game between the two teams. Hoot Flanagan returned the opening kickoff 30 yards to the Maroons' 40-yard-line. This was followed up by a few pass completions from Ernst to Berry, and some tough running by Tony Latone who finished the drive with a one-yard touchdown run.

With the Maroons' line dominating the line of scrimmage they quickly moved the ball deep into Yellow Jacket territory before the drive stalled. Much to the chagrin of the fans, Coach Rauch opted to go for a field goal and Berry converted.

The next time the Maroons got the ball, Latone took a handoff and crashed into a host of Frankford defenders. When he emerged from the bottom of the pile of tacklers, he was clutching his elbow and needed to be helped to the sideline. The team's star had been silenced and so were the fans, all fearing the worst.

The Yellow Jackets, sensing an opportunity to turn the tide of the first half began to methodically move the ball down field. Deep in Maroons' territory Ralph Homan dropped back to pass and at that moment Hoot Flanagan noticed Bob Fitzke of the Jackets sneaking out of the backfield and running a pass pattern. Flanagan jumped in front of Fitzke just as the ball was arriving and not only intercepted the pass but also ran it back 90 yards for a Maroons touchdown to give them a 16–0 lead at half-time.

In the locker room at half-time, Doc Striegel examined Tony Latone's injured elbow and determined that, at best, he would be lost to the team for the remainder of this game. Coach Rauch, adjusting for the loss of his star player, called on Jack Ernst and the passing game, which included a bigger role for Walter French and Charlie Berry, to hold off the Yellow Jackets, and hold them off they did. Ernst, "as cool as a cake of ice in the Polar Sea"[21] according to the Republican, proceeded to complete his first seven passes bringing the ball to the Yellow Jackets' one-yard-line before the team from Philadelphia ever knew what hit them. From there Latone's replacement at fullback, Barney Wentz, took the ball in for a touchdown. The Maroons now had a three-possession lead and the Yellow Jackets went to the passing game in an attempt to close the gap. This was to no avail as Hoot Flanagan once again intercepted a pass and this time ran it back 45 yards for a touchdown. Walter French made his presence felt in the fourth quarter. First, he caught a pass from Ernst and took it 30 yards for another Maroons touchdown. A few minutes later he caught another pass and this time raced 45 yards for the touchdown that closed out the Yellow Jackets. The Maroons had their revenge, coming away with a dominating 49–0 victory over their bitter rivals. "Against teams like Canton, Cleveland and Green Bay the Maroons followed the canon of good sportsmanship and eased up late in the game. But this was Frankford, and Shep Royle had it coming."[22]

After the Frankford game the Maroons fully expected that their next game would be against Notre Dame on December 12 in Philadelphia. The morning after the Yellow Jackets game the prognosis on Tony Latone's injury had improved and Doc Striegel was confident that with a week off that he would be ready for the game against Notre Dame. All seemed well with the world, however, here is where the story of the Maroons and the 1925 football season, takes a twist.

On November 26, Thanksgiving Day, while the Pottsville Maroons were handing the Packers a 31–0 defeat, Harold "Red" Grange, a three-time consensus All-American halfback at the University of Illinois turned professional signing a contract with the Chicago Bears. Nicknamed the "Galloping Ghost," it would not be an exaggeration to state that Grange was to football in the 1920s what Babe Ruth was to baseball. His first game, on Thanksgiving Day, was against the Chicago Cardinals at Wrigley Field. Over 36,000, the largest crowd to ever attend a professional football game were on hand to see him play but had to have been disappointed when the game ended in a scoreless tie. The tie left the Cardinals with a 9–1–1 record, and a one-half game lead over the Maroons in the standings.

Three days later, on November 29, while the Maroons were handing Frankford their beating, 20,000 people showed up to watch Grange and the Bears play the Columbus Tigers. Coming into the game the Bears had a record of 6–2–3 and had lost badly to the Cardinals the week before Grange joined the team. It was clear that George Halas and the Bears had struck gold with the signing of Grange, much to the chagrin of his crosstown rival Chris O'Brien, owner of the Cardinals.

Under the rules put in place before the 1925 season, teams could schedule games with each other even if they were not on the schedule at the start of the season, and as long as they were not played after December 20, they would count in the league standings. So it was, that O'Brien, looking to cash in on the fact that Grange and the Bears were departing from Chicago for a seven game, two-week road trip, reached out to Doc Striegel with a proposal O'Brien felt could draw a crowd like those turning out to watch Grange. O'Brien suggested that a game be played between the Cardinals and the Maroons on the following Sunday at Comiskey Park in Chicago. Doc, sensing an opportunity to win the league title on the field, accepted despite the disadvantage the logistics presented, and despite the fact that his team would be without Tony Latone, whose injury Doc knew would need another week to heal. They also faced the added pressure from the fact that "if they were to lose to Chicago, there was no guarantee Frank Schumann, the promoter of the Notre Dame game, wouldn't dump them in favor of the Frankford Yellow Jackets for the World Championship. Because of that scenario, many in Zacko's crew were convinced that the whole idea of a Cardinals–Maroons NFL title game had been brokered behind the scenes by none other than the nefarious Shep Royle."[23] None of that mattered to Doc. He accepted the challenge and "was about to call the league's bluff one more time, push his chips into the center of the table, and ask his team to do the impossible all over again."[24]

In the lead up to the game, newspapers in both Illinois and Pennsylvania billed the game as the league championship. Victory for the Cardinals, according to the *Chicago Tribune* "would clarify any dispute as to the championship. Pottsville claims the championship of the Eastern Division of the league. The Cardinals rule the Western end."[25]

The International News Service also weighed in on the significance of the two teams meeting writing "The national professional football title will be at stake when the Pottsville eleven, winners of the East Division of the National Professional Football League, and the Chicago Cardinals, winners of the Western Section, meet in the White Sox Park here tomorrow."[26]

On the morning of the game the *Chicago Tribune* reiterated this point "The National Professional Football League championship hangs in the balance today when the Chicago Cardinals and the Pottsville, PA eleven clash on the gridiron at Comiskey Park. A victory for either team carries the national title, for the Cardinals have swept over all opponents in the western half of the league while the Pottsville eleven holds the eastern crown."[27]

The Maroons boarded a train for Chicago on the morning of December 5 and as they approached Chicago, they ran into a major snowstorm that had hit the region and by game time the field was covered with snow and ice.

Only about 100 Maroons fans made the trip to Chicago and the rest of the faithful made their way to Pottsville's Hippodrome Theater where they were able to hear a rudimentary "play by play" of the game. A direct wire was installed from the playing field to the stage at the theater and, for a fee of 50 cents, fans could learn about the game within seconds. The telegrams from Comiskey Field consisted of game updates tapped out in Morse Code and read out to those in attendance.

Coach Rauch, in preparing for the game with the Cardinals, focused his defense on stopping their star player, halfback, John "Paddy" Driscoll. Driscoll had been one of the stars of the Great Lakes Naval Station team that had trounced French's Rutgers team back in 1918. He assigned the task to the Stein brothers, who were to shadow Driscoll almost to the exclusion of any other members of the Cardinals offense. If someone on the Chicago team was going to beat the Maroons on this day, it was not going to be Paddy. On the offensive side of the ball, Rauch was counting on the fact that the severity of Tony Latone's injury was unknown to the Cardinals and that their game plan would focus on stopping the straight ahead, smash mouth type of play that made the "Human Howitzer" the star he was in the league. Which is exactly what they did. The fact was that if Latone got in the game at all, it would only be as a decoy and with Latone out for the game, the running duties would be shared between Walter French and Hoot Flanagan.

Over 10,000 fans, despite the cold and snow, jammed Comiskey Field, including baseball commissioner Kennesaw Mountain Landis, who made a special point of wishing good luck to Walter French and Charlie Berry.

On the first series of the game Hoot Flanagan ran a reverse around the right but as he struggled to maintain his balance on the icy field, he fumbled the ball and it was recovered by the Cardinals at the Maroons' 40-yard-line. On the next play Driscoll drifted out of the Cardinals' backfield and caught a pass which brought the ball to the Pottsville 12-yard-line, however from there the Maroons' defense stiffened and the Cardinals' drive stalled. The rest of the first quarter played out the same way and ended in a scoreless tie. In the second quarter Jack Ernst fielded a punt and following his interference beautifully and breaking tackles he took the ball all the way to the Cardinals' five-yard-line. A few plays later, on third down, Barney Wentz took the ball the rest of the way for the game's first score. Berry kicked the extra point and the Maroons took the lead 7–0.

Back at the Hippodrome in Pottsville, the crowd was ecstatic with the news of the touchdown, however they would be brought back to earth when the news came across the wire that Hoot Flanagan was being helped from the field. Blocking for Wentz, Hoot had gone down hard on the frozen field and had broken his collarbone. Suddenly Walter French was thrust into the role of the featured running back.

When Walter entered the game in place of Flanagan the *Chicago Tribune* described what happened next: "Flanagan of the Pennsylvania team was taken off the field with a broken collarbone and the stage was set for the entry of Mr. French, the fast-running Army boy. French immediately got into action. He took the leather and raced downfield 30 yards before he skidded and was downed. A couple of line plays followed and then Mr. French got his second wind and took the ball again on another romp around the Cardinals' right end for 30 more yards and a touchdown. Three Cardinals tackled French in the course of his run, but he shook them all off. Berry again kicked the goal."[28] Down 14–0 the Cardinals tried to grab some momentum through the passing game with some success, eventually scoring a touchdown to cut the Maroons' lead to 14–7. "That ended the action except for a flash in the final period when Pottsville staged another big drive up the field with French tearing and ripping his way through the line and around the ends, and then Wentz dove off tackle for three yards and the final touchdown."[29]

For the Cardinals' right end, Eddie Anderson, Walter French's performance must have seemed like déjà vu. It was the same Eddie Anderson who, while playing end for Notre Dame in 1920, had incurred the wrath of Knute Rockne after Walter repeatedly beat him to the corner on his end runs.

The newspaper stories written after the game focused on two themes. The first was that the win by the Maroons constituted the league championship. The *Chicago Tribune* headline read "Pottsville Wins Over Cards and Takes Pro Title, 21–7." The sports section in the Philadelphia Evening Bulletin led with "National Title: Downs Chicago Cardinals 21–7, in East–West Play-Off of National Football League." The *Philadelphia Inquirer* headline read: "Maroons Conquer Cards, Take Crown." The *Evening Herald* in Pottsville shouted: "Maroons Are Now Hailed As the Champions."

The second theme, in the coverage of the game, was that its star was Walter French. The headline in the *Philadelphia Record* read: "French Scores TD, Runs Wild For Miners in Rout of Chicago, 21–7. Pottsville Player, who cavorts in the outfield for Athletics during the summer, hero in winning of National Crown." The *Chicago Tribune* summed up Walter's performance this way: "The whole show was centered around a slippery, cagey fellow named French, who gained quite a reputation as a back with the West Point eleven a few years ago … It was French more than anyone else on the Pottsville team who wrecked the Chicago title hopes. He bobbed up in play after play and the yardage he gained would make Red Grange sit up and check back in his notebook."[30] The *Philadelphia Inquirer* added: "the ex-Army gridder bucked the line. He hurled passes. He caught passes. He ran the ends. He punted. In each of these departments he showed so much skill that even the work of the brilliant Paddy Driscoll was overshadowed."[31]

Despite the lopsided score however, the Cardinals gave as good as they got physically during the contest. A number of the Maroons emerged from the game with injuries. In addition to Flanagan's season ending broken collarbone the Republican reported that "French's nose is not broken as was first feared, but he suffered a slight concussion of the brain from which he is expected to recover in a few days. Beck has an injured hand which may prove to be a fracture. Hathaway also has an injured hand and a black eye."[32]

For Walter this marked the second, documented time that he had sustained a concussion playing football. Although it did not appear to be as serious as the one in 1919, he did decide to remain in Chicago for a few days after the game to, as the newspapers reported, "spend a few days with relatives."[33] Conveniently one of the "relatives" was Beth's cousin Martha Dent who was a nurse.

The good news was that Latone's injured elbow was protected in the matchup with Chicago and the prognosis was that he would be ready to go in the upcoming game against what was officially being called the Notre Dame All Stars.

As the Maroons were making their preparations to play the game against the Notre Dame All Stars, Doc Striegel received a call from his nemesis Shep Royle. If Doc thought that the 49–0 drubbing the Maroons gave Royle's Yellow Jackets was the last he would hear from him for the season, he had another thing coming. Royle was calling to alert Doc to the fact that he was planning on filing an official protest with the league, objecting to the fact that the game against the Notre Dame All-Stars was being played in Philadelphia, at Shibe Park, and that Philadelphia was the "protected territory" of his team. He went on to say that he had already communicated with the league and that he was assured via telegrams, that his protest would be upheld.

Doc was furious. The game with Notre Dame had been agreed to prior to the game with Frankford back in November and it was anticipated that the game would draw a huge crowd and be a big financial win for all involved. He made two arguments to the league when he contacted them the day after Royle's call. First, was why this concept of a protected territory was suddenly being enforced. Chicago, he pointed out, had two teams in the same city. He also maintained that he had gotten a green light to play the game in Philadelphia during a phone call with Columbus Tigers' owner Jerry Corcoran, who was filling in for the league president while Carr was in the hospital having his appendix removed. In the end Corcoran denied ever having the conversation with Striegel, and as Royle had predicted, Carr notified the Maroons that if they went ahead with the Notre Dame game that they would be suspended from the NFL.

Doc was locked into the game with Notre Dame and Carr had to know that it would be impossible for him to pull the Maroons out of the game. Doc had to think too, that maybe when push came to shove, if the Maroons could win this game and in doing so call into question the conventional wisdom among football fans, that the college game was real football and that the professional game could not hold a candle to it, that maybe Carr would see what their effort had done for his league and go easy on them. In any event, the game would go on.

While tickets for the Notre Dame game sold briskly in Pottsville, the overall crowd on hand for the game was under 10,000, which was less than expected. In the first quarter both teams had trouble generating much in the way of offense. Each team managed only one first down in the period and both teams had passes intercepted. The offenses picked up their play in the second quarter. The Notre Dame All Stars made five first downs to three for the Maroons in the second quarter.

The Notre Dame game was a frustrating one for Walter French. Lost in the hoopla surrounding the presence of the Four Horsemen, was the fact that three lineman of the 1924 National Champion Notre Dame team, who were called the "Seven Mules," were also making their presence felt in the game and doing their best to stop Walter's end runs. The *Philadelphia Inquirer* reported "Wally French who had so completely been covered by his foes that he failed to get started often slipping on the soaked sod when a clear field loomed ahead was taken out in the final half."[34]

At halftime a telegram arrived for Doc Striegel and as the team rested up and strategized for the second half, Doc opened the message from the league office. Joe Carr had followed through on his threat. Because they went ahead with the game in Philadelphia, he was suspending them from the league, cancelled the rubber match they had scheduled for the next day with Providence making it impossible for them to claim the league championship that they had won on the field the week before and to make matters worse he was ruling that they had forfeited their franchise. One can only imagine the feeling in the locker room when Doc shared this news with the team.

Rauch replaced Walter French with Tony Latone at the start of the second half. It was time, he felt, to play some old school Maroons football, what we would call today a "ground and pound" style and see if the Notre Dame team could hold up.

Latone, following the bone crunching blocking of the Maroons' line and Barney Wentz, moved the ball deep into the Notre Dame territory. With the ball on the 18-yard line, and the Notre Dame defense gearing up for another run by Latone, Ernst took the snap and dropped back to pass and unnoticed, Latone slipped out into the flat and Ernst flipped the ball to him and Latone made the catch and walked into the end zone. Berry uncharacteristically missed the extra point kick and Notre Dame held on to a 7–6 lead.

On the next Notre Dame possession Harry Stuhldreher went back to pass but the Stein brothers and Duke Osborn broke through the line and forced him to rush his attempt, and the Maroons intercepted the pass. Back on offense, the Maroons, using the same strategy that got them their first score moved the ball down field to the Notre Dame five-yard-line where the Notre Dame defense stiffened. On fourth down, the Maroons decided to forgo the field goal and go for the touchdown. Ernst floated a pass to Berry for what looked like a sure touchdown but Charlie had the ball tip off his fingers and fall to the ground.

Undaunted, the Maroons' defense once again held firm and forced the Notre Dame team to punt the ball back with time running out in the game. Leyden boomed a 60-yard punt backing the Maroons up to their own eight-yard-line.

Notre Dame knew what was coming but was powerless to stop it. Latone ran the ball on five straight plays, Wentz took two carries and then the ball was handed back to Latone who in four carries had the ball to the Notre Dame 21-yard line. Finally, with only seconds left in the game, darkness falling and the ball on the 18-yard-line, Rauch sent Berry to kick the winning field goal. Herb Stein at center snapped the ball to Jack Ernst who caught it and placed it on Berry's favorite spot, and Berry, grateful for the chance to redeem himself after dropping a sure touchdown earlier, kicked the ball squarely, sending it over and through the uprights.

"Most of the fans at Shibe Park, even the ones from Pottsville, had come out for a fun day of football and a glimpse at the famous Four Horsemen. Instead, they were witness to a watershed moment in the history of American sports: the very moment that professional football surpassed college ball."[35]

From here the story of the NFL Championship of 1925 really gets murky. Two days after losing to the Maroons on December 6 the Chicago Cardinals announced that they had scheduled two more games to be played before the December 20 official end of the season. Unaware at that point that the Maroons would be stripped of the title, Chris O'Brien hoped that two wins over weak opponents would mean that the Cardinals would finish the season with the best record and thereby still lay claim to the title. A game was scheduled with the Hammond Pros the following Saturday and the next day they would play the Milwaukee Badgers. There was just one problem. Both of those teams disbanded when their season ended. Milwaukee, in fact, did not have enough players available to field a team when their game kicked off and had actually gone out and recruited high school players to fill out their roster, which was a major violation of the league rules.

O'Brien's motivation for going through all of these machinations was an attempt to set up a showdown with the Chicago Bears and their star player and world class drawing card Red Grange. However, Grange was injured in his next game and was shut down for the remainder of the season. The Cardinals beat Hammond and Milwaukee but Joe Carr launched an investigation into the use of high school players by Milwaukee. Ultimately the Milwaukee team was not suspended but its owner, Ambrose McGurk was forced to sell the team. Meanwhile Chris O'Brien and the Cardinals were fined $1,000 and put on probation which was essentially a slap on the wrist. Carr determined that O'Brien was not aware of the fact that the Milwaukee team was using high school players even though it was a Cardinal player, Art Folz, who was banned for life for his part in arranging for the schoolboys to join the team.

Never one to give up without a fight, Doc Striegel made one more attempt to change Carr's mind. He traveled to Columbus to beg the league president to reconsider his decision. The best Carr would agree to would be to bring the matter before the league owners at their next meeting on February 6, 1926. The meeting took place in the Hotel Statler in Detroit. Although Doc was allowed to be in the room for the meeting, Carr alone presented the facts to the owners. In his remarks, Carr once again addressed how important protecting a franchise's market was to the growth and integrity of the league. He also focused on the fact that "three different notices forbidding the Pottsville club were given and the management elected to play regardless" and in the final analysis this insubordination may have been what rankled him the most.

After the owners gave Doc a chance to present his side, they discussed the matter for 10 minutes and then voted to back Carr. The Maroons were still out of the league. A motion was then made and seconded to award the 1925 Championship to the Cardinals, who on the strength of their win over Hammond had the best record. However, just as the vote was taken, word arrived that the Cardinals' owner Chris O'Brien, who was not at the meeting, was informing the owners that the Cardinals would not accept the championship under these circumstances, at which point the matter was tabled and the 1925 championship was never awarded to anyone. In 1933, Charles Bidwill, a Chicago businessman, lawyer, and an associate of Al Capone, bought the Cardinals. Bidwill made his fortune as the owner of dog and horse racetracks. To that point in time the Cardinals did not have one title to their name so it is easy to understand why the new Cardinals' owner could not have helped himself from accepting the 1925 title. It would be the only title the team would win until 1948, one year after Bidwill died of pneumonia.

The story of the 1925 football season and the Pottsville Maroons, however, does not end there. Shortly after the owners meeting where the Maroons were kicked out of the NFL a presentation was made to the owners by Red Grange and his agent Charles C. Pyle. Grange and Pyle told the group that they had reached an agreement to lease Yankee Stadium and planned to put a team in New York. One can just imagine how uncomfortable this must have been for Carr and the owners. Carr had just waxed poetically about the importance of protected territories in his case against the Maroons and the owners had just unanimously agreed with him. Not to mention the fact that Tim Mara, owner of the New York Giants who held the "rights" to the New York market was in the room. However, Grange was by far the sport's biggest star and everyone wanted him in the fold. Carr and the owners were stuck, they had to back Mara, and stand behind the pronouncement that they had just made regarding protected territories in the Maroons' case and so they turned down Grange and Pyle.

Undeterred, Grange and Pyle announced that they would form their own league, the American Football League, for the 1926 season and the NFL found itself in a battle with Grange's league. AFL franchises were started in Boston, Brooklyn, Chicago, Cleveland, Los Angeles, Newark, and Philadelphia, in addition to Grange's New York entry, the Yankees. The Rock Island Independents were the only NFL team to jump to the new league.

Chris O'Brien and the Chicago Cardinals found themselves faced now with having to compete with two professional teams in Chicago, the Bears and the Bulls in the new league. To help keep the Cardinals solvent, Carr rescinded the $1,000 fine that had been levied against O'Brien for the Milwaukee game. Art Folz's ban from the league was also rescinded to keep him from playing for the rival league.

This left the Maroons, the best team in football, with no league and a prime target for Grange and Pyle. Remarkably, to keep the Maroons and the credibility they would bring away from the new league, Carr reinstated the Maroons for the 1926 season but there would be no change in the status of the 1925 title.

The cancellation of the planned game against Providence after the Four Horsemen game, although he did not know it at the time, meant that Walter French had played in his last football game on that December 12, 1925. It had been quite an experience. In a couple of months, he would be packing his bags and heading south for spring training with the A's.

In some telling of the tale of the Maroons and the 1925 season, in an effort to romanticize even more, an already remarkable Cinderella story, Walter French is depicted as "Little Walter" and a puny third stringer. The fact was, however, that Walter had been one of the stars of the team throughout the season. Only playing in nine games he finished the season with five touchdowns. Only Latone, who played in 12 games, and had eight touchdowns, Flanagan, who also played in 12 games and had seven touchdowns, and Berry, who played in 10 games, and finished with six touchdowns, had more than Walter did in 1925. Plus, his scores did not come on one-yard plunges. His touchdowns were long, break away efforts which averaged almost 30 yards each. In a league that had 20 teams in 1925, only nine players, including his three teammates, scored more touchdowns than did Walter French.

At the conclusion of the 1925 season Walter French, whose 5.4 yards per carry led the entire NFL, was named first team All-Pro by two of the recognized selectors at the time, E.G. Brands for *Collyer's Eye*, a sports journal published in Chicago and by the *Ohio State Journal*. He and Charlie Berry were the only two Maroons to be named All-Pro by more than one selector.

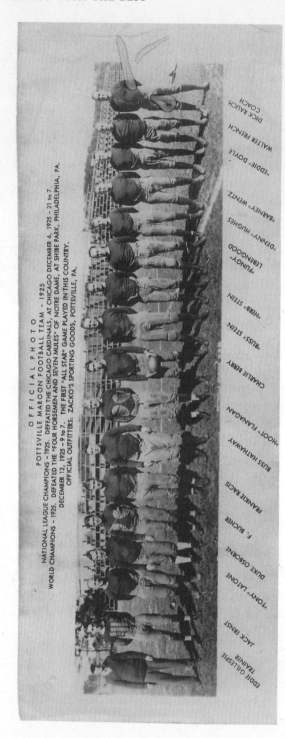

Pottsville Maroons official team photograph, 1925. The Maroons won the professional football title on the field, only to have it stripped by a controversial decision by Commission Carr. (Courtesy of Author)

CHAPTER 7

1926 and the Dutch Leonard Affair

When the calendar flipped to 1926 in January, Walter was back home in New Jersey spending time with his wife and baby daughter. The A's wouldn't head south for spring training until the second week of February but the "hot stove league" was already in mid-season form. In its preview of the upcoming season the *Miami News* noted that Connie Mack had only planned a couple of changes. "Only two changes are in prospect for the Philadelphia Athletics, runners up in the American League race last season. In right field, Walter French, erstwhile all-around Army stag, who played brilliantly toward the close of 1925 is slated to succeed Bing Miller."[1]

In his biography of Connie Mack, Norman Macht observed that in 1926 "Connie Mack had no holdouts; Cochrane had signed a three-year contract, starting with an 80 percent raise to $8,000 for 1926, $9,000 for 1927 and $10,000 for 1928. Simmons signed a new three-year contract doubling his salary to $11,000 for 1926." Lefty Grove was in the second year of his original contract and "just about everybody else received a satisfactory raise."[2]

Another subject of discussion in the "hot stove league" was the future of Connie Mack as the A's manager. Mack was turning 63 years old in 1926 and although he bristled when anyone ever speculated about his retirement the fact was, according to Norman Macht "Connie Mack was tired. One writer described him in the spring of 1926 as 'gaunt, wrinkled and gray.'"[3]

So, before the start of the 1926 season, Mack added Kid Gleason to the coaching staff. Gleason was born in 1866 in Camden, New Jersey. He started his major league career in 1888 playing second base and pitching for the Philadelphia Phillies. Over the next 20 years he played for the St. Louis Cardinals, Detroit Tigers, and New York Giants before returning to the Phillies to finish his playing career. After his playing days were over, Gleason got into coaching and was the manager of the infamous 1919 Chicago White Sox who were found to have thrown the World Series in what became known as the Black Sox scandal. It was determined that Gleason was not involved with throwing the Series but after managing the White Sox for a few more seasons he decided to retire and stayed retired until Connie Mack approached him about coming over to the A's.

100 • PLAYING WITH THE BEST

The A's arrived in Ft. Myers during the second week of February to start their training. On hand to meet the team was inventor Thomas Edison. "The Wizard of Menlo Park" owned a home and botanical laboratory in Ft. Myers and was a rabid baseball fan. He was particularly fond of the Philadelphia Athletics and was a close friend of Connie Mack. After being introduced to some of the players, he was handed a bat and took a couple of swings. During spring training, the team visited Edison and posed for a picture in front of his home. The copy of the picture currently on file in the archives at the Baseball Hall of Fame in Cooperstown, NY was a gift to the Hall of Fame from Walter French.

At the plate in spring training in 1926, Walter seemed to have picked up right where he left off at the end of 1925. The one part of his game that Mack wanted him to work on in camp was his fielding. Kid Gleason, in much the same way as Hans Lobert had at West Point, took Walter under his wing. The *Philadelphia Inquirer* reported that "Mack has a number of combinations in mind, all depending on whether Walter French will be in the regular line up when the race starts ... French simply cannot keep attention away from him because of his consistent batting while

Thomas Edison loved baseball and was especially fond of the Philadelphia Athletics. Manager Connie Mack and Edison were friends. In 1927, while in Ft. Myers, Florida for Spring Training, the team visited Edison's home and botanical laboratory. (Courtesy of French Family)

he is fielding and throwing much better than he did last season. Kid Gleason took him in hand during morning practice. He started hitting fungoes over his head. He made French run to get each ball. He never gave him an easy chance and also changed his style of catching balls. French always was timid to catch a ball with his hands high but held them down. Gleason broke him of this habit and now he is catching balls in orthodox style."[4]

It is easy to see why Walter responded so well to the suggestions of fellow New Jersey native Kid Gleason. Gleason was born less than 10 miles from where Walter was raised and was undoubtedly known to him. Today they are both in the South Jersey Baseball Hall of Fame.

As the regular season approached, the sportswriters were beginning to write their articles about the A's assuming that Walter had beat out Bing Miller as the starting right fielder. Billy Evans writing in his syndicated column commented that "with French in right field and Al Simmons in center, the Athletics will present the unusual spectacle of two players using baseball stances that are entirely unorthodox. Simmons pulls badly from the plate yet is one of the greatest batsmen in the American League. Some critics refer to him as 'foot in the bucket Simmons'. American League pitchers say a lot or worse things about him. French hits the ball with his feet wide spread. He doesn't step into the ball but rather hits from a flat-footed position. Opposing pitchers ridicule his style, but Walter does more than that to their offerings."[5]

On April 13, when Connie Mack filled out his lineup card for the first game of the 1926 season, Walter French was installed as the starting right fielder. He was batting third in the batting order between left fielder Bill Lamar and Al Simmons. The balance of the A's lineup that day included Max Bishop at second base, Joe Hauser at first base, Mickey Cochrane was catching, Jimmy Dykes was at third base; Chick Galloway was at shortstop and Eddie Rommel was the starting pitcher. Rommel was a 6'2", 197-pound, right-handed pitcher who spent his entire 12-year major-league career with the A's. His best year was 1922 when he won 27 games and he was coming off his second-best season in 1925 when he notched 21 victories.

The A's first opponent of the 1926 season were the defending American League Champion Washington Senators at Griffith Stadium. On the mound for the home team was Walter Johnson, who was starting his twentieth season. An opening day crowd of 25,000 including then Vice-President Charles G. Dawes braved the chilly weather. The Senators' player-manager Bucky Harris was presented with a floral piece, and Johnson was given a loving cup prior to the start of the game and after Vice-President Dawes threw out the first pitch, Walter Johnson took the mound.

It was clear from the outset that both starting pitchers had their good stuff on this day. Johnson held the Athletics hitless for the first four innings and Eddie Rommel was employing a "bend but don't break" strategy, as the Senators were getting their hits in the early going but they were unable to push across any runs. On and on the game went with both pitchers holding their opponent in check and after nine innings the game was still a scoreless tie. Both pitchers remained in the game and one of the greatest pitching duels continued. Twice the Senators had the bases loaded but Rommel was able to bear down and get out of trouble. As the game entered the fifteenth inning both starting pitchers were still in the game. After Johnson got the A's out in the top of the fifteenth, Bucky Harris opened the bottom of the inning with a single. He then advanced to third on a double by "Goose" Goslin and then scored the winning run on a single by Joe Harris.

Walter Johnson had struck out 12 A's while Rommel only struck out just one of the Senators. Johnson issued three walks in the marathon game, while Rommel gave up six. The Senators finished with nine hits off Rommel, while the A's had six off Johnson. It was the seventh opening day shutout of his legendary career.

For his part, Walter French finished the game one for five. His loan hit, a double, was the A's only extra base hit. He also made two successful sacrifices.

It is hard to imagine, in the way the modern game is played, a situation where the two starting pitchers would both complete a 15-inning game, let alone the fact that it was the first game of the season. Even more remarkable, by today's standards, the 15-inning game was completed in just a little over two and one-half hours.

After being shut out again the next day, the A's finally generated some offense in the third game of the series, as they cruised to a 9–2 victory. Once again batting third in front of Al Simmons, Walter had three hits in five at-bats and scored two runs. The Senators again won the fourth and final game of the series by a score of 4–3, but in this game, Walter had four hits in his five at-bats. For the first series of the season Walter had rewarded the faith placed in him by Connie Mack by collecting a total of eight hits in 18 official at-bats for a batting average of .444.

From Washington, the A's traveled to Boston where on April 17 they were victimized by another strong pitching performance. This time it was Red Sox right hander Howard Emke, who gave them fits, when he pitched a two-hit gem leading the home team to a 6–1 victory. The A's bounced back in the first game of the Patriot's Day double header with a 3–1 win behind the three-hit performance of Lefty Grove. In that game Walter reached base via a walk and scored one of the A's runs. After losing the second game of the double header the A's headed home with a 3–7 record.

In the A's first home game of the 1926 season, a 5–2 victory over the Senators on April 21, Walter had no hits but drove in one run with a sacrifice fly. He also reached base on a walk and came around to score a run. The A's then proceeded to lose two of the next three games against Washington.

Next on the schedule was a three-game series with the Yankees in New York. After losing the opener by a score of 7–2, the A's had to feel pretty good with Eddie Rommel going in game two. He came into the game with a 2–1 record, his loss coming in the epic, extra inning battle with Walter Johnson. As with most of the games in the first weeks of the season, Walter was starting in right field for the A's and batting at the top of the order. His counterpart on the Yankees, one Babe Ruth, was the cleanup hitter for what was to be known as Murderers' Row. Preceding Ruth in the Yankees' lineup was Lou Gehrig and behind him was Bob Meusel and behind him Tony Lazzeri. Only one pitcher had been able to last against the Yankee lineup to that point in the season and they had won nine of their first 12 games.

The Yankees hit Eddie Rommel hard. Writing in the *New York Times*, sportswriter James Harrison couldn't resist rubbing it in: "Mr. Rommel's control was excellent. He hit the Yankee bats with admirable consistency."[6] In the fifth inning, with the bases loaded, Babe Ruth hit a ball at A's second baseman Max Bishop so hard that Bishop was almost killed. As Bishop attempted to field the ball it struck him in the neck. The ball had been hit with such force that it rolled all the way to the wall in right field. When it was eventually chased down by Walter French, the bases had been cleared and Ruth was standing on second base.

At the plate Walter had a triple in the sixth inning and scored on an infield ground out. From an offensive perspective this game was typical for Walter in this part of the season. While his bat had cooled off from his torrid start in 1926, he was still getting on base, stealing bases, and most importantly scoring runs for his team.

After a slow start to the season the A's went on a winning streak. Starting on May 3, they won 12 of their next 13 games, including a sweep of the Yankees in Philadelphia. This pulled them to within three games of first place. However, by the middle of May, Walter was struggling at the plate and Connie Mack removed him from the everyday lineup relegating him to pinch hitting and pinch running.

On May 23, the A's were back in the nation's capital to play again against the Senators. By this time it must have become evident to his manager that Walter seemed to have a knack for hitting against Walter Johnson. To this point in his career he had faced him eight times and had four hits against him, and so Mack placed him back in the lineup, playing right field, and batting seventh. He responded by getting two hits in his two official at-bats. In his other two plate appearances he successfully executed a sacrifice bunt and was hit by a Johnson pitch. The A's won the game by a score of 5–3, knocking the Senators' ace out of the game in the eighth inning. Walter French had now faced the great Walter Johnson 10 times and had accumulated six hits.

Walter was back in the starting lineup to stay and the A's won four of the next five games against the Senators and climbed into second place in the American League, although they were still six games behind the Yankees, who were on a 16-game winning streak when the A's arrived for a crucial series on Friday May 28. In the series opener the Yankees sent their most dominant pitcher, Waite Hoyt to the mound to face Lefty Grove for the Athletics in the first game of a double header.

Chick Galloway knocked in the game's first run with a sacrifice in the second inning. Earlier in that inning Walter had singled but was later forced out at second, but in the process broke up double play which kept the inning alive for Galloway's

RBI. In the fourth inning Walter French knocked in what would prove to be the winning run in the A's 2–1 victory, when he hit a triple off the Yankee ace. Meanwhile Lefty Grove was keeping the Yankees in check and keeping them scoreless until the seventh inning.

By the end of May Walter's batting average was sitting at .294. With Walter's success, Connie Mack saw that Bing Miller was expendable and traded him to the St. Louis Browns for "Baby Doll" Jacobson in early June in a move that would solidify Walter's position as the A's regular right fielder.

The month of June was not a good one for the Athletics and their pennant hopes. They went 8–13 for the month and the team dropped to fourth place, 11 games behind the first place Yankees. However, when the two teams met on June 30, at Shibe Park in Philadelphia, the A's came away with a thrilling 5–4 victory, thanks largely to some sensational defensive play by Walter French in right field. With the Yankees leading 3–1 in the bottom of the sixth inning, the A's loaded the bases and their first baseman, Jim Poole, connected for a two-run double which tied the game. The Yankees took the lead once more in their half of the seventh when they pushed across one run to take a 4–3 lead. In the top of the ninth New York threatened to break the game wide open when they loaded the bases with two outs and future Hall of Famer Tony Lazzeri coming to the plate. Not as well-known as his teammates, Ruth and Gehrig, Lazzeri was a big part of "Murderers' Row." In his 13-year major league career he would average 171 hits, 17 home runs, and 111 RBI. He would finish 1926, his rookie season with 117 RBI, second on the team to only Babe Ruth. James Harrison writing in the *New York Times* described what happened next: "It was at this somewhat pulsing moment that Lazzeri put the wood to the ball and lifted it out toward right center on full wing. The count was three and two and all of the Yanks streaked for home with the pitch, but Lieut. French spoiled the happy scene by galloping back in his West Point style, sticking his glove skyward, leaping agilely and impaling the sphere."[7] In the bottom of the ninth inning Al Simmons drove in two runs to give the A's a much-needed victory. In his summation of the game Harrison wrote "Mr. Poole is entitled to several chaplets of laurel, but the lad who did as much to save the game was Walter French who's running one hand catch with the bases full choked off at least three runs."[8]

The thrilling, come-from-behind win over the Yankees seemed to spur the A's and they went on a streak winning 12 of their next 16 games. Although they were still seven games behind the Yankees, they had managed to climb back into second place. No one on the team contributed more to the team's winning ways than did Walter French. Walter hit .429 during the stretch and raised his batting average for the season to .329. Among the regulars only Al Simmons was hitting for a higher average.

However, their pennant hopes were not to be realized. The 1926 Athletics' season was marked by inconsistency. It seemed that every hot streak they put together was followed up by a losing streak of equal length and so after winning 12 of 16, they proceeded to lose 13 of their next 15 games and as the season entered its last two months, they found themselves back in third place, some 14 games behind the Yankees.

Although the A's could not mount a charge at the pennant, Walter continued to produce for his team and after getting seven hits in 12 at bats against the St. Louis Browns and Chicago White Sox, his batting average was raised to .326 which was tops on the team at that point of the season. The A's played out the rest of the season, never getting any further up in the standings than third place. Despite the team's poor showing, Walter French had to be happy about his performance in 1926. He finished the season with a .305 batting average, second on the team only to Al Simmons who, after a torrid last few weeks, had finished the season with a .341 average. Walter was third on the team in hits and scored 51 runs. As the season came to an end, he felt he had found his place as a regular outfielder on the Athletics and was looking forward to the 1927 season.

In October the Yankees faced off against the St. Louis Cardinals in the World Series. The series, which was won by the Cardinals in seven games, was highlighted by two performances. Grover Cleveland Alexander beat the Yankees twice in the series including a win in Game 6 and finished them off pitching in relief in game seven the very next day. The series is also remembered for the performance by Babe Ruth in Game 5 when he hit three home runs, a World Series record that has been equaled only four times since. Adding to the drama of that performance was the story of young Joey Sylvester, a New Jersey boy who had been injured in a fall. From his hospital bed he wrote a letter to the Yankees asking for an autograph from Ruth. According to the legend, Ruth wrote back and promised to hit a home run for Joey. Newspapers stories at the time, since disputed, claimed that the boy's condition miraculously improved after the Babe's performance.

The World Series would have been the final baseball story of 1926 if not for the unexpected news that Tris Speaker, player-manager of the Cleveland Indians, and Ty Cobb who held the same position with the Detroit Tigers, two of the game's greatest stars, had both announced that they were retiring from the game within a few days of each other. Even though both men were at the tail end of their brilliant, Hall of Fame careers, fans were shocked by this news because they were still among the game's best. As a player Cobb had finished the season with a .339 batting average and Speaker hit .306. As managers they were getting the job done as well. The Indians had finished the season in second place only three games behind the Yankees, and Cobb led the Tigers to a winning season, although they finished in sixth place of the American League.

The careers of Cobb and Speaker overlapped and depending on who you asked, one or the other was the game's greatest player, until Babe Ruth broke onto the scene. It would not be a total oversimplification to suggest that most fans felt that Cobb was the better hitter and base runner, at a time when base running was thought of on a par with hitting and fielding, while Speaker was considered the better fielder. However, one would be splitting hairs in either assessment. Until the last few years of his career Cobb ran the bases with reckless abandon and was considered the best at that aspect of the game. Speaker was such a superior defensive player that it was said that his glove was "where triples go to die." Except for cities of their major rivals, both men were enormously popular. So why, fans wondered, would these two legends of the game both decide to retire? Before the year was out, that question would be answered, as a major scandal was revealed involving both men.

Just before Christmas, the Associated Press broke the story that charges had been made by former Tiger pitcher Dutch Leonard that Cobb and Speaker had bet on a fixed game in 1919, which was the same year that the White Sox had thrown the World Series. The headline read "Charges Cobb-Speaker Bet On a 'Fixed Game'." It went on to speculate that the "Managers Supposed to have resigned in Face of Impending Scandal."

Hubert "Dutch" Leonard was a hard-throwing left-handed pitcher who broke into the majors with the Boston Red Sox in 1913. He had his best season in 1914 when he finished with a record of 19–7 and an earned run average of 0.97, which still ranks among the five best ERAs of all time and the lowest ever recorded in the American League. Among his teammates on the Red Sox were two other young pitchers, a 19-year-old rookie named Babe Ruth and Smoky Joe Wood, who had won 34 games for the Red Sox in 1912.

Leonard was just under six feet tall and was a well-built 185 pounds and it was said that he looked "more like a football player than a baseball player." His best pitches were a biting curveball, overpowering fastball and a spitball. When the spitball was outlawed in 1920 a handful of "grandfathered" pitchers were allowed to continue to throw the pitch and Dutch was one of them. His tremendous 1914 season was even more impressive when one considers that he suffered a wrist injury in early September and missed four or five starts that would have added to his statistics.

Leonard was given a $5,000 raise for the 1915 season but nevertheless showed up for the start of the season in terrible shape and saw limited action in the first six weeks. As if this was not bad enough, in May, in what was to become a pattern for Dutch, he was suspended from the team for insubordination. He accused his manager Bill Carrigan of mistreating his players. Although he did not return to the mound until early July, he still finished the season with a 15–7 record. The Red Sox won the pennant and Leonard defeated the Philadelphia Phillies, and future Hall of Famer Pete Alexander in Game 3 of the World Series, which was won by Boston in five games.

While Leonard's talent as a pitcher was undeniable, his value to his team was diminished by his poor attitude. He was always complaining about something and saying that he was being mistreated and taken advantage of in some way. His career was interrupted by World War I and when he returned to the game in 1919, he was included in a trade with the Yankees. Before accepting the trade, he demanded that Yankee owner Jacob Ruppert place his entire year's salary into a savings account. An enraged Ruppert, who felt his integrity was being questioned, refused to honor Leonard's demand, at which point he went back to California to pitch in the San Joaquin League. While back in California, in addition to pitching for the team in Fresno, he also focused on his farm, which he built into a very successful business. Teams, believing that his enthusiasm for farming had lessened the importance of baseball in Dutch Leonard's life, made no effort to acquire his rights from Fresno. Finally, in May, the Detroit Tigers purchased his rights for $12,000 and he soon joined the major league team and became a teammate of Ty Cobb.

In 1914, while Leonard was pitching for the Red Sox in a game against the Tigers, Cobb laid down a bunt and raced to first. Leonard came over from his position on the mound to cover first base but when it became apparent that both men would arrive at the base at the same time, Dutch veered off to avoid colliding with Cobb. Ty, who always approached the game with a "take no prisoners" attitude, was appalled by what he thought was a cowardly act on the part of Leonard, and he never forgot it. However, even if this had never happened, Dutch Leonard was simply the type of person that rubbed Cobb the wrong way. He had a "me first" attitude, was always making excuses when he pitched poorly, and worst of all he did not always give his best effort when he took the mound.

While Cobb was able to tolerate Leonard when they were simply teammates, that all changed in 1921 when Ty was named as the team's player-manager. Almost immediately upon assuming his new role Cobb started to come down hard on Leonard. If Dutch violated some team rule, that another player might have gotten a pass on, such as breaking curfew, he would always be subject to the harshest discipline.

"In 1925 ... the toxic relationship between him (Leonard) and Cobb resumed where it had left off ... they constantly clashed. Despite Leonard's success that year, Cobb accused Leonard of not putting forth his best effort and scolded the pitcher in front of the team. Both men were getting older and Cobb's long dislike of Leonard grew to new levels of hatred."[9] In July of that year Cobb kept Dutch in a game for the full nine innings even though he had given up 12 runs to the Athletics, the worst beating of his career. Finally, Cobb put Leonard on waivers, and it soon became apparent that no team was going to pick him up. At this point, in addition to his reputation as a malcontent, he was experiencing some nagging injuries that lessened his effectiveness.

One team that Dutch felt he might have had a chance to join was the Cleveland Indians, who were managed by Tris Speaker. Speaker and Leonard had been teammates for three seasons with the Boston Red Sox, but that didn't make any difference as Tris was not interested in the services of someone with Dutch's reputation. The 1925 season would be his last in baseball. He was just 33 years old.

In May of 1926 Dutch Leonard traveled from his home in California to Chicago to meet with American League President Ban Johnson. He was angry with both Ty Cobb, for releasing him from the Tigers, and Tris Speaker for not picking him up for the Indians when he was released. During the meeting with Johnson, Leonard claimed that prior to the final game of the 1919 baseball season, he met with Cobb, Speaker, and Smoky Joe Wood, who at this point was a member of the Indians, under the grandstand at Navin Field in Detroit. The Indians had clinched second place and were playing a meaningless game, for them, against the Detroit Tigers. The Tigers, on the other hand needed one more win to finish the season in third place, which would have awarded each man on the team a $500 bonus. Finishing fourth would get them nothing. According to Leonard, Speaker told them that he would have no problem getting his team to "lay down" against Detroit assuring the bonus for Cobb and his team. He went on to claim that the group figured that if the fix was in on the game anyway, why not get some bets down on the Tigers and cash-in even more on the caper. Leonard also claimed that Cobb had arranged for Fred West, an employee of the Detroit Tigers, to place the bets for them.

At this time Johnson, who had founded the American League in 1901 and had acted as its president since, was in a power struggle with then Baseball Commissioner Kennesaw Mountain Landis. Landis was a former federal judge whose handling of the Black Sox Scandal was credited with saving the game. Johnson felt that he should be the ultimate authority over the American League, while the owners and Landis felt the final say should reside with the Office of the Commissioner. So when Leonard also mentioned that he had in his possession two letters, one written to him by Cobb and a second one sent by Wood, that Dutch claimed proved that what he was alleging was in fact true, and that he planned to sell the letters to the highest bidding newspaper, Johnson was worried that the scandal would hurt the credibility of the American League and his own standing in the power struggle with Landis. To stop Leonard from selling them to the press, Johnson agreed to pay him $20,000 for the letters.

There are two interesting things about the letter that Cobb sent to Dutch. The first is that the tone of the letter gives no hint regarding the animosity that the two men felt toward each other. "Well, I hope you found everything in fine shape at home and that all of your troubles will be little ones"[10] he wrote. The second is that Cobb's letter never mentions a wager of any type let alone on a ball game. Instead, he references only a "business proposition"[11] and while one could say that the letter was written intentionally vague, the fact was that it was not the smoking gun that Johnson feared.

Wood's letter was certainly more damning as it laid out the details of the wager that they planned to make and the one that they were actually able to make. Taking such a sizeable bet so close to the day of the game made the bookies nervous and they only accepted a much smaller wager than what the men had originally hoped.

Wood wrote "if we ever have another chance like this we will know enough to get down early." Wood also seems to exonerate Cobb in his letter writing "Cobb did not get up a cent."[12] Finally, although Wood referred to the proceeds of the bet being split three ways, Wood, Leonard, and someone else from Cleveland, there is no specific mention of Tris Speaker in Smoky Joe's, nor in Cobb's letter as well.

After he bought the letters from Leonard, Ban Johnson kept Commissioner Landis in the dark about the entire matter, while he conducted his investigation. He paid private investigators to follow both Cobb and Speaker and to report on any suspicious activity that they might have observed. The surveillance revealed nothing with respect to Cobb, but the detectives reported that Speaker liked to gamble on the horse races.

Finally on September 9, Johnson convened a closed-door meeting of the American League owners at the league office in Chicago to brief them on the claim being made by Leonard. Much to his displeasure the owners voted to turn the matter over to Commissioner Landis for him to investigate and ultimately rule. For his part, upon learning of the case, the commissioner agreed that he would conduct his own investigation into the affair.

Johnson ignored the owner's action and continued to act as if he were the ultimate authority. He met with Cobb and Speaker and told them that they would have to resign their positions as player-managers and retire from baseball, a ruling, with which, oddly enough, they both complied.

Once the story hit the press, however, Ty Cobb went on the offensive. UPI reported that "in a tremendous voice Cobb rested his case 'with the baseball fans that have watched me play to win for twenty-two years.'" He admitted "I knew that something was afoot but I never bet a penny on an American League baseball game in my life and I did not have a cent on that game." Adding "the business deal mentioned in the letter to Leonard did not involve betting."[13] A few days later he charged Leonard with blackmailing the American League. "Cobb charges Leonard with Blackmail" read the headline in a UPI article on Christmas Eve. "Ty Cobb has hurled the charge of blackmail at Dutch Leonard and the American League." He was quoted as saying "I think the officials and the president of the league can tell you more about that than I can. It is sufficient for me to say that they paid money to a man that demanded it, and in so doing became parties to a blackmailing scheme." When asked by a reporter "what about the statement credited to Ban Johnson, president of the American League, to the effect that you and Speaker had 'seen the handwriting on the wall' and stepped down and out of baseball for that reason?" he replied "Oh well—what might one expect from a crowd that buys a blackmailer off for $20,000? ... it almost brings a fellow to the point of doubting an all-wise Providence, until he is brought face to face with the splendid spirt of loyalty I see exemplified by my friends, the public. And I may say that I have faith enough to believe absolutely that it is going to come out all right in the end."[14]

Landis planned to bring all the participants to his office in Chicago to hear all sides but Dutch Leonard refused to make the trip from his home in California. He told the Associated Press that he was afraid that he would be "bumped off" if he came to Chicago and so Landis traveled west and met with him there.[15]

While Landis was trying to conduct his inquiry without any outside interference, almost everyone had an opinion and most sided with Speaker and Cobb. Even politicians weighed in on the matter and it was not just members of their own congressional delegation. Senator James Watson, Republican of Indiana, issued a statement of support for the two stars. UPI reported that "As a lover of baseball Senator Watson, today expressed entire confidence in Ty Cobb and Tris Speaker against whom charges of throwing a game in 1919 have been placed. 'In my opinion, Ty Cobb, Tris Speaker, Eddie Collins and Walter Johnson, have done more to make baseball a clean game than any other men,' Watson said."[16]

After returning from his meeting with Leonard, Judge Landis brought in the other three men to question them and to hear their side of the story. Ty Cobb was the first to meet with Landis on December 20. After some preliminary questions Landis asked Cobb when he became aware that a bet was being put down on the ball game. Cobb claimed that his role was only to arrange for someone Leonard and Wood could trust to place their bet. Landis then questioned Cobb about Speaker. Ty maintained that he never spoke with Speaker about the game and vehemently denied having put any money on the game, nor had he ever had any intention to do so.

Landis then asked about the meeting under the grandstand at Nevin Field at which Leonard claimed that the plot to throw the game and to place the bets was hatched. Cobb was adamant that the meeting had never taken place and again maintained that his only involvement was in recommending West to assist with placing the bet. Cobb told Landis that when the story began to come out in the latter part of the 1926 season that he approached West and asked him if he had in fact made the bet for Wood and Leonard and that he admitted that he had. "Cobb's responses were carefully crafted and left Landis with nothing to hang him on about the affair, instead shifting all of the guilt on Wood whom Cobb asserted wanted to wager on the game. Cobb claimed to have been merely an intermediary to get Wood to West so that a bet could be placed. Cobb asserted that he only put money on two games in his life, losing $150 on the first two games of the 1919 World Series."[17]

For his part Tris Speaker told Landis that he had no knowledge of a bet on the final game of the season. He also denied the conversation under the stands where Leonard claimed that he offered to have his team "lay down" to assure the third-place finish for the Tigers. He also stated that he never spoke with Joe Wood about the matter until it came out that Wood had written his letter to Leonard.

From there Landis focused his line of inquiry on the game in question and some of the moves that Speaker made as manager. Here is where Speaker made the strongest case for his innocence. Speaker pointed to the fact that he played his regulars in the game, that they held Cobb to one hit, and reminded the commissioner that he himself had three hits in five at bats.

Next to meet with Landis was Joe Wood. Landis went right to the line in the letter Joe had written to Leonard where he explained that the proceeds from the bet were divided three ways. Who was the unnamed "friend from Cleveland" that was in on the bet? Landis asked. Wood replied that the friend was not in baseball and refused to provide the Commissioner with the individual's name.

Before leaving Landis, both Cobb and Speaker insisted that the commissioner release to the public all of the evidence in his possession including the testimony that they had just given. The next day Landis complied with the request releasing all of the information that he had along with the transcripts of the men's testimony, and that of Leonard from their meeting in California. He also announced that he would render his decision on the fate of Cobb and Speaker over the winter.

Landis realized that he was in a tough spot. For starters, public opinion was squarely behind the two ballplayers. Leaders in politics and business all expressed their support for them. Even Babe Ruth, who had a love-hate relationship with Cobb came out in their defense. "This is a lot of bull," he told a crowd in San Francisco, adding "I've never known squarer men than Cobb and Speaker."[18] In addition to the wave of support the players were getting, Landis was also faced with the fact that if the men were not exonerated it would not only put a stain on their reputations and legacy, but also it would call into question the integrity of the game of baseball which he had worked so hard to re-establish after the Black Sox Scandal. Finally, at this time, there were some rumblings that a group of businessmen were contemplating the establishment of a new league and the Commissioner did not relish the notion that two of the game's biggest stars might wind up in a rival, startup league.

Finally, on January 27, 1927, Landis issued his ruling clearing both men. This meant that "Ty Cobb and Tris Speaker, two of the most famous outfielders in the history of baseball, have been placed on the reserve list of the clubs they formerly managed. They have been completely exonerated of any wrongdoing."[19]

While Landis, in his ruling, had indicated that Cobb and Speaker would now be the property of their former teams, both Cleveland and Detroit gave permission to the players to entertain offers from other teams. In other words both men were being released.

There was no shortage of teams with an interest in Tris Speaker and Ty Cobb. "On hearing the news, Connie Mack reacted like a teenager turned loose in a mall with an unlimited credit card."[20] Coming into the 1927 season the A's had a pretty set outfield but in Connie's mind Cobb and Speaker still had some good years left and that they would add two big names to draw fans. He was not alone in that belief. "The line quickly formed ... The White Sox and Yankees were interested in Speaker but not Cobb. The Browns wanted Cobb, not Speaker. Jack Dunn offered Cobb $25,000 to come to Baltimore."[21]

The team most interested in Speaker was the Washington Senators. Clark Griffith, the team's owner, was the first to make an offer to Speaker and after some back-and-forth negotiations Griffith agreed to all his conditions and he accepted the offer. He would be paid $30,000 for the 1927 season. Connie Mack reached out and said that he would top the Senators' offer but Speaker said that he had given his word to Griffith and that he felt duty bound to honor it.

With Speaker out of the equation, Mack made a big push to acquire the services of the man nicknamed the "Georgia Peach." Connie sent a letter saying that he was coming down to meet with Cobb and his home in Augusta, Georgia. When he arrived on February 4, he learned that Dan Howley, manager of the St. Louis Browns, was also in town to meet with Cobb. "That evening Cobb invited them both to his home, where they enjoyed a pleasant, noncommittal evening with their coy host and his family." The next day the three men boarded a train for the northeast for a series of sportswriter's dinners in New York and Philadelphia. During the train ride, Mack met with Cobb in his drawing room. "Mack probably put his offer on the table—a $10,000 signing bonus, $50,000 salary, a cut of exhibition games (which would earn him an additional $5,350.83) and $15,000 if the A's won the pennant."[22] After the dinner in New York Cobb traveled to Philadelphia for that city's event and met with Connie Mack in his office at Shibe Park and then he headed over to the Adelphi Ballroom in Philadelphia for the writer's dinner. When it was his turn to address the writers, Cobb first thanked them for inviting him. He mentioned that he was particularly touched by the fact that the invitation had come prior to the decision by Judge Landis that reinstated him to baseball. He then added "I am happy to announce I will be associated with the Athletics this season"[23] and with that, on February 7, 1927, Ty Cobb officially became a member of the Philadelphia Athletics and a teammate of Walter French. That association would have a major impact on the trajectory of his career and not in a positive way.

CHAPTER 8

1929 and the Team that Time Forgot

One would think that adding a big name like Ty Cobb to a team would be plenty for one franchise to handle, but Connie Mack was not done making moves to improve the Athletics. In addition to the "Georgia Peach" he picked up two future Hall of Famers in Zach Wheat, in a trade with the Brooklyn Robins, and the signing of free agent second baseman Eddie Collins. Sportswriter Don Q. Duffy wrote that "seven successive seasons in the American League cellar convinced Mack that the quickest road to the top was experienced material—the more expensive the better ... Ponder these three names Tyrus Raymond Cobb, Edward Towbridge Collins and Zachary Davis Wheat. A year ago, they were in other parts, but for 1927 they are members of Connie Mack's Athletics."[1]

The A's were not the only team making moves, and Cobb, Collins, and Wheat were not the only big names changing teams. It was as if everyone expected that it would take a special team in 1927 to win the pennant and World Series. In the American League the Senators had added Tris Speaker to their team and in the National League the St. Louis Cardinals added 15-year veteran middle infielder Rabbit Maranville to their World Series championship roster. The New York Giants traded future Hall of Famer Frankie Frisch and Jimmy Ring to the Cardinals for their superstar player Rogers Hornsby. Players were not the only new faces on teams, of the 16 managers in major league baseball in 1927, eight were either new to the job or new to their team.

With the addition of Cobb and Wheat, the Athletics went into spring training with five established major league outfielders, plus three additional players Mack had signed from the minor leagues. The holdovers from the 1926 roster were Al Simmons, Bill Lamar, and Walter French. Other new faces in addition to Cobb and Wheat were Dave Barbee, Alex Metzier, and Max West. There was also now a bottleneck in the infield as well. Max Bishop who had been the A's second baseman was now vying with Eddie Collins for his position, and Chick Galloway the A's shortstop was now in competition with Joe Boley for whom Mack had purchased from the Baltimore Orioles for $100,000.

It is hard to imagine that Walter did not feel a little threatened by the addition of Cobb and to a lesser extent Wheat, but there is no evidence that he ever mentioned it to anyone in 1927. He had been the team's second leading hitter in 1926, and his star was on the rise, while Cobb's best days were behind him. Making it a little easier to swallow for Walter was the fact that his salary had been raised from the $5,000 he earned in the previous season to $7,500 and although it was only one-tenth of what Cobb was being paid, it did represent a sizeable increase.

Another indication that his position was secure was the reaction of Connie Mack to Walter's request, toward the end of the 1926 season, to once again join the Pottsville Maroons in the National Football League in the offseason. There was no giving in on Mack's part this time. Walter's football playing days were over as long as he was a member of the Athletics' organization. Instead of playing football, in the offseason, Walter took a job as the head coach of the Atlantic City Roses, a team in the professional Eastern Football League.

It also must have made him feel better each day when reading the newspapers because, in their coverage of spring training, the sportswriters were not all convinced that it was a forgone conclusion that the starters from 1926 would not keep their jobs. In an article from March 10, sportswriter Elwood Rigby speculated as to who should bat in the leadoff spot in the lineup: "It is almost a sure bet that Mickey Cochrane will be number one man in the batting order … when either Walter French or Max Bishop are playing, Cochrane no doubt will be moved down the ladder."[2] Adding that "Mack has another exceptionally good boy to put at the top of his batting order in Walter French, who is doomed to see bench duty most of next season because of the acquisition of the great Ty Cobb. French is probably the fastest man on the Athletics' team. He is a left-handed hitter and gets down to first with amazing speed."[3] Adding an element of uncertainty with respect to the outfielders was the health of Al Simmons. Simmons was a limited participant in the spring training exercises and practice due to a ruptured muscle in his right shoulder.

As spring training progressed to include practice games it became less and less certain that the new acquisitions were better than the players that had been with the A's in 1926. Davis J. Walsh, Sports Editor for the International News Service, did not pull any punches about what he and others had observed: "Walter French May Beat Ty Cobb for A's Berth" read the headline. "Neither Ty Cobb nor Eddie Collins will start the season in regular positions with the Philadelphia Athletics unless they can prove they are better men than men now sitting on the bench more or less by courtesy." Mack, Walsh wrote, "candidly admitted that to date some of last year's team have looked better."[4]

Walsh claimed that Collins's range had diminished to such an extent that he "can't cover more than a quarter of an inch around second and Cobb has not been hitting." "I paid a lot of money to build up the team this year," Mack told Walsh, "But if my 1926 men prove to be better players, they will get the call regardless of box office values."⁵ Both Cobb and Collins assured the A's fans that they would be ready to go when the season started.

Also not so sure about Cobb was syndicated columnist Billy Evans. "How valuable will Ty Cobb be to the Philadelphia Athletics this year?" he wrote. "My answer is going to be a rather negative one … Ty Cobb has lost much of his speed. I don't believe that even Ty would give you an argument, if you insisted that he had dropped at least two steps in going to first in comparison to his best days."⁶ In addition to losing a step on the bases, Evans also pointed to another deficiency in Cobb's game, "Cobb can no longer get the quick start on a fly ball that was once his custom, neither can he cover the wide territory that he could when in his prime."⁷

As opening day rolled around it seemed that all of Connie Mack's pronouncements that when filling out his lineup, he would make his decision without concern for "box office value" seemed to ring hollow. In the season opener against the Yankees on April 12 a record-breaking crowd of 65,000 fans packed Yankee Stadium to see the league's top pennant contenders. When Mack posted his lineup Max Bishop was on the bench in favor of Eddie Collins at second, Chick Galloway sat while the newly acquired Joe Boley started at shortstop, and Ty Cobb started in right field while Walter French sat the bench.

Mack selected Lefty Grove as the starting pitcher who was opposed by Yankee ace Waite Hoyt. Both pitchers looked sharp and the game was a scoreless tie until the bottom half of the fifth inning when the Yankees broke the game open by scoring four runs helped by A's fielding errors by Mack's new men Collins and Boley.

In the top of the sixth Ty Cobb beat out a bunt flashing some of his old speed. He then advanced to third on a single by Sammy Hale and he scored on a fielder's choice. The A's scored one more run in the sixth to make it a 4–2 game. The Yankees however, put four more runs on the board in the bottom of the sixth inning to finish the scoring. In the ninth inning Walter French was put into the game to hit for Joe Boley and failed to reach base.

The next day was more of the same for the A's as they lost to the Yankees by a score of 10–4. In this game, Babe Ruth, who was removed from the first game due to illness, came back with a vengeance going two for four with a triple and two runs scored. Cobb had another productive day going two for four with one run scored.

In the third game of the season the two teams combined for 26 hits and 18 runs but the game ended in a 9–9 tie, when the game had to be called for darkness.

In the final game of the series the Yankees once again handed the A's a beating, this time by a score of 6–3. In the first inning Babe Ruth brought the crowd to their feet when he hit his first home run of the season. There would be more where that came from this season.

Walter French went into the final game of the Yankee series as a pinch runner and came around and scored his first run of the season. It is not hard to imagine what was going through his head as the first few weeks of the season were being played. His expectations for the 1927 season had to have been high given his success in 1926. In the first month of the season however, he saw very limited action, used exclusively as a pinch hitter, pinch runner, and occasional late inning defensive replacement for Ty Cobb. Making matters worse was the fact that the three men who were emerging as the regular outfielders had all started the season very hot at the plate. In the first week of May, leftfielder Bill Lamar was hitting .357, Al Simmons in centerfield was hitting .410 and Ty Cobb in Walter's rightfield position was hitting .409.

On May 5, the A's were in second place with a record of 11–7, only one-half game behind the first place Yankees who were sporting a record of 12–7. The A's faced off against the last place Red Sox at Shibe Park. With the Red Sox trailing 2–1 in the eighth inning Ira Flagstead hit a pinch hit, two-run home run to give the visiting team a 3–2 victory. But the lead story of this game was not the dramatic outcome. In the eighth inning Cobb crushed a pitch high and far into right field. The ball was hit so high that the *Boston Globe* reported that it went over the housetops on 20th Street. Umpire Red Ormsby called the ball foul. Cobb and Al Simmons, who was in the on-deck circle when Cobb hit the ball, rushed the umpire screaming their disapproval. The argument went on for 10 minutes and then Ormsby ejected Simmons. At this point Cobb made some comments to Ormsby and he was ejected from the game as well. However, Cobb refused to leave the field and then grabbed Ormsby and began shaking him. It was not until A's coach Kid Gleason subdued him did Cobb leave the field.

Upon learning about the incident in Philadelphia, American League president Ban Johnson suspended Simmons and Cobb "indefinitely" and both men were out of the lineup when the A's played the Cleveland Indians at Dunn field the next day. Instead, Connie Mack had Bill Lamar in left field, Zach Wheat in right field and starting for the first time in 1927, Walter French in center field. He had one hit in five at-bats, with an RBI. He also made a good play in the outfield throwing out George Burns, who was attempting to go from first to third on a single. Cleveland however won the game 11–10.

Cobb and Simmons were also out of the lineup in the second game of the series with Cleveland, another loss for the A's, this time by a score of 4–2. Once again batting in the leadoff spot for the A's Walter French had two hits, a single and a double, in three official at-bats, along with one walk. The two A's stars were still not in the lineup when the team faced Cleveland for the final game of the series, yet another loss, this time by a score of 6–1. Walter French once again was in the leadoff spot in the lineup and playing centerfield. He went hitless in three plate appearances.

At this point in the season the Athletics had a record of 11–10 and had dropped into fifth place in the American League but were still only 2.5 games behind the first place Yankees who were 14–8.

The next game for the A's was one of the most anticipated games of the 1927 regular season. It would mark Ty Cobb's return to the city of Detroit and Navin

Field. There was only one problem, both he and Simmons were still suspended for their actions in the game against the Red Sox.

The timing of the suspension of Simmons and Cobb just days before the big series in Detroit was not good for Walter and his chances for more playing time. Clearly Ban Johnson, still fuming about being overruled in the Dutch Leonard Affair, was looking to throw the book at both players over the ruckus they caused in Boston, by suspending them indefinitely. However, pressure began building on Johnson to reverse himself or at least end the suspension at three games, which would allow Cobb to play in Detroit. Leading the protest was Connie Mack who argued that Ormsby, realizing that he had made a bad call, apologized to Cobb. "I want Ormsby to explain why he apologized to Ty for putting him out of the game and then made a report to Ban Johnson that apparently inflamed him,"[8] Mack wrote. Hundreds of telegrams came into the league office, mostly from Detroit where the Tigers had planned a full day of festivities honoring Cobb. Finally, Johnson got a last-minute report from the second umpire working the game in Boston, Brick Owens, in which he claimed that he never saw Cobb strike Ormsby. Ultimately Johnson issued a last-minute reprieve saying, "I do not see how I can keep Cobb out of the game any longer considering Owens' report." Simmons was also reinstated but Johnson did require that each player be fined $200 "payable by personal check within forty-eight hours."[9]

Ban Johnson's reversal was joyously received in Detroit where the largest weekday crowd, nearly 30,000 strong, in the history of Navin Field, prepared to celebrate Cobb's return. Both Simmons and Cobb were eligible to play in the game. James Isaminger writing in the *Philadelphia Inquirer* described the scene this way: "Probably no other player in baseball history was as regally honored as was the Dixie Daredevil, who was the lion of the city of automobiles from 1905 to 1926, came back today in his twenty-third season of high-pressure baseball, still the acclaimed monarch of the American League attack and wearing the regalia other than Detroit's for the first time in his career overlapping two long decades." Cobb was given a testimonial luncheon, a "high grade" automobile, a chest of silver, a big cowboy sombrero, and a floral piece shaped like a huge corncob.[10]

The game, which seemed like an afterthought to the crowd on hand that day, was won by the Athletics by a score of 6–3. Walter French, although not in the starting lineup, was sent up to hit for Cobb in the eighth inning and stayed in the game to play right field. In his one at bat, he hit a two-out single which scored Eddie Collins and moved Bill Lamar to third. Al Simmons then drove both men in with a double that put the game on ice.

For the remainder of the month of May, Walter French was relegated to entering the game as a late inning defensive replacement for Cobb. In some of the games he would get one at-bat but nothing more. It didn't help that all three of the men playing ahead of him were still among the league's leading hitters. On May 31,

Cobb was hitting .381, Bill Lamar .337, and Al Simmons was hitting .399. At this point in the season the A's were in third place with a record of 22–20, and six games behind the first place Yankees who had a record of 28–14. In second place were the Chicago White Sox with a record of 27–17.

Although he was the leading pinch hitter in the American League in 1925, Walter had shown in the last month of that season and again in 1926 that when used regularly he could be a very effective offensive player. But with so few opportunities to hit at this stage of the season, his batting average dipped to .174. He played in only four games from May 31 to June 18. In one he went in as a pinch runner and the other three as a defensive replacement for Cobb. He only came to bat three times over that span.

Finally, coming into a double header at Shibe Park against the Washington Senators, after Cobb landed himself on the injured list with a strained side, Walter was inserted into the starting lineup for both games. He was batting second and playing right field. The game got off to a rough start for Walter when his throw to the plate sailed over the head of Mickey Cochrane, allowing Goose Goslin of the Senators to score an unearned run in the top of the first inning. However, he made up for his miscue by hitting the ball in both games, as the *Philadelphia Inquirer* reported "French atoned for his sinful conduct by belting the ball hard in both games. He had two singles in the first game and a single and a triple in the second. The long lick scoring two runs and taking all of the fight out of Washington."[11]

Pitching in the second game for the Senators was Walter Johnson. Johnson was pitching in the final season of his illustrious Hall of Fame career. It would be the last time that Walter French would square off against the "Big Train." His two hits brought his lifetime average against one of the greatest pitchers in the history of baseball to .381.

The following day, with Cobb still nursing his injury, Walter started both games of a second doubleheader against the Senators and went hitless. He played the whole game the next day and again went 0 for 4.

Next on the schedule for the Athletics was a series against the New York Yankees. At this juncture of the season, not even the halfway point, it was becoming obvious that the Yankees were in the process of putting together an historic run. They sat atop of the American League with a record of 44–17, a full 10 games ahead of the A's who had worked their way back into a virtual tie with the White Sox for second place. Head-to-head games between the two teams would be crucial if Mack's team was to have any chance at catching the Yankees.

On June 25 the two teams squared off in a double header, necessitated by a game having been postponed in May due to rain. There were over 50,000 fans in attendance at Yankee Stadium. In what James Isaminger described in the *Philadelphia Inquirer* as "their boldest stroke of the year"[12] the Athletics swept both games from the Yankees. The first game by a score of 7–6 and the second game by a score of

4–2. Walter started both games and had one hit in three tries in the first game, with a successful sacrifice thrown in and one hit in four at-bats in the second game. In both games he came around and scored a run. Spirits were lifted in Philadelphia. "The Athletics seemed to serve notice," Isaminger noted "that there will be a keen pennant fight in the American League after all and with the halfway mark in the race not quite reached there will be plenty of chances to overhaul the gifted bat bearers of the Yank cast in the last half of the race."[13]

On the following day another sellout crowd was on hand for another double header. In the first game, Walter French collected three hits in five at-bats and scored two runs as the A's took their third straight game from the Yankees. The Yankees bounced back in the second game winning by a score of 7–3 on the strength of Lou Gehrig's twenty-second home run of the season. Slowly but surely, Walter's batting average was starting to rise after he collected one more hit in the second game. In the eight games that he had started since Cobb's injury, he had hit safely in six of the games, collecting nine hits in total.

Unfortunately, the A's still had two more games to play against the Yankees before the series would be over. The Yankees won the first game by score of 6–2 and the next day they won by a score of 9–8. The Yankees had come back and despite the fact that they had won the first three games, the A's were essentially right back where they started when the series began, 10 games out of first place. Walter was hitless in the first game but bounced back the next day going two for four.

On July 2, Cobb returned to the starting lineup and Walter was relegated to pinch hitting once again, coming to the plate only two times over the next nine games. Finally, on July 11 he was inserted into the lineup replacing Bill Lamar in left field. He responded with one hit in four trips to the plate and the Athletics defeated the St. Louis Browns by a score of 7–6. He remained in the lineup the next day against the White Sox in Chicago, collecting three hits and scoring one run in an 8–5 A's loss. However, except for one appearance as a late inning defensive replacement for Zach Wheat, he was relegated to the bench again until July 21. On that day he played left field and hit in the seventh spot in the order. He had one hit and scored two runs as the A's defeated Cleveland 8–3 and he played long enough in the next game to come to bat twice, although he went hitless.

At this point in the season the Athletics were mired in fourth place in the American League, already 18 games behind the Yankees, when they lost their best player and the leading hitter in the American League, Al Simmons. The Associated Press reported that "Simmons injured his groin sliding into second base" and that "physicians had advised him today to remain inactive until the middle of August. Manager Connie Mack switched Ty Cobb to center field, placed Zach Wheat in left and Walter French in right against Detroit as a result of Simmons' absence."[14]

Walter responded with one of his best games since joining the Athletics. He finished the game, a dramatic 13-inning affair, with four hits in five trips to the plate. He also scored a run and had one run batted in. With the A's trailing by one run in the bottom of the ninth inning Walter led off with a long double. Eddie Collins came up as a pinch hitter for Boley and laid down a perfect sacrifice bunt which sent him to third base. Bill Lamar followed with a single, scoring Walter with the tying run. In the thirteenth inning Jimmy Dykes won the game with a walk off home run.

The Tigers bounced back the next day in the first game of a doubleheader, with a 10–4 win. In this game Walter French, again batting seventh and playing left field had three hits in four at-bats and scored one run. In the second game he went two for three including a triple, with four runs batted in, two with two outs, as the A's won 5–2. He had also raised his batting average, once as low as .174, to .288.

As the calendar switched over to August, Walter had to be pleased about the turn of events that gave him the opportunity to play every day. In the seven games that he had played since Simmons' injury he had nine hits. Meanwhile the Yankees were running away with the American League with a record of 73–28. They were followed by the Washington Senators and Detroit Tigers, with the Athletics still stuck in fourth place.

Next on the schedule for the A's was a series at Shibe Park against the Yankees on August 9. By this point Walter had expected to see his name on the manager's lineup card each day but he was not ready for what he saw on this day. No longer was he hitting seventh in the A's lineup. Connie Mack had moved him up to the third spot in the order just ahead of Ty Cobb and Mickey Cochrane. So, the three, four, and five hitters for the Athletics, considered the meat of any team's batting order, were Walter French, Ty Cobb, and Mickey Cochrane respectively. The *Philadelphia Inquirer* reported that "Mr. Mack promoted Fritz French to third place in the batting order and the young Jersey lightning showed his appreciation by smashing out two singles and a double."[15] Hitting third he went three for five, with two runs scored and two runs batted in as the A's drubbed the Yankees by a score of 8–1.

Still hitting in the third spot in the lineup the next day against the Red Sox, Walter collected two more hits, scored three times, and knocked in two runs as the A's won by a score of 12–2. As designed, the three, four, and five hitters for Philadelphia, French, Cobb, and Cochrane, drove in eight of the team's 12 runs.

Walter stayed hot the next day, August 11, with two hits in four at-bats with a run scored to back up the pitching of Howard Ehmke who shutout his former team, Boston, 4–0 in the first game of a doubleheader.

After the second game, which the Red Sox won by a score of 2–0, Walter along with Mickey Cochrane and Jimmy Dykes were transported to the town of Catasauqua, PA, a suburb of Allentown located in Lehigh County. The occasion was the town's annual carnival. The players were expected to meet with fans, sign autographs, and participate in some of the different activities.

Originally, Ty Cobb was supposed to attend with Dykes and Cochrane but he was a last-minute cancellation and Walter was tabbed to go in his place. Walter said he would be happy to do it as long as he was able to get back to Philadelphia in time to catch the last bus to Moorestown, NJ where he lived with his wife, who was pregnant at the time, and his daughter Fran. George Bellis, who was one of the organizers of the event and who was driving the players back to Philadelphia, promised Walter that if he did not get him back to catch the last bus at midnight, he would drive him the rest of the way, a trip of about 15 miles. One of the featured events at the carnival was a dog show, specifically for bird dogs used by hunters and Walter performed as the judge of the contest. One can only surmise that Cobb, a legendary hunting enthusiast, was originally supposed to serve in this role, and given that Walter was filling in for Cobb, he was enlisted as the judge, despite how little he knew about the subject.

As Walter expected, Bellis did not leave Catasauqua with the players until 11 o'clock. Even today one would be hard pressed to make the trip to Philadelphia from Catasauqua, a distance of about 65 miles, in an hour. After dropping Dykes and Cochrane off in the city, true to his word, Bellis started driving Walter to his home in Moorestown.

When they were about halfway, in the town of Merchantville, NJ, they came upon the bus that Walter was supposed to be on. It had been involved in an accident with two of its occupants injured. Witnesses said that a speeding touring car had cut off the bus attempting to squeeze between the bus and a trolley car. The bus driver, credited with preventing an even worse outcome, took evasive action, maneuvered his bus over the sidewalk, having it come to rest in the front yard of the home of former Congressman Francis Patterson. The driver of the car was charged with reckless driving. According to a newspaper account of the incident "French turned to Bellis and said, 'I'm glad you kept me at Catasauqua as late as you did, or I would have been in that bus.'"[16]

However, if the late night or the close call bothered Walter French, you could not tell by his performance in the game the next day, where he had two hits in five at-bats and one run batted in. It was much the same in the final game of the series the next day when he led the A's with three hits and three runs batted in.

The following day against visiting Cleveland he had one hit in five at-bats but that hit resulted in knocking in a run with two outs. In the second game of that day's doubleheader he led the A's offense going two for five with three runs batted in. In fact, French, Cobb and pitcher Jack Quinn drove in all of the eight runs that the team scored in their 8–0 victory.

On August 17, Walter had two hits in four trips to the plate and raised his batting average to .302. In addition, the A's were starting to win a higher percentage of their games than at any other time of the season. No one was going to challenge the Yankees but a second-place finish and the bonus money that went with it, which seemed unlikely earlier, was now within reach.

The Athletics stumbled the following day, losing 2–1 to Cleveland, but Walter remained hot with two hits in four at-bats. Next for the A's were the White Sox and Philadelphia got off to a fast start. In the first inning Max Bishop led off with a single. He then advanced to second when Sammy Hale grounded out. Walter French then smacked a single and drove in Bishop with the game's first run. Ty Cobb then singled moving French to second. This brought up Mickey Cochrane, who hit a pop ball in foul territory along the third base line, which was dropped by the White Sox third baseman Willie Kamm giving Cochrane new life. Mickey then hit the next pitch over the right field wall for a three-run home run, scoring Walter and Ty Cobb ahead of him.

On August 25, French, with three hits in four at-bats, Cobb, who had five hits in five chances, and Cochrane, who had two hits in five trips to the plate accounted for 10 of the 14 hits the A's had in a 6–1 win over St. Louis. Walter's batting average was now at .317. Moreover, the A's were quietly putting together a winning streak and had moved into third place only 1.5 games behind the second place Detroit Tigers. The A's won again on August 26 beating St. Louis 7–0 and again Walter had three hits, and in what was becoming a regular occurrence scored one run and knocked in another.

On August 28, in a crucial head-to-head matchup with the Detroit Tigers, Walter led the way to a key A's victory with three hits all of which resulted in him coming around to score in a 9–5 win.

As August came to an end, the Athletics had finally moved into second place and were now three games ahead of the third-place Tigers. While the difference between second and third place to a modern-day baseball fan, in an era with playoffs and Wild Card teams, may not seem significant, it meant a great deal financially to the teams involved. The A's had 21 wins against only seven losses in the month of August, and since moving Walter French to the third spot in the lineup on August 9, they had gone 17–4 for the rest of the month of August, an almost identical record to that of the Yankees over the same span. No one on the A's was more instrumental in putting this run together than was Walter French.

However, if the A's were feeling pretty good about themselves, the Yankees put that right in the first game of September by beating them at home by a score of 12–2. Babe Ruth hit his forty-fourth home run and Lou Gehrig hit two, his forty-second and forty-third. Walter French still continued to perform well, getting one of the only six hits the A's got off of Yankee Ace Waite Hoyt.

The next day Lefty Grove blanked the Yankees by a score of 1–0, holding "Murderers' Row" to only four hits.

On September 6, a familiar name was back in the Athletics' lineup. Walter started the game as had been the case for almost a month, batting third and playing right field, but after he came to bat twice, Al Simmons was sent in to replace him in the first game of a double header that was won by the Washington Senators. Walter was back, however, for the second game and went two for four as the A's took the Senators behind the pitching of Eddie Rommel by a score of 4–0.

The following day, September 7, the A's had an exhibition game against a team in Allentown, PA. Playing these exhibition games during the season was not an unusual occurrence for the A's. The *Philadelphia Inquirer* noted that "Connie Mack had booked another one of his hoodoo exhibition games."[17] Earlier in the year Ty Cobb had been injured in one such game in Buffalo, NY. Pitching for the Allentown team was "Beezer" Stauffer, a local baseball legend. With Al Simmons, just back in the lineup the day before at the plate, "Beezer" tossed up one of his slow, tantalizing curve balls at which Simmons took a mighty cut and came up with nothing but air, and in the process twisted his ankle. He stayed in the game but he was not in the lineup when the Athletics squared off the next day against the Tigers. The A's won the game easily by a score of 9–1. Walter was back in his normal spot in the lineup and had one hit and one run scored.

Walter continued his excellent play, the Athletics continued to win, and Al Simmons still had not been near the field since his mishap in Allentown. Finally on September 14, Simmons went in and played left field late in the game that the A's won 5–4 against the White Sox. In that game Walter had two hits in five at-bats and came around to score twice. By this juncture of the season Connie Mack's team was secure in second place with a seven-game lead over the Detroit Tigers.

Finally on September 15, Al Simmons was put into the starting lineup, only as the left fielder, Walter French continued to start in right field and despite the presence of Simmons who was hitting nearly .400 at the time of his injury, continued to bat third in the A's lineup. Simmons had one hit in the game, Walter French had two.

Slowly but surely, Simmons began to regain his form. On September 19 he had three hits, including his fifteenth home run of the season, and he knocked in three runs bringing his season total to 105 as the A's defeated the St. Louis Browns by a score of 4–1.

When the Athletics beat the Browns again the next day by a score of 7–3, both Simmons and French went two for four and each man scored a run.

On September 22, Walter French for the first time since Simmons injury was not in the A's lineup when they faced the Cleveland Indians in a game won by Philadelphia by a score of 4–3. He was back in the lineup a few days later, no longer hitting third but down in the lineup hitting seventh. A new name appeared in the box score for the Athletics, catcher Jimmie Foxx, who Mack was converting to a first baseman, in an effort to get both his bat and that of Mickey Cochrane into the everyday lineup.

On September 27, Walter had one hit with one run batted in, in a 7–4 loss to the Yankees. In that game Babe Ruth hit his fifty-seventh home run, a three-run shot off of Lefty Grove.

As the 1927 season came to an end, Connie Mack, like all of his contemporaries in the American League, was already pondering what moves he would have to make to keep up with the Yankees. One wonders if one of the options he considered was keeping Walter French in the regular lineup. In the 52 games he started from

August 2 through the end of the season, Walter batted .325. In that stretch he had 21 multiple hit games and overall played outstanding defense. More importantly the Athletics won 40 games against 16 losses. A closer look at the 40 games played from August 9, when Mack moved Walter to the third spot in the order through September 21, his last game hitting third, the Athletics went 31–9, which was even a better record than the Yankees over the same span.

As bad as the season had started for Walter French, he had to feel pretty good about the way it ended and his prospects for the 1928 season. Most observers believed it to be unlikely that Cobb would return for his twenty-fourth season. He would be 41 years old in 1928. There was even some speculation that Connie Mack, who would turn 66 years old in the offseason, may retire. "Late in the season," Norman Macht wrote in his biography of Mack "everywhere the Athletics went the writers renewed the speculation about Connie Mack's retiring. The presence of Eddie Collins a logical successor, fertilized the guesswork."[18]

The *Journal Gazette* of Mattoon Illinois reported that "the chance to become a sure enough big leaguer has apparently caused Walter French of the Philadelphia Athletics to cut down on professional football. I note where he has signed to assist in coaching football at Swarthmore ... now with a chance to become a major league star, French has decided the chances taken in football are not in keeping with the possibilities offered in baseball."[19]

Confident that he would find himself as one of the regular outfielders in 1928 Walter headed off to his offseason job coaching football at Swarthmore College under head coach Roy Mercer. Mercer was a graduate of the University of Pennsylvania, who was a star on the football and track teams. He was a member of two U.S. Olympic Teams, 1908 and 1912. He earned his MD at the University in 1913 and served on the staff of two Philadelphia hospitals, while coaching football at the same time. In 1955, he was elected to the College Football Hall of Fame.

Even though the A's 1927 season ended on a high note and with a second-place finish, there was little cause for celebration. The A's had won 91 games and still finished an amazing 19 games behind the eventual World Series champions Yankees. If the 1926 season had not convinced everyone that the game had gone through a cosmic change, the 1927 season brought the message home in a brutal fashion. The 1927 Yankees completely dominated their competition, and for Connie Mack the message was clear, the game of baseball had changed and he and his team needed to change with it. The Yankees had outscored the A's by 135 runs even though the teams had an almost identical team batting average. During the season the Athletics, as a team, hit 56 home runs, compared to 158 for the Yankees. Babe Ruth alone had 60 and Lou Gehrig finished the season with 43 home runs and 175 runs batted in. Al Simmons, the Athletics' leading home run hitter, had a total of 15 by comparison. After his team lost both games of a double header to the Yankees by identical scores of 21–0, Joe Judge, first baseman for the Washington Senators spoke for a lot of the American League when he observed "those fellows not only beat you, but they tear your hearts out."

The Yankees domination also drove down attendance at Shibe Park. Although finishing in second place meant a lot financially to the A's players, being so far out of first place for all but the very start of the season badly hurt attendance. In 1926, when the team finished in third place, 714,508 people attended games at Shibe Park, the second-best attendance in the league. In 1927 however, finishing second only attracted 605,529 a drop of 108,979 fans which represented only the fourth best attendance in the American League.

One of the rumors that was floating around in early October was that there were two trades in the works, one with the White Sox and one with the Senators. The first trade would have the White Sox sending Bib Falk and Johnny Mostil to the Athletics for Al Simmons. The second called for the Senators to trade Goose Goslin to the Athletics in exchange for Bill Lamar and Walter French. Both rumors turned out to be false and Tom Shibe issued a statement denying any knowledge of a trade being considered involving any of the three members of the Athletics. However, while there was no truth to the rumor that Mack planned to trade for Falk, Mostil, and Goslin, on December 27, Mack made the first of what would be a number of offseason moves in an effort to keep up with the Yankees. Bing Miller, with whom he had parted in 1926, as Walter French developed into a dependable everyday player, had had a good season in 1926, batting .326 after arriving with the St. Louis Browns and he followed it up in 1927 by hitting .319 and knocking in 75 runs in the process. When the Browns indicated that they were prepared to accept pitcher Sammy Gray, who had a respectable 9–7 record for the A's in 1927, in a trade, Mack jumped at the chance to bring Miller back to Philadelphia.

Then on February 1, 1928, the Washington Senators announced that they were releasing Tris Speaker. For most outside observers it appeared to be the end of the road for the 40-year-old star. He was not alone. In fact, a number of sports stars who had come to prominence in the decade of the 1920s had either announced their intention to retire or were expected to do so soon. Famed sportswriter Carl Finke, from Dayton, OH in his weekly column "Finke Thinks" wrote that the winter of 1927–28 would go down as the "most retiring in all history of sport." He went on to cite the announced retirements of Walter Johnson, boxing great Jack Dempsey, U.S. Polo team captain Devereux Milburn, tennis great Bill Johnston, and Tad Jones longtime head football coach at Yale before finally adding "Ty Cobb and Tris Speaker apparently are through with the big show."[20] On February 5, The *Sioux City Journal* added "The expected passing of Tris Speaker from the major leagues will mark also the exit of the greatest fly chaser in baseball."[21]

That same day however, unbeknownst to the sportswriters, Connie Mack interrupted his Florida golfing trip to place a call to Speaker with an offer of $15,000 to join the Athletics, an offer the 40-year-old accepted.

When Ty Cobb ultimately did retire after the 1928 season he was asked if he had any regrets looking back on his 24-year career. The only regret he would acknowledge was that he hadn't played his entire career with the A's and Connie Mack. In his Mack biography Norman Macht wrote that "Ty Cobb's admiration for Connie Mack was genuine. Watching him manage men on a daily basis, Cobb recognized in Mack what he himself had lacked as a manager."[22] Grantland Rice once ask Ty how he would rate Connie Mack as a manager and as a man. Cobb replied that Mack was "about the best I have ever known. He is smart and square. He understands baseball and men ... the ballplayer who won't work his head off for Connie Mack isn't much good."[23] And so it was that Connie Mack was able to prevail upon Ty to put off his retirement for one more year.

Before he joined the Athletics the word was that Ty Cobb was a difficult teammate. However, the A's players who had gone up against Cobb, seemed happy to have him. Jimmy Dykes, himself a hard-nosed player, recalled with a smile how when he first broke into the major leagues and was playing second base, whenever he passed him on the field, Cobb would say to Jimmy "you stink." Dykes had a tremendous amount of respect for Cobb. Cobb had been the hero of some of the younger players on the A's like Max Bishop, who told Bill Dooly, "Ty was my big hero ... I read everything I could lay my hands on about him."[24] Bishop, a natural right hander, learned to bat lefty because Cobb hit left-handed. Al Simmons benefited from Cobb's guidance, especially when it came to hitting tough left-handed pitchers. Cobb was known to offer stock tips to players usually recommending that they buy stock in Coca-Cola and those that listened to him were glad they did. Cobb and Mickey Cochrane became particularly close and lifelong friends.

Numbered among the A's that got along well with Ty Cobb was Walter French. Walter's daughter Fran recalled meeting Cobb when she visited her father while he was playing for the A's and how he let her sit on his lap. Walter was also one of the A's that followed Cobb's stock tips and purchased shares of Coca-Cola. He and Cobb would be seen together in the clubhouse or on the field before a game. Ballpark errand boy Jim Morrow told how Cobb, Grove, and French would sit in the right field corner bullpen and send him for ice cream or a candy bar and "never give me the money to pay for it and they would holler, don't let Mr. Mack see you."[25]

On February 27, James Isaminger reported in the *Philadelphia Inquirer* that "in all probability Ty Cobb will announce in a few days that he will play another season with the Athletics. Connie Mack talked to the Peach in Augusta, GA over the long-distance phone tonight and at the end of the conversation he told reporters that Cobb wanted a day or two to discuss the Athletics' offer with his family." Mack, however, declared that negotiations were proceeding satisfactorily and that he expected Ty to sign a 1928 contract. Three days later it became official. Ty Cobb had signed with the A's for the 1928 season. "It took a long campaign to get Ty for another season," Mack said. "He had virtually retired from baseball and didn't want to play, but I showed him how useful he would be to me next season and moreover give us a chance for the pennant and he finally relented." Then Mack spoke the words Walter French must have expected but still dreaded hearing "Cobb, Speaker and Simmons! What an outfield that will be to electrify the nation."[26]

The final straw came a few days later when it was announced that Mack had signed first baseman and outfielder Mule Haas who had played for the Pittsburgh Pirates' organization. Haas was the perfect fit for the type of team Mack felt he needed to compete with the Yankees, a big, strong, powerful hitter.

However, "electrifying the nation" would have to wait because when Al Simmons showed up at spring training in Fort Myers he was "crippled with rheumatism" and "could hardly walk." Mack suggested that he could be out of the lineup until summer or perhaps all year. When the team travelled north to start the season, instead of suiting up, Simmons was admitted to the Methodist Hospital in Philadelphia.

A crowd of 25,000 were on hand at Shibe Park for the Athletics' opening day game against the New York Yankees on April 11. The outfield for the Athletics consisted of Ty Cobb in right field, Tris Speaker in centerfield, and Bing Miller, filling in for Simmons, playing left field. The Yankees behind Ruth and Gehrig picked right up where they had left off the previous year as they easily defeated the A's by a score of 8–3. The next day was more of the same as the Yankees once again beat the home team by a score of 8–7. Walter French went hitless in his one at bat as a pinch hitter

Members of the 1928 Philadelphia Athletics outfield. Left to right: Walter French, Ty Cobb, Tris Speaker, Bing Miller, and Mule Haas. Missing from the photo is Al Simmons. (Courtesy of Author)

while Cobb, Speaker and Miller once again played the outfield. The A's then lost their next two games to the Senators and once again got the season off to a slow start.

Over the next few weeks, the team ran into some bad weather and were way behind the other teams in the American League in terms of the number of games they had played. Of the six games they were able to get in, they won each of them and as the calendar flipped over to May, the Yankees were in first with a record of 10–3, followed by Cleveland at 12–6, St. Louis was in third place at 11–8, and the A's at 6–4 were in fourth place. For his part, Walter French had only made the one pinch hit appearance in the entire month of April.

After going winless in their first four games, however the A's got hot and by the middle of the month of May they had a record of 16–7 and were in second place 2.5 games behind the Yankees who were 21–5. Mack continued to stick with the outfield of Cobb, Speaker, and Miller. His pinch-hit appearance in the second game of the year was still the only time that Walter did not spend on the bench.

Then on May 21, in the sixth inning of the first game of a double header between the Athletics and the Washington Senators, Bobby Reeves, the Senators' shortstop hit a fly ball into the gap between left and center. Bing Miller and Tris Speaker both went for the ball and collided just as Miller was about to catch the ball, sending both men sprawling in the ground. Speaker was knocked unconscious and Miller sustained what looked to be a serious injury to his shoulder. Walter French was sent in to replace Miller and Mule Haas went in for Speaker. Haas had three plate appearances, going hitless in two at-bats, and reaching on a base on balls. Walter came up four times, knocking out two hits, one of which drove in a run in the A's 4–3 win.

In the second game of the doubleheader, with the A's clinging to a 1–0 lead in the fourth inning, courtesy of a Jimmy Dykes home run, Walter French came to bat with two outs and smacked out a double scoring first baseman Joe Hauser with what would prove to be the winning run. Later in the game his perfect throw from right field beat Senators' pitcher Bump Hadley to the plate saving another run. The 2–1 victory meant the doubleheader sweep allowed Mack's team to stay only 3.5 games behind the first place Yankees. The next day Walter was back in the starting lineup and again had two hits in five at-bats, scoring one run in the process.

Next on the schedule for the A's was a doubleheader against the Yankees. The first game was a makeup of a game from April that was postponed due to extremely cold weather. Walter was in the lineup in right field as he had been in the previous few games and Tris Speaker back from his injury was in centerfield. Bing Miller made an appearance in the game as a pinch hitter. Walter went hitless in the game but did drive in one run in the 9–7 loss to the Yankees. Another name that appeared in the A's lineup for the first time was Al Simmons, who pinch hit for Walter in the seventh inning, and got one hit, a single, and just like that Walter's narrow window of opportunity in the 1928 season closed. In the remaining games with the Yankees, he only appeared once as a late inning defensive replacement for Speaker. New York swept the series and took a commanding seven game lead in the American League with a record of 30–7.

Finally on May 28th, in the A's thirty-seventh game of the year, Connie Mack got to start his dream outfield starting Cobb in rightfield, Speaker in centerfield and Simmons in left but the Yankees still won 11–4. However, from that point on, when the dream outfield was not playing, Miller and Haas were Mack's first choices to replace any of the regulars and Walter French remained the odd man out.

Over the next several weeks Walter continued to see limited action. From the end of May until the Fourth of July, nearly halfway through the season, Walter came to bat as a pinch hitter 10 times and came in as a late inning defensive replacement for Speaker or Cobb, coming to bat only twice in that capacity and in total he had three hits. While he was spending his time sitting on the bench the A's were falling further behind the Yankees who at this point had a 12-game lead over the Athletics.

In July it appeared that Mack had given up on his "dream outfield." The regular outfielders were now Ty Cobb in left field, Bing Miller in center field, and Al Simmons in right field. Any mention of Tris Speaker was in the role of a pinch hitter, who along with Mule Haas, appeared to be Mack's go to men off the bench. Walter French made his first appearance on July 12, when he was used as a pinch hitter. He hit a single in a 4–3 loss to the White Sox.

On July 17 Ty Cobb had to leave the game against the St. Louis Browns after being hit by a pitch. Walter went into the game in right field and had one hit in two at-bats. The next day Walter got the start in place of Cobb, who was still recovering. He played right field and batted in the leadoff spot. He responded with two hits in five at-bats and he also scored a run as the A's defeated the Browns in the second game of a doubleheader by a score of 4–3.

Cobb was back in the lineup on July 25, when the A's defeated the White Sox by a score of 16–0. He came to bat three times and had two hits and scored three runs. He then came out of the game and was replaced by Walter French, who in turn went two for two with a run scored and one run batted in. At this point he had raised his batting average, albeit on a small number of chances, to .318. In the second game of the doubleheader, he went in for Cobb as a defensive replacement. The next day he did the same but did not get to bat. On July 27, he was sent in to pinch hit for the A's shortstop Joe Boley. He remained in the game playing left field and came to bat three times. He had two hits, a single and a double, scored one run and had one run batted in as the A's defeated the White Sox 7–4, raising his batting average to .333.

Over the next few games Mack's outfield began to consist of Simmons, Haas, and Miller and however he was shuffling his lineup, it was working. The A's had gone 25–8 in the month of July and had cut 6.5 games from the Yankees' lead.

In the month of August, Walter French appeared in 11 games, 10 as a pinch hitter, in which he had one hit in with one run scored and one run batted in. He also came in as a defensive replacement for Al Simmons. In that game he came to bat once, hitting a double which drove in a run. The A's had gone 19–9 for the month and had shaved another 4.5 games off of the Yankee lead. Going into the last month of the season only two games separated the first place New Yorkers from the second place Athletics. St. Louis in third place was 17 games behind the A's. The Athletics followed with a record of 15–10 in September and finished the season in second place only 2.5 games behind the Yankees who had won 101 games to Philadelphia's 98 wins. The Yankees went on to win their second consecutive World Series sweeping the St. Louis Cardinals in four games.

In the month of September, Walter appeared in only seven games, five as a pinch hitter. He finished the season with a .260 batting average. He had appeared in only 48 games and only had 76 plate appearances. It was the most time he spent on the A's bench since his first season with the team. In a letter to a friend written some 50 years later he acknowledged that "1928 was a very disappointing year for me, as I had to compete with Cobb and Speaker. Both were over the hill. Sitting on the bench just wasn't my cup of tea."

As Walter reflected on the 1928 season and his role on the Athletics, he had to feel frustrated. What more could he do? When he played on a regular basis his numbers were as good as anyone on the team. What's more, when he was in the lineup the team's record, as seen in 1927, was a winning one. Contributing to his frustration had to be the knowledge that the game of baseball had changed and the skill set valued in a player earlier in the 1920s was not the same as what teams wanted and needed as the decade came to an end. Some 50 years later in an interview with sportswriter Greg Lathrop that feeling of frustration with the turn of events in 1928 was still present for Walter. Replying to a question about the acquisition of Bing Miller, Mule Haas, and Tris Speaker in 1928 he said "That left me sitting on the bench. That was one of my biggest gripes. I had a big year in '27 and they still took on those other players."[27]

Since the 1926 season Walter had been earning $7,500 per year, an amount which was supplemented by bonuses when the team finished high in the standings. And so, frustrated by his lack of playing time and feeling the pressure of now having a wife and two daughters to support, he announced that he was retiring from baseball on November 1, 1928. The *Chester County Times* reported with Chicago as a byline, "Walter French, for six years an outfielder with the Philadelphia Athletics, may have played his last major league baseball game. French has entered business in Chicago and has asked Connie Mack to put him on the voluntary retired list."[28] The Chicago business in question was Sears and Roebuck and his role was an unspecified "desk job." Two days after Walter announced his retirement, Connie Mack announced that he had asked waivers on Ty Cobb and Tris Speaker and both men retired.

His stint working for Sears would be the only job that Walter French ever held to that point in his life that was not in professional sports or the military and it did not last long. Within a few weeks of accepting the position, he realized that he had made a big mistake and that a desk job too was "not his cup of tea." As he thought about it, he realized that, as much as he hated it, sitting on the A's bench was preferable to sitting at a desk all day. It may have been nothing more than that, but according to Walter he also had a dream that the A's were going to win the pennant and beat the Chicago Cubs in the World Series and that there would be some World Series winnings in his future. "I worked hard all day," he told sportswriter Harold C. Burr, "and did a lot of sleeping at night. Ordinarily I was too tired to dream, but one night something funny happened, something significant. I dreamed a tall thin man was holding something out toward me. I looked closer and saw it was a $5,000 bill. When I woke up, I didn't have the five grand, but I had an idea ... the tall thin guy was Connie Mack. It was a World Series check he was holding for me to take ... Walter French couldn't ignore such a series of suggestions. He threw up his job with a yell, wired Connie Mack, got Judge Landis to reinstate him, and bought a ticket to the Fort Meyers training camp of the Athletics."[29]

How much the dream really had to do with his decision is unknown but on March 28 the Associated Press reported that "Walter French, Philadelphia Athletics outfielder, who retired from baseball last fall has been reinstated by Commissioner K.M. Landis and will report to the club in Philadelphia April 6, manager Connie Mack announced today. The former Rutgers and Army football star had terminated his professional baseball career to enter business."[30] Connie Mack agreed to keep Walter's salary at $7,500 for the 1929 season.

In its preview of the upcoming season the *New York Times* rated the Yankees and the A's as the teams to beat in the American League. Today it is hard to find a list of baseball's greatest teams that does not include the 1929 Athletics, but in the days before the start of the season many of the prognosticators were giving the edge to the Yankees because of the results of the head-to-head meetings between the two teams in the last two seasons. In 1927, the Athletics were 8–14 against the Yankees while they were 83–63 against the rest of the American League. It was even worse in 1928 when they only finished 2.5 games out of first place, Philadelphia was 92–39 against the rest of the American League, while only 6–16 against the Yankees. The *New York Times* correctly stated that the A's needed to get over the "apparent wholesome respect it has shown in the past for the Yanks when the two meet in hand-to-hand conflict."[31]

Unlike the previous two seasons, the Athletics got off to a fast start in 1929. By the end of May they were sitting in first place with a record of 29–9, five games in front of the second place St. Louis Browns, and eight games in front of the third place Yankees. With the exception of the pitchers and Max Bishop, all of the A's starters were hitting above .300, led by Jimmie Foxx at .434, Mickey Cochrane at .384, and Al Simmons at .346.

By May 31, Walter French had yet to start a game. He had two appearances as a pinch runner and four as a pinch hitter. On May 23 the Athletics were playing the Washington Senators and found themselves down 8–0 in the second inning. After George Earnshaw and Ossie Orwell failed to record an out in the first inning, Connie Mack brought in Bill Shores to pitch. In the fourth inning with the Athletics trailing 8–4 they loaded the bases and with Shores scheduled to bat Mack sent up Walter as a pinch hitter. He hit a double which scored three runs, and later came around himself with the tying run. The A's scored another run in their half of the fifth inning and came away with a 9–8 win.

On May 26, Walter got some good news from New Brunswick with the announcement that he had been named, along with 15 other athletes, to the Rutgers Athletic Hall of Fame. His induction class included his former teammates Paul Robeson and Don Storck. Some 90 years later, in 2019, he would enter the school's Hall of Fame a second time, posthumously, as a member of the 1919 basketball team.

The Athletics continued to dominate their opponents in the American League, including the Yankees. In the month of June, Walter French continued to be used sparingly. He went into a game against St. Louis on June 7 as a defensive replacement and got two hits in three times up and scored one run. He next appeared on June 16 as a pinch hitter and knocked in a run with a sacrifice fly against Cleveland. He pinch hit in the first game of a double header against the Yankees on Friday, June 21, but did not reach base, in a game the A's won 11–1. The Yankees bounced back in the second game, winning 8–3.

Unlike today, where a doubleheader means that the same two teams will play each other on the same day, with usually one game being played in the afternoon and one at night, before two different crowds, for two admissions, doubleheaders, until recently, were two games played on the same day, in front of the same crowd and for one admission. On the weekend beginning on Friday, June 21, in addition to that day's doubleheader, the two teams played two games on Saturday and one on Sunday. Over 186,000 fans packed Yankee Stadium to watch the series. The A's won three of the five games.

By the halfway point of the season, the Athletics, with a record of 53–18, had built up an 8.5 game lead over the defending American League Champions. However, it was more of the same for Walter French in the second half of the 1929 season. He had a total of 10 at-bats in the entire month of July. His highlights were few and far between. On July 16, he was sent in as a pinch hitter in the top of the tenth inning in a game in Cleveland that was tied 5–5. Walter smashed a single to center field, which scored Dykes with what would turn out to be the winning run.

By August 1, the Athletics had built their lead over the Yankees to 10.5 games. Walter only came to bat five times in the first three weeks of the month of August. Finally, on August 21, Connie Mack announced that he was giving Al Simmons a few days off to visit his family and rest his legs, and so on that afternoon Walter

French made his first start of the season against the St. Louis Browns playing left field. In the top half of the fifth inning Walter hit a long fly ball toward the gap between left and center fields. Thinking he had just made a long out he tossed his bat in disgust and started running toward first base. He then realized that the two Browns' outfielders, Fred Schulte, and Heine Manush, were both yelling "I've got it." When neither man yielded, they collided and the ball rolled toward the wall. The newspapers reported that French "tore around the bases" for an inside the park home run.

Two days later he filled in for Simmons again in Chicago. The Athletics lost to the White Sox but Walter had a successful sacrifice in the first inning, moving Max Bishop from first to second. He later drew a walk and singled to center. However, Al Simmons' break was indeed to be a short one as he was back in the lineup on August 24. The rest apparently did him some good as he went three for four and knocked in two runs.

At this point in the season the Athletics were running away with the American League Pennant. They held a commanding 13.5 game lead over the second place Yankees. Offensively the team was led by Jimmie Foxx who was hitting .376, while Al Simmons was hitting .365, Mickey Cochrane .326, Bing Miller .337, and Mule Haas .305. After a tough series with the Senators, the A's squared off against the Yankees in a three-game series during the first week of September. If the Yankees were to have any hope of making the pennant race interesting, they would have to sweep the series. However, unlike in the previous two seasons where the Yankees dominated the Athletics in their head-to-head meetings, Philadelphia crushed any hope the Yankees might have had coming into the three-game set. The A's swept the series and outscored the Yankees 26–10 and in the process, extended their lead to 14.5 games with the regular season in its final weeks. By September 12, the race was over as the Athletics had clinched the pennant. At this point Connie Mack had started to rest some of his starting players. On September 20, Mack inserted Eric McNair, a late season call up from the A's minor league team in Knoxville, TN, at shortstop in a game against the Tigers. McNair responded by getting three hits. With the game tied in the bottom of the tenth inning, Bevo LeBourveau was walked. McNair then hit a ground ball to short forcing LeBourveau out at second. McNair then stole second base. Walter French was then put in to pinch hit for Al Simmons, and he singled home the winning run.

Walter's last appearance in the 1929 regular season was on October 6, in a game against the Yankees. He first entered the game as a pinch hitter for pitcher Rube Walberg, and then stayed in the game relieving Bing Miller in right field. He finished the year with one hit in two at-bats and scored one run.

As the season came to an end the Athletics had won the pennant by 18 games over the defending American League champions. The concern the experts had at the beginning of the season about the "wholesome respect" the Athletics had shown to the Yankees in their head-to-head matchups in past years, turned out to be unfounded in this campaign, as the A's finished with a record of 14–8 in games with New York. They had taken over first place in May and had never relinquished it. Their pitching staff boasted of three of the league's best pitchers, Lefty Grove who finished the season with a record of 20 wins against only six losses, George Earnshaw who finished at 24–8, and Rube Walberg who turned in a record of 18–11.

Matched up against the Philadelphia club in the 1929 World Series were the Chicago Cubs. Although the Cubs were not as dominant in the regular season as were the Athletics, they walked away with the National League pennant in an impressive way. They finished with a record of 98–54, some 10.5 games ahead of the second place Pittsburgh Pirates. The Cubs were led by future Hall of Famers Rogers Hornsby and Hack Wilson. Hornsby, playing in his first season with the Cubs, had 229 hits in the regular season and knocked in 149 runs. Wilson had 198 hits, including 39 home runs and he knocked in 159 runs. The ace of the Cubs pitching staff was Pat Malone. Malone was a right-handed pitcher from Altoona, PA, in his second season in the major leagues. He finished the 1929 season with a record of 22–10.

In the lead up to the World Series the oddsmakers had installed the Athletics as slight, 11–10 favorites to win the title. It was also announced by Commissioner Landis that NBC had been selected to broadcast the Series. Graham McNamee, who is often credited with originating play-by-play sports broadcasting, was selected to call the games for the network.

The Athletics checked into the Edgewater Beach Hotel located near Wrigley Field on the north side of Chicago prior to the start of the series. When Connie Mack spoke to reporters from his suite at the hotel he was willing to discuss any topic but refused to reveal the name of his starting pitcher for game one. Joe McCarthy, manager of the Cubs had announced that Charlie Root would start the game for his team. Root was a 30-year-old right-handed pitcher, in his fourth season of a 16-year career with the Cubs. Root finished the regular season with a record of 19–6.

Even though Connie Mack would not discuss who he was going to name as his starting pitcher the newspapers were convinced that his silence was just some gamesmanship on his part and his choice would ultimately be one of the two aces on his staff either George Earnshaw or Lefty Grove. The *Boston Globe* ran a story on the front page of its sports section stating that Earnshaw would likely be Mack's choice to face Root, while UPI proclaimed that either Earnshaw or veteran Jack Quinn would get the start. Speculation was that because the Cubs had a lot of success against lefthanders during the season, Mack was leaning toward starting a righthander like Earnshaw or Quinn. "You'll know my pitcher fifteen minutes before the game," Mack told the reporters. The A's pitchers most mentioned as starting possibilities were Grove (if Mack opted to go with a lefthander) Earnshaw, and Quinn.

The Philadelphia Athletics arrive in Chicago for the start of the 1929 World Series. Walter French is in the front, on the right, holding a suitcase. (Courtesy of French Family)

However, despite giving the impression that he was still making up his mind on who would start the game for the Athletics and would not decide until just before the start of the Series, Connie Mack had known for two weeks who would get the call and it was none of the names being bandied about. He had made the decision to start Howard Ehmke, the 35-year-old right hander, who had only appeared in 11 games all season. In fact, only three people in the world knew of Connie's plan, Mack, Eddie Collins, and Ehmke himself. Years later Connie Mack recalled that Ehmke told him that his one regret in his baseball career was that he had never won a game in the World Series. "Howard," Mack said, "You're going to pitch that game in the series. You stay home and work out here in Philadelphia. When the Cubs come here in their final games with the Phillies, go to every game and study their hitters carefully." Mack told him that he was to tell no one. Mack figured that "a major surprise at the outset would break their spirit, so my strategy was to nullify the Chicago plan of campaign at the start."[32] He felt too, that if Ehmke could pull off the improbable and win Game 1, that it would cause the Cubs to doubt their chances against the A's big three Earnshaw, Grove, and Walberg. It was also true that the Cubs were a great fastball hitting team, and when on his game, Ehmke was an off-speed pitcher with a big breaking slow curveball and was likely to give the Cubs trouble.

On game day Mack had still not named his starting pitcher as the players took the field for their warmups. "At one point Ehmke sat down on the bench next to Mack. 'Is it still me Mr. Mack?' he asked. 'It's still you,' Mack said. Fifteen minutes before game time, Ehmke took off his jacket and started to warm up. Jaws dropped in both dugouts and among the 51,000 fans in attendance. Grove and Earnshaw stared at each other in disbelief. Ehmke hadn't pitched in weeks." Sitting near Mack, Al Simmons reportedly asked his manager "Are you going to pitch him?" to which Mack replied, "do you have any objections to that?" "No," Simmons replied, "if you say so it is alright with me."[33]

Over the next two hours Howard Ehmke put on a clinic on how to pitch to the hard-hitting Cubs team. Years later, Cubs Shortstop, Woody English told *Sports Illustrated* that he recalled that Ehmke "looked like he didn't give a damn what happened. He threw that big, slow curveball that came in a broke away from the righthanded hitters."[34] Given that all but one of the Cubs players was right-handed, Ehmke's style was perfect. "Ehmke was a change from the guys we were used to, who threw hard," English told *Sports Illustrated*, "not that many pitchers used that stuff against us."[35]

In fact, both pitchers were performing well and the game was scoreless when the Cubs came to bat in the bottom of the sixth inning. The Chicago fans were excited as their number two, three and four hitters were scheduled to bat. Woody English who had hit .276 during the regular season was leading off the inning followed by Rogers Hornsby who had hit .380 and Hack Wilson who had hit .345. Unfazed, Ehmke proceeded to strike out all three of them.

In the top of the seventh inning, Root retired Al Simmons on a fly ball to centerfield. This brought up first baseman Jimmie Foxx. Foxx, in his fifth major league season, had improved on his breakout year of 1928 and in 1929 had emerged as a star in the league and a prolific power hitter, recording 33 home runs and 118 runs batted in. Foxx crushed a Charlie Root pitch over the fence in centerfield, some 400 feet from home plate, to give the Athletics a 1–0 lead.

In the bottom of the seventh inning the Cubs mounted a threat. Kiki Cuyler led off with a single followed by a single from Riggs Stephenson which put men on first and second base. Charlie Grimm then laid down a perfect sacrifice bunt which moved Cuyler to third and Grimm to second with only one out. This brought up Cliff Heathcote with the go-ahead run-in scoring position. Ehmke got Heathcote to hit a harmless fly ball into short left field for the second out without either runner advancing.

At this point Cubs manager Joe McCarthy inserted future Hall of Famer Gabby Hartnett into the lineup to pinch hit for Charlie Root. Hartnett had been used on a very limited basis during the 1929 season as he tried to recover from an arm injury. Ehmke struck out Hartnett, his twelfth strikeout of the game, to end the inning and the Cubs threat.

Joe Boley led off the top of the eighth inning for the Athletics by grounding out to shortstop. This brought up Howard Ehmke, and even though Philadelphia was clinging to only a one-run lead, Mack had no plans to fix what wasn't broken and sent Howard up to bat for himself. He immediately hit a single to right field. However, Max Bishop and Mule Haas each flied out to end the inning and stranded Ehmke on first.

Howard made short order of the Cubs in the bottom of the eighth inning, when he got Norm McMillan and Woody English to fly out to centerfield and rightfield respectively. This brought up Rogers Hornsby again but Ehmke retired him on a ground ball to second baseman Max Bishop.

In the top of the ninth inning Mickey Cochrane led off the inning with a single to center field. Then on two consecutive plays Cubs shortstop Woody English committed two errors on balls hit to him by Al Simmons and Jimmie Foxx, which loaded the bases. Then Bing Miller lined a single to centerfield scoring Cochrane and Simmons and moving Foxx to third base. Jimmy Dykes and Joe Boley then reached base on a fielder's choice when Foxx and Miller were both thrown out at home plate.

After Howard Ehmke made the final out for the Athletics in the top of the ninth, he came out to pitch the bottom half of the inning. Hack Wilson led off for the Cubs and bounced back to the mound where Ehmke threw him out at first. Kiki Cuyler then hit a ground ball to third where Jimmy Dykes fielded it cleanly but made a wild throw to first, allowing Cuyler to get to second base. Riggs Stephenson then hit a single scoring Cuyler. Stephenson advanced to second when Charlie Grimm hit a single. Pinch hitter Footsie Blair hit a grounder to Dykes who threw to second for out number two. McCarthy then sent Chick Tolson up to pinch hit for pitcher Guy Bush who had gone into the game when Root was lifted for a pinch hitter. With Stephenson on second and two out, Tolson represented the tying run. Seemingly impervious to the pressure of the situation, Howard Ehmke struck him out to end the game. It was Howard's thirteenth strikeout which, to that point in time, was a World Series record, breaking the previous record of 12 set by Ed Walsh of the White Sox in the 1906 World Series. It still ranks in the top four of all time. Only Bob Gibson, Sandy Koufax, and Carl Erskine have struck out more than 13 batters in a World Series game.

In the wake of the performance by Howard Ehmke the sportswriters were focused on Mack's decision to start him. Was it a further sign of Connie's genius or was it just a lucky hunch on his part? Frank Getty, Sports Editor at United Press International concluded that "knowing Mr. McGillicuddy for one of the smartest men in the national pastime, one is inclined to credit him with just some touch of super-strategy."[36] Looking back on it years later Mack would write "It was one of the greatest thrills in my life to see Ehmke pitch that game and break a world's record. He smashed the record that Big Ed Walsh had held for twenty-three years."[37]

For Game 2, Mack selected George Earnshaw to start for the Athletics against Pat Malone. This game would lack the drama of Game 1 as Jimmie Foxx got the scoring going in the third inning when he hit his second home run of the series, a three-run shot to deep left field. The A's scored three more runs in the fourth inning to take a 6–0 lead. However, in the bottom of the fifth inning the Cubs offense finally came to life. After Woody English flied out to third, Rogers Hornsby singled to centerfield and Hack Wilson did the same. Earnshaw then struck out Cuyler and for a moment it looked like he would get out of the jam without any damage but then Stephenson, Grimm, and Zach Taylor wrapped out consecutive singles and three runs came across for the Cubs. Having seen enough, Mack replaced Earnshaw with Lefty Grove who struck out Gabby Hartnett to end the inning. At this point the Cubs manager Joe McCarthy took Malone out of the game and sent in Hal Carlson.

Both teams failed to score in the sixth inning but in the top of the seventh Jimmie Foxx hit a leadoff single. He was then moved to second on a sacrifice bunt by Bing Miller and scored on a Jimmy Dykes single. Now staked to a 7–3 lead, Grove retired the side easily in the Cubs half of the inning. In the top of the eighth inning Carlson retired Max Bishop and Mule Haas before walking Mickey Cochrane. The next batter, Al Simmons then blasted a home run deep into the seats in right field to give the A's a 9–3 lead. Lefty Grove did his job and recorded the last six outs, game two was in the books and the Athletics were heading back to Philadelphia with a 2–0 lead in the series.

However, any thought that the Cubs would go quietly was disproved in Game 3. The A's bats went quiet as Guy Bush, who won 18 games in 1929, held them to one run. George Earnshaw, having only pitched into the fifth inning in Game 2, got the ball to start the game for the Athletics. He gave up three runs in the sixth inning on hits by Hornsby and Cuyler.

Frank Getty noted that Philadelphia lacked "Pep." He went on to observe that the "Mackmen did not show to advantage in their first appearance before their own fans yesterday. Jimmie Foxx, the versatile first baseman, who was the hitting hero of the game in Chicago, couldn't bat a ball out of the infield. Al Simmons went hitless. Jimmy Dykes, the most popular of the whole lot with the Shibe Park fans, had the misfortune to contribute the misplay which helped along the three-run Chicago rally in the sixth inning."[38] The Athletics left 10 men on base in the game.

The next day, Jack Quinn, who many had speculated would get the start in Game 1, was selected by Connie Mack to pitch in Game 4. Again, it appeared that Mack was trying to keep the Cubs right-handed hitters off balance. Quinn had finished the regular season with a record of 11–9, so there were more accomplished options available to the manager. Charlie Root, the Cubs game one pitcher was back on the mound for the visiting team.

The confidence level of the Cubs and their fans was sky high as game time approached. The *Chicago Tribune* had published a list it called "Ten Reasons for

Elation for the Cubs." One of the reasons listed was "Malone and Blake, as well as Root, believe that they have discovered how to pitch to Simmons and Foxx both of whom batted .000 against Bush"[39] in game three.

The game was scoreless until the fourth inning. After Hack Wilson flied out to deep right field, then Kiki Cuyler singled and with two out Cubs first baseman Charlie Grimm homered into deep right field to give the Cubs a 2–0 lead. The score remained the same until the top of the sixth inning when the Cubs got to Quinn in a big way. Successive singles by Hornsby, Wilson, Cuyler, and Stephenson resulted in two more runs for Chicago and chased Jack Quinn from the game. Replacing Quinn was Rube Walberg. Walberg, as noted earlier was a left-handed pitcher who was one of the best for the Athletics in 1929 with a record of 18–11. The first man Walberg faced was Charlie Grimm and he hit a single which brought in two more runs. Zach Taylor followed that up with a run scoring sacrifice fly and the Cubs were up 7–0. Eddie Rommel replaced Walberg in the seventh inning and after Woody English flied to left, Rogers Hornsby hit a triple and two batters later Cuyler drove him in with a single giving the Cubs an 8–0 lead. By this time the Cubs were beginning to mock their opponents. "In the dugout Bush had been celebrating each run by donning a blanket as if it were a headdress and doing what one writer described as a 'mock Indian war dance' along the Cubs bench."[40] Things could not get any worse for Connie Mack and his team as it appeared the Cubs would even the series and, in the process, re-establish their home field advantage.

What happened next was something that no one in attendance or listening to the game on NBC would ever forget. Later Connie Mack would call Game 4 the most unforgettable of his career.

When they came to bat in the bottom of the seventh inning, the Athletics had managed only three hits off Charlie Root all game. The meat of the A's order was scheduled to bat in the inning, with Al Simmons leading off. Simmons got the inning off to a flying start when he slammed Root's pitch to the opposite field depositing the ball deep in the seats in left field. Jimmie Foxx and Bing Miller then hit back-to-back singles and stood on first and second. Jimmy Dykes followed that up with a single of his own which scored Foxx with the second run and moved Miller to second. Joe Boley got the A's fifth consecutive hit of the inning which, in turn, drove in Miller and sent Dykes to third base. After George Burns made an out pinch hitting for Eddie Rommel, Max Bishop hit a single to center which scored Dykes, with the fourth run of the inning. At this point Cubs manager Joe McCarthy pulled Root from the game and replaced him with Art Nehf. The first batter to face Nehf was Mule Haas who crushed a ball to deep center field. Hack Wilson raced back to the wall in center field and briefly lost the ball in the sun. When he was finally able to locate the ball, it was inches from the ground and bounced away from him. Haas raced around the bases for an inside-the-park home run with Boley and Bishop scoring in front of him. Just like that the Cubs lead, which once seemed insurmountable, was down to one run and there was still only one out.

Nehf then walked Mickey Cochrane which closed the book on his day. McCarthy replaced him with Sheiff Blake. The first batter Blake had to face was Al Simmons batting for the second time in the inning. He singled through the left side of the infield moving Cochrane to second base. This brought up Jimmie Foxx who had singled earlier in the inning. Foxx once again hit a single scoring Simmons with the tying run. Blake was then removed from the game and replaced by Pat Malone. Malone hit the first batter he saw, Bing Miller, with a pitch which loaded the bases. With still only one out, Jimmy Dykes hit a double to left field which scored Simmons and Foxx. Malone then struck out Joe Boley and George Burns to finally end the inning. The Athletics had scored 10 runs. "When the score was shown on the scoreboard at Franklin Field where thirty thousand people were watching a Penn-Virginia Poly football game, all action on the field stopped. The spectators went berserk. Players on both sides stood and watched to see what would happen next. Thousands more stood cheering in disbelief outside of City Hall and newspaper offices, watching metal figures moving around the bases."[41]

To start the eighth inning Mack sent Lefty Grove to the mound. Grove induced a ground ball out from Charlie Grimm and then proceeded to strike out Zach Taylor and Gabby Hartnett to end the inning. The A's got two more hits in their half of the eighth inning but failed to score. Lefty Grove was back out to face the Cubs in the ninth inning and was not to be denied a chance to close out the game and to firmly put the Athletics in the World Series driver's seat. He struck out Norm McMillan swinging and Woody English who looked at a call strike three. He then got Hornsby to fly out to right field to end the game.

The Athletics fans went crazy when Grove recorded the final out. Meanwhile the reporters who had been covering the game and who had been busy rewriting their stories to account for the miracle ending, began to rush the field in hopes of getting a comment from Connie Mack about what had transpired. Stan Baumgartner, one-time Athletics and Phillies pitcher turned sportswriter, wrote that the manager bounded up the stairs to the clubhouse shouting the game was the greatest thrill he had had in all his years of managing. The next person Mack encountered was Bob Paul, sports editor of the *Daily News*. Paul recalled that Mack grabbed him by his jacket lapels and yelled "Wasn't that marvelous? Did you ever see such hitting? No team in the world can stop them now."[42] Later Mack was sitting alone in his office when Rud Rennie of the *New York Herald Tribune* stopped in to see if he could get any last words. He came back downstairs after only a short stay and told his fellow reporters that "the old gentleman is pretty well fatigued" and that "he just murmured to me 'I guess that seventh inning was a little too much for me'. I think you better not go up there."[43]

Game 4 was the lead story in all of the next day's newspapers. Damon Runyon wrote "this isn't a baseball fairy story. It really happened no matter what you may think about it. With the score 8–0 against them going into the seventh inning the Philadelphia Athletics ran up ten tallies to beat the Chicago Cubs 10–8 in Game 4 of the 1929 World Series. All right, all right, say I'm a liar if you want to. But I can prove it by the box score if there is room in the paper to print it."[44]

The newspapers also reported that in scoring 10 runs in one inning of a World Series game, the Athletics had made history by breaking the previous record held by the New York Giants when they scored eight runs in one inning in the series with the Yankees in 1921.

From the Chicago perspective, Edward Burns writing in the *Chicago Tribune* summed up the feeling of all Cubs fans writing that "It remained for our beloved Cubs to furnish the greatest debacle, the most terrific flop in the history of the World Series and one of the worst in the history of major league baseball games of all types."[45] In addition, a loss like this one had to have a goat and that honor fell to Hack Wilson, whose mishandling of the Mule Haas fly ball, led to the inside-the-park home run that tied the score at eight. "Losing a ball in the sun usually is condoned, but Hack had had his warning that his sunglasses were not adequate. He muffed an easy fly in the fifth, which should have caused him to get smokier equipment. But he did not, and as a result he and his mates were blown higher out of the water than any other club ever has before."[46]

The prohibition on playing games on Sunday in Pennsylvania was still in effect in 1929 so Game 5 of the World Series would not be played until Monday, October 14. To this point Walter French had not stepped on the field in the entire series. Not once did he pinch hit, pinch run, or enter the game to play defense, as had been the case during the regular season. In fact, it had been over a week since he last saw any action, a pinch-hit appearance against the Yankees in the season's final game. Knowing how much he despised sitting on the bench it stands to reason that he was bitterly disappointed by the fact that to that point he had had no role. What would have kept up his spirits however, as the Athletics were one game away from winning the series, was the payday that he knew awaited him from the winning player's share which was based on the total revenue from ticket sales for the series. In the dream that he maintained caused him to reconsider his retirement and rejoin the team, his winner's share was $5000 but in actuality it would be more than that amount.

Feelings were still running hot between the two teams after Game 4. Both teams had been riding each other hard, first the Cubs when they had built up their 8–0 lead, and then the Athletics when they turned the table in the seventh. In fact, the language had gotten so rough that Commissioner Landis visited with both managers before Game 5 and warned them that a repeat performance would result in the offending player losing their world series share, and if it was not possible to identify the offending player that he would hold the managers responsible.

Cubs manager Joe McCarthy chose Pat Malone to be his team's starting pitcher for Game 5. Malone had pitched to only four batters in the fateful seventh inning of Game 4 and had pitched well in Game 1. Now with an additional day of rest, the Cubs were confident that he would give them a good game. For the Athletics, Connie Mack once again looked to Howard Ehmke, which set up a rematch from Game 1.

The game was scoreless until the fourth inning when with two outs Cuyler hit a double to right field. Ehmke then walked the next batter Stephenson and then Charlie Grimm hit a single to centerfield which scored Cuyler with the game's first run and moved Stephenson to third. Zach Taylor followed that up with another single to center scoring Stephenson to make the score 2–0. At this point Mack removed Ehmke from the game and replaced him with Rube Walberg, who struck out Malone to end the inning.

For his part, Pat Malone was pitching a masterpiece against Philadelphia, allowing only one hit in the first four innings. Finally, in their half of the fifth inning Jimmie Foxx reached base on an error with one out. Bing Miller then got the A's second hit sending Foxx to second base. At that point however, Malone retired Dykes and Boley on fly balls to end the inning and the threat. Another opportunity appeared to be in the making for the A's when Mickey Cochrane led off the seventh inning with a walk, this time Simmons popped out to third base and Jimmie Foxx hit into a double play.

The score remained 2–0 as the Athletics came to bat in the bottom of the ninth inning. To that point Malone had only given up two hits. Woody English at his position at shortstop recalled that "Malone could throw really hard, and he was throwing really well. All we needed was three more outs and we were back in Chicago for the last two games. It looked like we had it salted away."[47]

With Rube Walberg scheduled to lead off the bottom of the ninth inning, Connie Mack sent Walter French up to pinch hit. Malone made short order of Walter quickly striking him out on four pitches, a predictable outcome given the fact that he had not stepped on the field in over a week and had seen very limited action in the last month of the regular season.

There are a couple of versions of what Walter told his teammates when he returned to the dugout after being bested by Malone. In Norman Macht's biography of Connie Mack he writes that when French came back to the bench he said "that fellow has everything," referring to Malone. However, famed sportswriter Stoney McLinn writing in the *Philadelphia Evening Ledger* told a different version of the story to his readers. "I have heard Connie Mack tell several times," he wrote, "that it was a remark made by French as he carried his bat rather shame-facedly back to the dugout which had a lot to do with the subsequent rally. 'Malone hasn't got a thing',

French told the boys on the bench, 'I ought to be shot at sunrise for fanning'. The other Mack boys who heard this remark believed him."[48] One can only speculate on the impact of whatever scouting report he delivered, but what happened next is World Series history.

Max Bishop followed Walter and hit a single into left field. This brought up Mule Haas. On his first pitch to the A's centerfielder, Malone made his first mistake of the game. He later recalled that the pitch "simply strayed away from me." It was a waist-high fastball that "strayed" right down the middle of the plate and Haas did not miss it, knocking it over the right-field wall to tie the game. After Mickey Cochrane grounded out, Al Simmons hit a double to right-field. Malone and the Cubs decided not to pitch to Jimmie Foxx and to take their chances with Bing Miller. Malone threw Miller four fastballs, which he took without swinging, two were for strikes. At this point Malone and Miller were engaged in the typical mind game that a pitcher and hitter in a big spot would find themselves. Miller figured that normally in this situation the next pitch would be a curveball but concluded that that was what Malone would expect him to be thinking, and so he braced himself for another fastball. He guessed right and smacked Malone's pitch on a line over the head of Rogers Hornsby in right field, bringing home Simmons with the winning run.

The Philadelphia fans went wild with joy. They ran down on the field and mobbed the players attempting to carry off Simmons and Miller. A photo which appeared in a *Sports Illustrated* story about the 1929 Athletics shows the reaction of the fans and players at the moment Simmons touches home plate with the winning run. The players are out of the dugout, embracing one another and jumping for joy. Jimmy Foxx described the scene from his perspective saying that "we carried on like a bunch of college boys and our spirit was all of that. There was a delirium of ecstasy and I think that the only person in the park who was not unduly excited was President Hoover, but the President is like that, and my guess is that he got as big a thrill out of it as anyone."[49]

Seated in the President's box at the game was Philadelphia Mayor Harry A. Mackey. When the final run was scored, Mackey leaped from the box and ran into the Athletics' dugout to celebrate with the players. When he returned to the President's side, he noticed that Hoover had given up any pretense of neutrality, usually the posture taken by the nation's chief executive on such occasions, and he was cheering the Athletics with the rest of the crowd. He leaned over and yelled to Mackey "Well Mr. Mayor, you will give me credit for having been neutral for most of the game."[50]

The next day the Athletics' players started arriving, in small groups at Shibe Park, to clean out their lockers, but there was one more important piece of business that they needed to resolve and that was the distribution of the World Series winner's money pool. The players voted that all of the 25 eligible members of the team would get a full share, as would coaches "Kid" Gleason and Earl Mack along with trainer E. E. Ebling. For Walter the decision to return to the team for the 1929 season turned out to be a wise one. Despite the fact that his role was a limited one, with his World Series winner's share of $5,831.30 on top of his annual salary of $7,500, 1929 was the most financially successful year of his life to that point.

It is hard to envision today, but the distribution of the winner's pool dominated the sports pages in the days immediately following the World Series. Writers were speculating on what each player's share would turn out to be, and who among the players would be getting a full share. They even quizzed the players on what they intended to do with their money. When they got to Walter, he jokingly boasted that "I am going to buy myself a new saddle and spurs, so I can give those National League nags a good ride in the next series." His classmates from West Point would have found this to be funny given his track record at the Academy in the equestrian department. Despite his ability to master almost any athletic endeavor he could not manage to stay on a horse, to the point where he both feared and hated horses. However, when pressed by reporters to be serious, he sheepishly admitted that when it came to money matters, he "took his orders from Mrs. French." For Walter the World Series winner's check was literally a dream come true.[51]

Connie Mack stopped in the locker room and addressed the team. He asked them to stay in Philadelphia for the banquet being held in their honor on Thursday at the Penn Athletic Club. Although most of the players intended to head home, out of respect for their manager, they all changed their plans and attended the big testimonial. Over 1,600 fans attended the event. The dinner was sponsored by the City of Philadelphia, the Philadelphia Chamber of Commerce, the Philadelphia Sporting Writers Association, and the Penn Athletic Club. Connie Mack was presented with an "electric clock" and the players and coaches were each given gold watches.

CHAPTER 9

The Stock Market Crash, Dizzy Dean, and The Dixie Series of 1931

On Thursday, October 24, 1929, just one week after the Athletics' championship celebration at the Penn A. C., at some point mid-morning, the stock market experienced a wave of selling. Banking executives and other experts assured everyone that the losses sustained in this sell-off were temporary and that the resulting drop in stock prices was too low and that they would rebound. Things remained calm on Friday but on Monday, October 28, the Dow declined by 13 percent. The following day, now referred to as Black Tuesday, the market dropped by another 12 percent. By mid-November the market had lost half of its value and was continuing to slide. Although the stock market crash, and the Great Depression that was to follow would have a major impact on the national pastime, it was not evident in those last few months of 1929, apart from the impact that it had on individual members of the league's teams. Mickey Cochrane, for example, was quoted as saying that he would now be using his World Series check to "pay off the margin on his stocks."[1] Years later Walter French, in an interview with sportswriter Jim Baily, recalled that "most of us on the A's lost most of our investments when the stock market crashed."[2]

On December 3, 1929, Connie Mack announced that Walter French, along with pitcher Lefty Yerkes, and infielder Jimmy Cronin were being sent to the Portland Beavers of the Pacific Coast League in exchange for two pitchers Percy Mahaffey and George Snider. The Beavers became a farm team of the Philadelphia Athletics in 1924 after A's owners John and Thomas Shibe purchased the team along with its ballpark, Vaughn Street Park. In 1929, the Beavers changed their name to the Portland Ducks for one season and they finished in last place. The Beavers were formed in 1903 and were one of the charter members of the Pacific Coast League. In the early 20th century the Pacific Coast League was considered by many to rival the big leagues and was often thought of as a third major league. According to the Baseball Hall of Fame over 60 Hall of Fame players got their start in the PCL.

When word reached Walter about his move to Portland, he was spending the winter in Birmingham, AL. The *Prattville Progress* reported that "Mr. and Mrs. Walter French have purchased the W.N. Smith home and lands in northeast Prattville and will make their home here. Mr. French is a member of the Philadelphia Athletics and ranks as one of the star players of the United States. His native home is New Jersey. Mr. and Mrs. French are quite a desirable asset to our town and will be met with a warm welcome by all our people."[3]

Seemingly unfazed by the news from Philadelphia, Walter confirmed that he had used his World Series bonus money to purchase a farm near Prattville, AL. "When baseball gets through with me, I am going to settle down in Alabama and live the life of a farmer" he told the Birmingham News. "However," he continued, "I hope this will be sometime yet to come as I love to play baseball and would like to finish up my career in the Southern League."[4]

Playing in the Southern League would have to wait. Walter headed off to Portland to join the Beavers who were coming off a dismal 1929 season where they finished with a record of 90–112. The season ran from late March to October. Due to the more moderate climate in the region, the regular season schedule for the teams in the Pacific Coast League called for each team to play between 170 and 200 games in the season.

In early April, Sid King sportswriter for the Eugene Guard was giving his scouting report on the team and wrote "Walter French, noted especially for his speed is another acquisition from the Athletics as are Jimmy Cronin and Caroll Yerkes. With these men on hand manager Larry Woodall has some chance of turning out a winning combination and if he does, he will just about own Portland after this year."[5] Of the 33 players on the Beavers Roster in 1930, 21 had played in the major leagues.

One of Walter's teammates in Portland was Carl Mays. Mays was a right-handed pitcher who had a 15-year major league career which included seasons with the Red Sox, Yankees, Cincinnati Reds, and the New York Giants. He won 20 or more games five times with his best season being 1921 when he won 27 games for the Yankees. Many experts say that Mays was one of the best pitchers not to be in the Hall of Fame.

Sadly, Mays is most known for one pitch he threw to Ray Chapman, shortstop of the Cleveland Indians on August 16, 1920. Mays was, what is still called today, a submarine ball pitcher, which means that rather than throw with an over-the-top arm slot, or with even a sidearm delivery, Mays released the ball below his waist, in an underarm fashion. He was also known to throw a spitball and to take advantage of any blemishes to the baseball to get even more movement on his pitches.

The scene was the Polo Grounds in New York, and Mays was pitching for the Yankees against Cleveland. Chapman was the leadoff batter for the Indians in the fifth inning and on the first pitch by Mays he was struck squarely in the head. Tris Speaker, who was in the on-deck circle and the home plate umpire Tommy Connolly immediately called for help realizing that his injury was serious. Mays later said that when the ball hit Chapman it made a noise so loud that he thought it had hit his bat and so when the ball bounced back in his direction, he picked up the ball and threw to first. Chapman was rushed to the St. Lawrence Hospital where at just before five o'clock the next morning he died. The newspapers reported that Carl Mays was overcome with grief when he was told of Chapman's death.

Chapman's death resulted in some important rule changes for baseball. From that point on, umpires were required to replace balls that had been blemished or scuffed up in any way. Previously one or two balls would be used for an entire game regardless of its condition, resulting in a softer, discolored ball, the path of which became harder for the batter to see as the game went on. Fans were even required to return balls hit into the stands until 1921. After the rule change, any blemish on the ball required the umpire to replace it, which meant that the batter had the advantage of hitting a harder and easier to see ball. After 1920 the spitball was also banned. The repercussions of the death of Ray Chapman marked the beginning of the end of the Dead Ball era in baseball.

The 1930 season for the Beavers was even worse than it had been in 1929. The team finished in last place with a record of 81–117. However, for Walter French, the season was a very successful one. After playing such a limited role for the A's in 1929 he played in a team high 160 games for Portland and came to bat 644 times. He led the team in hits with 199 and finished the season with a batting average of .309.

Over the next few years, the impact of the Great Depression on baseball, as with the rest of society, would be severe. A few new innovations to the game would be born out of necessity due to the decline in attendance at games after the 1930 season. One of those innovations came in 1930 with the introduction of night baseball. The first game in organized baseball, played under permanent lights took place in Independence, Kansas on April 28, 1930, between the Muskogee Chiefs and the Independence Producers of the Western Association. A few days later in Des Moines, IA another game was played under permanent lights. In the Negro League night games were also played in the early days of the decade using portable lights that the teams brought along with them. Starting in 1930 teams like the Kansas City Monarchs began traveling with their own set of lights so that they could stage the more lucrative night games at home and on the road. Major League Baseball, however, did not introduce night baseball until 1935. One of the earliest adopters of night baseball was the Pacific Coast League who started playing games under the lights in certain cities in 1930. On June 10, 1930, the league's first night game was played in Sacramento, California between the Sacramento Senators, and the Oakland Oaks. By the end of 1931 every park in the league would be equipped with lights for night games.

In early September the Portland Beavers played a night game against the Los Angeles Angels at Wrigley Park. The Angels were purchased by Chicago Cubs owner William Wrigley in 1921 and after trying to get the city of Los Angeles to improve the existing home of the Angels, Washington Park, he built a new ballpark modeled after the Wrigley Field in Chicago and named it Wrigley Park. The ironic thing about the fact that Wrigley Park was one of the earliest venues to play night games, is that Wrigley Field in Chicago was the last to do so, not introducing night baseball and lights until 1988 when the Cubs hosted the New York Mets in August of that year.

In the Sunday, September 7, 1930, edition of the *Los Angeles Times*, their rotogravure section was dedicated to covering the series between the Angels and the Portland Beavers. The three-game series played under the lights earlier in the week was labeled the "Night Blooming" Series. Featured on the entire top half of the front page of the rotogravure section was a picture of Walter French at bat for the Beavers awaiting a pitch. Also pictured is Angels Catcher Bill Skiff and Umpire Monroe Sweeney. "Night Baseball" read the headline "A Horsehide that Goes Out Nights." The full caption read "Fielder French of Portland ready to take a swing at a night evader, while catcher Skiff of Los Angeles and Umpire Sweeney apply the owl eye to the on-coming baseball. Taken during the current Wrigley Park 'Night Blooming' series."[6]

The photo was taken by legendary Los Angeles photojournalist E. J. Spencer. Spencer came to prominence in 1912, when a man named Carl Warr walked into the City Jail in Los Angeles. Strapped to his body was a contraption attached to numerous sticks of dynamite. He sat down in the outer office of the police chief and threatened to explode his device. The police tried to negotiate with Warr as others cleared the building of the staff and of those prisoners housed in the jail. Hearing word of this event, E. J. Spencer rushed to the scene and then calmly walked into the jail where he came face to face with the "mad bomber" who kept threatening to detonate his device. Spencer calmly set up his camera on a chair and took Warr's picture. He then gathered up his equipment and left the building. A short time later the police subdued Warr and defused his bomb. The next day Spencer's photo ran on the front page of the *Los Angeles Examiner* under the headline "Examiner Photographer Hazards Death to Snap the Dynamiter."

Despite the impact the Great Depression was having on the United States' economy, attendance at Major League baseball games remained high in 1930 topping 10 million for the first time ever. However, attendance plummeted in 1931 and 1932, with gate levels dropping by nearly 70 percent over that two-year span. Attendance would not top 10 million again until 1945.

Sensing what was coming, teams began to pare down their rosters. Major League teams reduced their rosters from 25 players to 23 during this period. Trying to economize, minor league teams such as those in the Pacific Coast League looked for ways to reduce their payrolls.

The annual meeting of the National Association of Professional Baseball Leagues was held in Montreal Canada the first week of December in 1930. The reason for holding the meeting north of the border was to allow the attendees to enjoy an alcoholic beverage without being in violation of the Volstead Act which prohibited the production and sale of alcohol in the United States. There were two big story lines. First, was the ongoing debate between the major leagues and minor leagues over what was called the "Universal Draft," the practice which allowed the big-league clubs to draft players from high school, college and minor league teams for as little financial outlay as possible. The second big story coming out of the meeting was the sudden death of William Frazer Baker, owner of the Philadelphia Phillies, who passed away from a heart attack while attending the meeting.

Lost in these stories was an announcement that Thomas Turner, President of the Portland Beavers had released both Walter French and Jimmy Cronin and so despite having turned in a great season in 1930 Walter was given his walking papers by the Portland club. Reflecting on it years later, Walter told the *Arkansas Gazette* that "I think maybe they let me go just because they did not want to pay my travel expenses to the West Coast the next Spring. The Depression was on and I was living in Alabama at the time, and they did not want to pay my travel expenses."[7]

A few weeks later, the tragic news reached Walter that his oldest brother, 39-year-old Joseph French, had taken his own life on New Year's Eve. Joseph had graduated from Rutgers and was considered one of the most knowledgeable arborists in the South Jersey area. At the time of his death he was working at the Willowdale Farm and living on site with his wife Helen, in what is now Cherry Hill, NJ. He had a history of depression and had been hospitalized for what was called at the time "a nervous breakdown." After leaving a note to his wife saying that he found no "use in living" and that he considered himself a "failure" he took a shotgun to on the outbuildings on the property and shot himself.

After returning from his brother's funeral Walter began to contemplate his options for the upcoming season. He was about to contact the Southern League team in Birmingham when he saw an item in the *Sporting News* saying that the Little Rock, Arkansas team was looking for players. The *Sporting News* was first published in 1886, and although it eventually branched out to cover several sports, its primary focus was on baseball, to the point where it was known as the "Bible of Baseball" and so it was a good resource for out of work ballplayers looking to catch on with a team. Walter contacted the Little Rock Travelers and on March 27, 1931, the Associated Press reported that "Manager Harry Strohm of the Little Rock Travelers says he expects to give Southern pitchers plenty to worry about this year. Starting the tentative batting order is Walter French, center fielder, a newcomer who hit .310 with the Portland, Ore., Pacific Coast club last year."[8] Walter was paid $800 per month to play in Little Rock.

The 1931 Travelers were the last club to play at old Kavanaugh Field which had been built in 1907 and previously known as West End Field. The field had been best known for being the spring training site for the Boston Americans led by their star pitcher Cy Young in 1907 and 1908.

Walter started in centerfield for the Travelers and usually batted in one of the first three spots in the order. He quickly became a fan favorite due to his style of play.

He ran the bases hard and his play the field was outstanding. He soon established himself as the best player on the Travelers. Consistently having multiple hit games, stealing bases, and making one great catch after another.

One team that he played particularly well against was the Birmingham Barons, with whom they were battling for first place throughout the season. On May 16, he had three hits in a 6–5 win over the Barons. He also had an outstanding day in the field as reported by the *Birmingham News*. "Walter French, one of the smartest outfielders seen here this year, went hither and yonder to take hits away from the Milans. He raced over in deep right center for Eisemann's wallop in the second, hoofed it over in left center for Eisemann's second drive in the fourth, and outraced Moore's drive in deep right center in the ninth"[9] the newspaper reported. On June 17 he had three hits in a game won by the Barons by a score of 5–4 but once again Walter showcased his defensive abilities. "Walter French raced from center over into right center to take a triple away from Andy Moore in the eighth. Moore cracked one right on the nose and it headed as straight as a bullet travels for the wire fence. French came sprinting across the outfield like a streaking comet catching the ball with his extended gloved hand, not more than three feet off the ground."[10] Birmingham manager Clyde Milan told the *Birmingham News* that "French's catch of Moore's low liner was as fine a catch as I ever saw."[11] On August 25, the Travelers beat the Barons by a score of 9–4 and according to form, Walter once again had three hits and made a great play in the outfield. "There might have been a great deal more trouble in the eighth however, had not Walter French turned in one of the best catches of the season to rob Woody Abernathy of an extra base hit," the *Birmingham News* reported. "Two men were on base at the time and both of them would have scored, had that ball escaped Walter."[12]

On August 31, the Travelers played a doubleheader against the first place Birmingham team, winning the first game 11–3 and the second game 7–2. Walter led the way for his team collecting six hits in the two games.

When the 1931 season came to a close Walter French ended up leading the Southern League with 674 at bats and 235 hits for a batting average of .345 which was in the top 10 for the league. He also had 51 stolen bases which led the league. His 235 hits for a single season remained the team record for 50 years. He was named the Travelers' Most Valuable Player for 1931.

The sweep of Birmingham in the final series of the season turned out to be too little too late for the Travelers as they finished the season in second place behind the Barons, who were headed for the Dixie Series against the Houston Buffaloes, winners of the Texas League. The Dixie Series, sometimes referred to as the "Little World Series," was the annual matchup of the winner of the Southern League with the champions of the Texas League.

While the rest of the Travelers were cleaning out their lockers and heading home for the offseason, a trip home to Prattville would have to wait for Walter French. The rules at the time for the Dixie Series allowed the two teams participating, if they so desired, to select an "extra" player from some other team in their respective leagues. For Birmingham the choice of an "extra" was made easier when Andy "Scrappy" Moore announced that he would be leaving the team to start his new job as head football coach at the University of Chattanooga, now called the University of Tennessee at Chattanooga. With Moore's departure the Barons needed a centerfielder and what better choice could they make than Walter French who had played so well against them in the regular season. On September 8, the *Birmingham News* reported that "Walter French will take Andy Moore's place in the Barons' lineup in the Dixie Series. The Houston and Birmingham clubs reached an agreement on Monday whereby both could add an extra man to their roster for the series. Houston will select a pitcher to replace Tex Carelton who suffered a broken index finger on his pitching hand. Walter French, who is the leading base thief on the Southern League should fit right into the Barons' lineup ... French is considered the greatest all-around centerfielder in the league and his speed should come in handy."[13]

The smart money was on the Texas League champion Houston Buffaloes. They had won 108 games in 1931 against only 51 losses. Houston was a farm team affiliated with the St. Louis Cardinals and two of that organization's top prospects were the team leaders. Pitcher Dizzy Dean, at the time a 21-year-old rising star in the Cardinals' organization, had won 26 games for the Buffs in 1931. The future Hall of Famer would go on to be one of the best pitchers in the game, winning 30 games in 1934, and a key member of the famous Cardinal team nicknamed the "Gashouse Gang." Always a colorful character, one of Dean's favorite expressions was "it's not bragging if you can back it up."

Also on the Cardinals in 1934 was Dizzy Dean's brother Paul, also a pitcher. Before the season started Dizzy predicted that he and his brother would win 40 games during the season. That was the year that Dizzy won 30 games and his brother Paul won 19, which more than backed up his prediction.

Dizzy was not the only future Hall of Famer on the Houston club. Outfielder Joe "Ducky" Medwick led the Buffs with a .305 batting average and 19 home runs on the season. Medwick too would be a member of the "Gashouse Gang" and part of the Cardinals' team that won the World Series in 1934.

The first game of the Dixie Series was played on September 16. Squaring off were the young star pitcher for Houston, Dizzy Dean and 43-year-old Birmingham pitcher Ray Caldwell, who was coming off a 19-win season. Caldwell had started his career in 1908 with the New York Highlanders, who eventually became the Yankees. His won-loss record over his first four years, 32–38, was deceiving because he received some of the worst run support any pitcher had ever seen. At one point he pitched 52 consecutive scoreless innings and over that span his team did not score a single run. By 1914, Caldwell had hit his stride and finished that season with a record of 18–9 with a 1.94 earned run average. Sportswriters were singing his praises. Grantland Rice compared him to Christy Mathewson and there was even a rumor that the Washington Senators had contemplated offering to trade Walter Johnson for Caldwell. Caldwell was every bit as colorful as his young opponent, but his career was hampered by alcoholism. Pitching for the Cleveland Indians in 1919, in a game against the Athletics, he was one out away from a complete game victory when a storm rolled in off Lake Erie. Just as he was about to pitch to what he hoped would be the final batter, he was struck by lightning. When his teammates got to him, they recalled later that his uniform was smoldering. Tris Speaker, the Indians' player-manager, called for medical help, but Caldwell refused to leave the field until he got the final out.

Game 1 proved to be a great pitching duel with both pitchers holding their opponents scoreless into the eighth inning. Finally, Bill Bancroft hit a double off Dizzy Dean in the bottom of the eighth inning to score the game's only run and giving the Barons a 1–0 lead in the series.

Houston bounced back in Game 2 behind the pitching of 25-year-old Dick McCabe, who was the player borrowed from their Texas League rival in Fort Worth, before the start of the series. McCabe pitched a brilliant game and shutout the Barons 3–0 to even the series at 1–1.

To this point in the Dixie Series, Walter French, despite all the hype around his selection as the Barons' "extra player," had yet to play but before Game 3 the *Birmingham News* announced that the Barons' Manager Clyde Milan planned to insert Walter French into the lineup hoping to get the team's offense untracked. "Walter French, the borrowed outfielder from Little Rock will start in centerfield for the Barons and bat in second place" the newspaper reported. "It will be up to Walter French to start the Barons off hitting, something they haven't done with any regularity to date in the series."[14]

Game 3 however, was more of the same for the Barons as they were once again shutout, this time by a score of 1–0 behind the pitching of 42-year-old George Payne, who had finished the regular season with a record of 23–23 and a 2.75 earned run average. In its wrap-up of the game the *Birmingham News* reported that "Walter French, Art Weis, and Judge Abernathy made sensational catches, but they didn't give Hasty any help with their bats." The catch made by Walter came on a ball hit to deep centerfield by Joe Medwick. "French went up in front of the temporary bleachers in right center and took Medwick's powerful line drive out of the darkness."[15]

Now down two games to one the Barons were faced with the prospect of having to beat Dizzy Dean to prevent themselves from going down three games to one. Once again Walter French was in the lineup playing centerfield and batting second. He did manage one hit against Dean but it was nowhere near enough as Dizzy shutout Birmingham by a score of 2–0.

It is hard to overstate how bad the offense was for the Barons to this point in the series. They had been shutout in three of the first four games, and in the one game that they were not shutout they had only scored one run. So dismal was their offense during that four-game stretch that they had only 36 balls hit out of the infield.

On the following day, Clay Touchstone, a right-handed pitcher who finished the regular season with a record of 15–11 with a 4.76 earned run average, saved the day for the Barons. He held Houston to one run and sent his team back to Alabama with a chance to tie the series with a 3–1 victory.

In Birmingham for Game 6, the Barons' bats finally came alive as they roughed up four Houston pitchers for 23 hits and 14 runs, as they defeated Houston by a score of 14–10. Walter French had his best offensive game of the series finishing with three hits in six trips to the plate. He also scored three runs. In one inning, in his typical fashion he singled, stole second and came around to score on a double by Butch Weis.

Back in Houston on September 25 the stage was set for a climactic Game 7. Once again Dizzy Dean was on the mound for the Buffs and Clyde Milan tabbed right-hander Bob Hasty to pitch the game for the Barons. Walter French was playing centerfield and batting second.

Dean got off to a hot start striking out five batters in the first two innings but on this occasion, he could not keep the Barons off the scoreboard. As the Barons came to bat in the top of the ninth inning, they clung to a slim 3–2 lead. To that point in the game, Walter French had one hit in four trips to the plate. When he came to bat in the ninth inning there were two men, Bill Eisemann and Bob Hasty, on base. To that point of the game the *Birmingham News* reported that Walter and Dizzy Dean had been "carrying on a hot kidding match"[16] as both players were verbally needling each other from the bench. Walter planted a swinging bunt down the third base line and Eddie Hock in his haste to get the speedy French made a wild throw to first which got past the first baseman and rolled into right field. Eisemann and Hasty both scored. Walter was not credited with a hit for his effort but the *Birmingham News* maintained that he "should have had a hit, as he had Hock's throw beat by a step."[17] After the Barons got one more insurance run off Dizzy Dean, Clyde Milan sent Bob Hasty out to finish the game. After getting the first batter to foul out, Eddie Hock laid down a perfect bunt for a single and advanced to second when Hasty threw low to first base attempting to get him out. The next batter, Earl Smith, singled to centerfield which brought Hock home. After he had given up a hit to the next batter, Clyde Milan had seen enough and replaced Hasty with his game one pitcher Ray Caldwell. The first batter Caldwell had to face was Joe Medwick and the veteran pitcher struck out the future Hall of Famer. He then induced Peel to hit a routine ground ball to second to end the game and gave his team the Dixie Series title. The series in 1931 marked the twelfth playing of the Dixie Series and the Barons' victory was only the third time the team from the Southern League had won.

By the spring of 1932, the Great Depression was dramatically impacting all segments of American society. Attendance at Major League baseball games had dropped from 10.1 million in 1930 to 8.4 million for the 1931 season. Ballplayers at every level of organized baseball were being forced to take significant pay cuts. Although their second-place finish in 1931 drove their attendance to 113,738, up from the 78,688 fans that saw the sixth place 1929 team play, the Travelers' players were forced to accept a pay cut. Years later, Walter recalled that "when I first went to the Southern League, the established players were making $700–$800 per month. Because of the Depression we all took a cut down to about $300–$400 the next year. That was it; take it or leave it."[18]

Night baseball also debuted in the Southern Association in 1932. Nicknamed "Moonshine Baseball" the Associated Press stated that night baseball was "at the cross-roads in the Southern Association as the stepchild of hard times and is in good standing in only two cities—Atlanta and Little Rock. Night baseball started down in Arkansas when the Little Rock Travelers needed some customers and figured a few nightstands might attract some weary bridge players, the capital crowd, and others. It was successful and the Travelers are going to stick with it."[19]

Walter French had an equally impressive season in 1932 for the Little Rock club. He played in all of the team's 152 games, came to bat a team leading 628 times, collected 211 hits, also tops on the team, and included 25 doubles, eight triples, and three home runs for a team leading batting average among players with at least 100 at bats of .336. The Travelers finished in third place with a record of 77–75 and attendance had dropped lower than it had been in 1929 with only 72,856 fans attending games in the newly constructed Travelers Field.

Walter was back for the 1933 season with the Little Rock Travelers which began on Sunday April 11 at Memphis where they were visiting the Memphis Chicks.

It should be noted that hitting a home run was a very rare occurrence for Walter French. In his major league career, he only had two homers and he hit 17 in the minors. Most of those were inside the park home runs.

On opening day Memphis scored the game's first run in the second inning and pushed across another in their half of the third. The Chicks maintained their 2–0 lead into the top half of the sixth inning. With Travelers' outfielder George Gerken on base, Walter French came to the plate. On one of the first pitches he saw, he swung hard and made perfect contact with the ball, driving it over the fence in deep right field, to tie the score. The game went into extra innings and the Travelers scored a run in the top of the tenth inning and held the Chicks scoreless in their half of the inning to win the opening day game.

Almost immediately following his performance in the season's first game, Walter found himself mired in a batting slump. Looking back on that period years later he recalled that "I was not going good for Little Rock, but it was just a slump like players go through."[20]

The general manager of the Travelers beginning in 1931 was Ray Winder. Winder had served in administrative positions with several minor league teams before coming to Little Rock beginning in 1921 with the Chickasha Chicks in Oklahoma. What Walter saw as "just a slump" Winder must have seen as something else, because a few weeks after his heroics on opening day, Walter was notified that he had been traded to the Knoxville Smokies.

The announced trade of the team's most popular player did not sit well with the Little Rock fans. Their displeasure only got worse as Walter promptly came out of his slump in his first days in Knoxville.

The *Knoxville Journal*, on the other hand, expressed the joy that the fans in Knoxville felt with this new addition to their ballclub. "The announcement that Walter French, fresh from Little Rock ranks, has been added to the Knoxville roster comes as a rare treat. French, a daring baserunner and ball hawk extraordinary, packs plenty of the thing called color,"[21] the paper reported. The Associated Press reminded the fans that "French led the Southern Association in 1931 and 1932 in the largest number of hits and in 1931 for stolen bases."[22]

The owner of the Smokies was a man named Col. Bob Allen. His title was not earned in the military but was a social title given at the time to prominent citizens and those considered to be "Southern Gentlemen." Allen had played professional baseball for several teams as a young man and did some managing as well before becoming a success in the lumber industry. Allen had been the owner of the Little Rock Travelers but sold the team in January of 1931, just before Walter's arrival there, and purchased the Nashville Volunteers for $50,000. The Volunteers soon found themselves in last place in the league. Attendance was dismal and Allen soon became "cash strapped" and so in June, he sold the club to Faye Murray, another Nashville businessman. However, in December of 1931, he and his son Edgar, who had joined his father's business, purchased the Mobile, Alabama franchise and moved it to Knoxville before the start of the 1932 season.

From the minute Walter stepped on the field in a Knoxville uniform his batting slump ended. Sportswriter Bob Murphy, writing in the *Knoxville Journal*, said "a good slogan for everyone to adopt would be as French goes, so goes the Smokies."[23] He continued "of all the colorful athletes ever to wear a Smoky uniform the most colorful of all is now cavorting at Smithson Stadium. Walter French is the name." The cause of all the praise from Murphy was the fact that in his first 16 trips to the plate for Knoxville, Walter had 13 hits and there were two disputed plays where he was called out at first where hometown fans were convinced that he had been safe. "That same French," Murphy wrote, "has stolen more bases since he joined the club than the rest of the team has totaled all season. He has fielded like a demon, thrown out two men at the plate on successive days, scored almost every time he got on base, and in short served as a real inspiration to a Knoxville team that has been kicked about something terrible all season."[24]

Meanwhile, the Great Depression was keeping down attendance at all levels of professional baseball. In 1933, in an effort to boost attendance, a Major League All-Star game was conceived. Given the opportunity to vote for their favorite players, the game drove up fan interest in the sport when it was hard for the average person to afford to attend a game. The *Chicago Tribune* held a contest to award a $500 prize to the fan who could come the closest to picking the starting teams. The game was played at Comiskey Park in Chicago and all the proceeds from the game went to a charity supporting retired ballplayers facing financial ruin due to the effects of the Great Depression. The crowd at the game, estimated to be 49,000 saw the American League win the game by a score of 4–2, with a two-run home run in the third inning by Babe Ruth being the game's highlight. Of the 42 players, managers, and coaches participating in that first All-Star game, 25 would eventually wind up in the Baseball Hall of Fame. Among Walter French's former opponents on the field were Ruth, Lou Gehrig, and Tony Lazzeri. Of his former teammates with the Athletics Jimmy Dykes, Al Simmons, Lefty Grove, Jimmie Foxx, Eddie Collins, and manager Connie Mack all took part in the game.

Back in Knoxville, Walter French continued his excellent play throughout the year. In early August, with the team in first place, Smokies' owner Col. Allen, was praised for the moves he made earlier in the season adding offensive stars like Walter French and Bill Allington and pitcher Climax Blethen. Associated Press writer W. J. Davis called Allen's efforts "one of the most remarkable pieces of work done this year in minor league baseball." The Knoxville team was what their hometown paper the *Knoxville Journal* described as the "sensation of the second half of the season."

On Sunday, August 6, the Smokies honored Walter French between the games of a doubleheader with the Birmingham Barons. "Honor to whom honor is due" the *Knoxville News-Sentinel* reported, "That's the reason that they are going to hand a bouquet of orchids to Walter French, the Smokies' right-fielder, and the Southern League's most versatile player, when the Taylorites meet the Birmingham Barons in a double-header at Caswell Park starting at 2:00 p.m. today. Frenchy, who is practically tied for the league batting honors, is the leading base-stealer and who also hovers close to the top in several other departments. He has been a spark plug since he became a Smoky. He will be presented with a wristwatch between the doubleheader today for having led all members of the club in hitting in their last home stand."[25]

As the season wore down, however, the Smokies' hot streak came to an end and they finished in third place. Walter finished the year with a .351 batting average and his hit total was tops in the league for the third consecutive season. In December when the post season awards were announced for the Southern Association, Walter French was named the league's Most Valuable Player. The MVP was decided by a vote of the sportswriters who covered the Southern League, and was sponsored by the *Sporting News*, which was still the official baseball publication of the time. He received 41 votes from the writers, a full 10 votes clear of Lance Richbourg, of Nashville who received 31 votes. James Isaminger, veteran Philadelphia sportswriter reported the news to the local fans in the Delaware Valley. "Walter French, (Fritz to many Moorestonians) one of Connie Mack's forgotten outfielders is still good enough to be named the most valuable player of his league,"[26] he wrote.

Although the Smokies were not in contention in either half of the next season, Walter was once again a contender for the league's Most Valuable Player. He led his team in hits with 180, which was fifth best in the entire league, and finished with a batting average of .311. Marvin Thomson, sports editor of the *Knoxville Journal* laid out a compelling case for Walter. "You can't name a player in the league who has meant as much to his team, who has fielded as sensationally, who has delivered in as many pinches, who has been the sparkplug and inspiration to his team's drive …" he wrote. "Who has stolen as many bases as Wally French?" he continued, "Who has got as many hits? Who has featured with as many thrilling catches? Who has been a bigger inspiration to his team than Walter French?"[27]

While all teams in organized baseball were looking for ways to economize during the Depression years, Colonel Allen took it to the extreme. "Allen believed in running his baseball operation like a bank. While some owners relied on giveaways and promotions to attract fans, Allen felt that the product on the field should be the main attraction."[28] Walter's assessment of Allen was that he was "the tightest man that ever ran a ball club." After two seasons, in which he was the league's MVP and a top contender for the honor in another season, Allen told Walter that he was going to cut his salary for the 1935 season.

After refusing Colonel Allen's offer, Walter returned to the town where he began his professional baseball career when he caught on with the Williamsport Grays in the Eastern League.

CHAPTER 10

Outlaw Ballplayer

Although, as Walter would recall years later, there was no money to be made in Williamsport, he had another successful season. He played in 133 of the team's games, collected 171 hits including 16 doubles and eight triples, and finished the season with a .307 batting average.

Meanwhile there was some drama unfolding back at West Point with the Army Athletic Association, the ruling body for everything related to the Academy's sports programs. The baseball coach at West Point, Harry E. "Moose" McCormick, after 10 seasons on the job suddenly found his position at risk. McCormick had been a star athlete at Bucknell, played in the major leagues with the New York Giants and appeared in two World Series, in 1912 and 1913. He had led Army to winning seasons in all but three years of his tenure. But there was something in his coaching style that rubbed the Graduate Manager of Athletics at West Point the wrong way.

In the Spring of 1935, Major L. D. Worsham appealed to the Army Athletic Association not to renew McCormick's contract which was coming up in a few months. In a statement which became part of the Association's meeting minutes, Worsham, West Point class of 1916, explained that "I have carefully observed Mr. McCormick as a baseball coach for the past three years. I have spent afternoons watching his practices and have sat on the bench at practically every baseball game during the past two seasons. Mr. McCormick has many admirable qualities. He is clean morally and appears to be loyal to the Military Academy. He has certain defects which I think outweigh these qualities. I have never seen him assume responsibility for an error in judgement. The blame is always passed to the particular member of the team who was involved. He criticized players with a sharp tongue during the progress of an intercollegiate contest. At the end of last season, I had a long talk with him, trying to induce him to save his corrections until the Monday following the game. He has not done this this past season. The time has come when we should change baseball coaches, and I therefore recommend that Mr. McCormick's contract be not renewed."[1]

Harry McKenzie Roper, a 1st lieutenant and the "Officer in Charge of Baseball" however, took issue with Worsham's position. In his defense of McCormick he wrote that "the coach believed that he obtained better results by such a procedure than by the other alternative of postponing his corrections until the next day. I felt that if he believed this procedure best and as long as he does not humiliate a cadet, he should not necessarily change his methods ... I therefore recommend that his contract be renewed for whatever time the members of the Athletic Board recommend."[2]

At the next meeting of the group, Roper's position prevailed and McCormick's contract was renewed but only for one year as opposed to the multi-year renewals he had been given in the past. The Association meeting minutes reflect that "careful consideration was given by the Athletic Board to the renewal of the contract with Mr. H. E. McCormick as baseball coach. All members of the board, with the exception of Major Worsham, whose minority report appears below, recommended that Mr. McCormick's contract be renewed effective September 1, 1935, at his present salary of $4,200 per year. They consider him clean morally, loyal and a good influence on the cadets on the baseball squad."[3]

At the end of 1935, however, Major Worsham would get his wish. "Moose" McCormick announced that he was going to retire. The newspapers reported that "Moose" was retiring to devote more time to his insurance business. How much of an impact Worsham's effort to remove him had on his decision is impossible to know, but there now was an opening for a baseball coach at West Point for the next season. The Athletic Board acted quickly to name McCormick's replacement. Explaining why it was important to name a successor as soon as possible the board stated that "if the man selected is an active baseball player, he might take this into consideration before signing a contract to play professional ball. The board recommends that Mr. Walter French, an ex-cadet, who has more than thirteen years of service in professional baseball, be offered a contract to succeed Mr. H.E. McCormick as baseball coach at an annual salary of $3,800."[4]

The offer was accepted and the Associated Press reported that "Walter French, professional baseball player who formerly played baseball and football at West Point has announced he will retire after next season and coach the Cadet baseball team in 1937."[5]

While he may have retired from "organized" baseball, Walter still had one more stop to make as a player before hanging up his spikes and taking over the baseball team at West Point. Not unlike the way the Anthracite football league in the coal region, which gave birth to the Pottsville Maroons, provided a distraction from life in the mines through football, the Carolina Textile League and the Western Carolina Textile League, provided the same service to those working in that industry's mills, during the Great Depression, through baseball. In 1936, the leagues merged and went from being a loosely organized, semi-pro circuit to a full time, independent baseball league that would challenge the dominance of organized baseball.

The Great Depression had taken its toll on professional baseball. At the major league level teams had reduced their rosters from 25 players to 23. Moreover, by 1932 the number of professional baseball leagues had dropped from 36 to 13. So, if a player lost his job when his major league club reduced their roster, there were fewer places for that player to go to get picked up by another team. To make matters worse, the presence of the reserve clause in ballplayer contracts at the time meant that the player was still bound to their team until they retired or were released. Therefore, there was no shortage of talent available to be tapped by an upstart independent league.

The attraction of joining such a league for the players was financial. In many cases, top players, even former major leaguers like Walter French, could make more money than they were being offered by the farm teams of their former organizations. In addition, the players were offered offseason jobs in the mills. "A player in organized baseball faced an uncertain future; he might be sent up or down at any time, moving not just from town to town but state to state, and when the season was over, he could be on his own in a strange place, looking for work through the winter. Or he could jump his contract with organized baseball, come to the Piedmont, command a salary equal to what he earned in organized ball, settle there for as long as he liked, be guaranteed an off-season job right in that hometown and be idolized as a community hero."[6]

Jake Wade, sports editor of the *Charlotte Observer*, in describing the Carolina League, wrote: "the league abides by the rules and general plan of organized professional baseball. The ball they hit is standard and bears the league president's signature. The carefully chosen umpires are uniformed, draw regular salaries, and work under strict supervision. The only difference is the players are not strictly chattels as in organized professional baseball. They can leave at a moment's notice and go to an organized professional league, but they cannot jump from one club to another in this circuit."[7]

The new league was almost immediately viewed as a threat by organized baseball. Players were being "pirated away with the lure of higher wages, more enthusiastic fans, hero status in community life and an off-season career."[8] Organized baseball could not sit still. If the Carolina League succeeded, what would stop another independent league from starting up in another region of the country? It could jeopardize the monopoly that they had held over the players for years.

Judge W. G. Bramham, president of the National Association of Professional Baseball Leagues issued a warning to players contemplating joining the new league: "The Carolina League, composed of Concord, Kannapolis, Salisbury, Shelby, Hickory, Forest City, Charlotte, and Valdes is harboring and playing players under contract or reserved with organized ball. All such players are placed on the ineligible list, and all players and clubs in organized ball are notified that the playing with or against ineligibles, or with or against clubs playing or harboring ineligible players, will bring about the ineligibility of any and all players who fail to observe this warning."[9]

At the end of the 1935 season, future Hall of Famer, pitcher Herb Pennock, by then the head of the Boston Red Sox farm system created a stir which ultimately gave the upstart league a big boost. Charlotte was one of the largest cities in North Carolina and it did not appear that the Carolina League would be able to place a team there with the Red Sox farm team, the Charlotte Hornets, firmly entrenched in that city. Faced with disappointing attendance results, Pennock insisted that Charlotte add Sunday games to its schedule for the 1936 season. The people of this region were very much against any commercial enterprise operating on Sundays. (Laws permitting Sunday commerce in this region were not passed until 1960.) Believing that he could break the will of the locals, Pennock threatened to move the Red Sox franchise out of Charlotte if Sunday games were not permitted. The response of the Charlotte City Council to Pennock was to call his bluff and tell him to do what he had to do. Pennock promptly moved the team from Charlotte.

A Charlotte cotton broker by the name of Barron Hinson had been waiting in the wings to see how the Red Sox dispute with the city would be resolved and as soon as the Red Sox confirmed that they were leaving, Hinson announced his plan to put a Carolina League team in Charlotte. "It was a coup of head-spinning proportions for the league. Charlotte—the area's biggest city, ten times the size of the biggest textile league towns and home to the area's largest daily newspaper, the *Charlotte Observer*—was committing to play in an upstart league, completely outside the control of organized baseball. Charlotte's presence promised both a boom to attendance and a huge automatic boost to the league's publicity, not to mention the added credibility of just having a town that size as a member of the league."[10]

The entry of Charlotte convinced the other owners that their plan to offer full-time professional baseball, outside of organized baseball, could work, and so on March 4, 1936, the Carolina League was born. Nine clubs made up the charter members of the new league: Concord, Salisbury, and Kannapolis from the old Carolina Textile League; Hickory, Shelby, Valdese, Conover, and Forest City/Rutherford County of the Western Carolina League; and the former Red Sox affiliate Charlotte.

After learning that he had secured the head coaching job at West Point, Walter was considering his options as to what he would do to earn a living and support his family while waiting to start his new job in September, when representatives of the Concord Weavers of the new Carolina League reached out to him. Rusty McCall, who the Weavers thought would be one of the stars of their team had been reactivated by Albany in the International League just before the start of the season which meant that the Concord team needed an outfielder. Walter accepted the spot with the Weavers and was with the team on opening day.

It turned out that the Albany team changed their mind on McCall and he returned to Concord. This gave the Weaver's manager Bobby Hipps one of the best outfields that the area had ever seen, with McCall in center field, French in right field, and one of the top sluggers from the 1935 season, Jeff Bolden in left field.

The Weavers played their home games at Webb Field, a converted high school facility in Concord, that was named for a former superintendent of Schools. In addition to a grandstand that went behind home plate from first base to third, three new bleachers were constructed for the 1936 season. Two of the bleachers were designated for white fans while a third for Black fans. This brought the capacity of Webb Field to 3,000 fans.

Opening day for the season was held on Friday, May 8, with the first pitch at 4:15pm. Hoping for a crowd of 1,000 fans for the game, the Concord officials were thrilled when 1,800 turned out for the game with the Charlotte Hornets. The Weavers won by a score of 4–2, with Walter French making an immediate impact on his new team. With his team trailing 1–0 in the bottom of the first inning, Walter slammed a triple and then scored on a wild pitch to tie the score.

The first big series of the season for the Weavers was a two-game set against the Kannapolis Towelers in Concord. "Coddle Creek" Taylor, the ace of the Kannapolis pitching staff was on the mound for the visiting team and beat the Weavers by a score of 4–2. The next day the Towelers defeated the Weavers by a score of 12–2. In the two games Walter French had four hits, and even at this early stage of the season he was establishing himself as one of his team's best players and a fan favorite. Although the two losses moved the Weavers back to second place in the standings, team officials were thrilled by the record-breaking attendance at both games.

By June 4, Concord, Kannapolis, and Valdese were tied for first place all with identical 15–8 records. The Charlotte Hornets were only one game back. The ongoing battle with Kannapolis for first place created a heated rivalry between the two teams. As another big head-to-head matchup was approaching, the Kannapolis management tried to put a stop to ticket scalping by holding off on the sale of reserved seats until the day before the first game.

Concord swept the two-game series winning the first contest by a score of 7–2. The next day the Weavers topped Kannapolis by a score of 9–3 on the strength of an all-star performance on the part of Walter French. Leading up to this series Walter had been playing center field for the Weavers but was moved to left field with the arrival of Sammy Payonski who was moved to center. Walter came to bat five times in this game and had three hits. He knocked in two runs and scored three times. One of his runs came in the first inning when he was trapped between second and third base. He dashed back and forth evading being tagged out until eventually the Towelers' shortstop threw the ball away and he came around to score. However, it was not his hitting or base running that made the highlights of this game but his excellent play in the field. The Charlotte news described two of his best plays of the game: "Watt's hard drive looked like two bases in the third but French took it in almost on top of the bank." In the seventh inning "he climbed the bank in left to pull down Miller's hard drive."[11]

If Walter thought he had played with some colorful teammates in his years in professional baseball and football, that experience paled in comparison to what he found in the Independent Carolina League. It attracted an interesting collection of rogue characters whose backgrounds ranged from former preachers to an ex-con. The experience of young George Barley reveals a great deal about the type of individuals that gravitated to the outlaw league. After his sophomore year in high school, Barley was approached by a Yankee scout who wanted him to sign a contract which would have him leave high school to pitch in the minor leagues. Barley declined, saying that he wanted to go to college, specifically Duke University. The problem was that Barley's family could not afford to send him to Duke and so he reached an agreement with the Yankees where they would pay him $200 per month while he was in college in exchange for Barley signing with whatever team the Yankees required for $200 per month once he graduated. So, Barley stayed in high school and spent his summers playing semi-pro baseball against a variety of teams including some of the professional Negro League teams. Eventually, while attending Duke, he signed to pitch for Kannapolis at a weekly salary of $85 which was more than the Yankees were going to pay him and more than his father was making at the time. Years later he described the environment in the Carolina League: "This was an entirely different group of ballplayers than I had ever played with before. I had played against the Cuban All-Stars, the Kansas City Monarchs, and so forth, but I had never been on the same team, in the same dressing room, with so many rough characters …"[12] He also recalled that there was a lot of drinking going on amongst the ballplayers: "Bethel Rhem, for example, had a night table and at night before he went to bed he would place a bottle of gin and a package of cigarettes on it … first thing he did when he woke up in the morning was take a swig of gin and smoke a cigarette."[13]

One colorful character who was the hottest pitcher in the league by mid-June was Charlotte's ace Charles M. "Struttin Bud" Shaney. On June 20, he was in the midst of a nine-game winning streak, all of which were at home. Naturally this raised some eyebrows and rumors started to float that "Struttin Bud" was cheating. In his column in the *Concord Tribune,* Dick Montague wrote: "It's remarkable how old "Strutting Bud" Shaney has managed to chalk up nine straight victories this season. And just last season he was washed up."[14] The truth was that Shaney didn't mind the fact that people were accusing him of cheating. He thought it gave him a psychological advantage. So convinced was Weavers manager Bobby Hipps that Shaney was up to no good that he would take some of the balls used by Shaney and saw them in half to see if there was anything inside that was not supposed to be there. Strutting Bud's streak finally came to an end after 17 consecutive victories. Later in 1936, Bud became the Hornets' player-manager.

By the halfway point of the season Walter French had established himself as one of the best players in the league. Besides his stellar play in the field, he was hitting .339 and his 75 hits were second most in the league only behind his teammate Art

Hord, who had 84 hits and Walter was tops on his team and near the top of the league in runs scored.

The Weavers finished the first half of the season in first place ahead of the Kannapolis team. In early August the two teams met in a doubleheader in Concord. The Towelers won the first game by a score of 2–0. In that game, Walter made another amazing play in the outfield. He robbed "Razz" Miller of an extra base hit with a sensational catch up against the wall in left field which saved two runs.

Glenn "Razz" Miller was a farm boy from Rockwell, NC who was recruited literally while plowing his father's field by the coach from Lenoir-Rhyne College, a Lutheran school in Hickory, NC. While at Lenoir-Rhyne he was one of the leaders of the school's baseball team which posted a winning record in each of his four seasons. After graduating from college Miller entered the Lutheran Theological Seminary and eventually served as a minister of the Calvary Lutheran Church in Concord beginning in 1934. With the church's permission he played in the semi-professional leagues a few nights a week but struggled when he felt his role as a minister conflicted with that of a professional baseball player. In particular, he felt that he could not, on the one hand, be a man of the cloth and at the same time back up his teammates when fights broke out, which was a regular Carolina League occurrence. So he resigned from the ministry in May of 1936, joined the Kannapolis team and became one of the leading hitters in the league.

At the opposite end of the spectrum from "Razz" Miller was a player who joined the Charlotte Hornets on July 12, 1936, by the name of Edwin "Alabama" Pitts. After being honorably discharged from the Navy in 1930, Pitts, a newlywed at the time, found himself broke and unemployed in New York City. He and an accomplice were implicated in a number of grocery store robberies. Convicted of armed robbery, Edwin was sentenced to eight years in the notorious Sing Sing prison, which was located about 35 miles north of Manhattan. While in prison he came under the influence of Warden Lewis Lawes, a noted prison reform advocate and champion of prisoner rehabilitation. One of Lawes's initiatives was the establishment of prison sports teams and Pitts became the star player on the Sing Sing baseball team. His on the field exploits, most notably his play in an exhibition game with the Yankees in September of 1933, soon garnered him the attention of the New York sportswriters.

Besides being an outstanding athlete, Pitts was also a model prisoner and Warden Lawes eventually arranged for his sentence to be reduced to five years. He was released in September of 1935. Initially, W. G. Bramham, President of the National Association of Professional Baseball Leagues, was adamant that Pitts, a convicted criminal, would not be allowed to play on any team in organized baseball, but eventually he succumbed to pressure from the likes of Dizzy Dean and others, and Pitts was permitted to play professional baseball.

When the 1936 season began, Pitts was playing for the York, PA team in the New York–Penn league. Then for no apparent reason, beyond wanting to get out of the northeast and the opportunity to make more money, he showed up on the Charlotte roster midway through the season. He made an immediate impact for the Hornets and quickly became one of the league's best hitters.

Walter's season was coming to an end as he was preparing to report to West Point to start his new job on September 1. In addition to coaching the baseball team, he was going to coach the school's freshmen football team, so his presence was required on campus by early September. French's "play in the Carolina League established him, in one year, as the best outfielder in the league."[15] He was hitting better than .370 and led the league with 147 hits when his last game was played. The Weavers held a special "Walter French Appreciation Day" to send him off, presenting him with a valise in recognition of his contributions to the team.

Walter had made a conscious decision to finish his playing career in what he knew was an outlaw baseball league, and one that was sure to raise the ire of organized baseball. At this point Walter had been in professional baseball for 13 years. He knew that he and his fellow outlaws were doing nothing less than challenging the sacred "reserve clause" which bound ballplayers to their team even after the expiration of their contract. Whether he would have made the same decision without the knowledge that he had a job waiting for him at West Point, we will never know, but the fact is that he did challenge a system that would not be abolished until 1975 when through the efforts of the Major League Baseball Players Association, the reserve clause was removed from player contracts.

In January of 1937, organized baseball dropped the other shoe and announced that it had banned 27 players for life for playing in the outlaw Carolina League the previous year. When the list of banned players was published it included six of the 1936 Concord Weavers: Ken Chitwood, Johnny Hicks, Art Hord, Charles Mundy, Hobart Scott, and Walter French.

CHAPTER 11

Coach French

When Walter French stepped foot back on the campus of the United States Military Academy as the school's new varsity baseball coach and coach of Army's plebe football team, in early September of 1936, it marked almost 14 years to the day from when he was discharged by the Academic Board for deficiencies in his studies. It had to have been with more than a little satisfaction that he made his return. He was taking over a team that had been 4–9 in 1936 under "Moose" McCormick, including a painful 11–10 loss to Navy.

The *Howitzer*, the student yearbook, reported that "Walter French returned to the Academy, this time as the head coach of baseball."[1] Shortly after arriving back on campus, Walter began to institute a number of changes aimed at improving the team's fortunes in the upcoming season. In addition to making some changes to the team's lineup, he had two batting cages installed in the gymnasium. Previously baseball practice had been held in Riding Hall in the winter months, but starting with the 1937 season, the new batting cages in the gymnasium were large enough to permit batting practice in the cold months before the season. The extra practice allowed the team to get off to a fast start.

Although the season started in early April, bad weather kept the team from playing a home game until May 1. The team's first opponent was Yale and Army won the game easily by a score of 8–3. A week later the team traveled to New Jersey to take on a tough Princeton squad who they defeated in a pitcher's duel by a score of 1–0. On the mound for West Point was a pitcher that Coach French would lean heavily on throughout the 1937 and 1938 seasons by the name of Andy Lipscomb. Lipscomb pitched a nine-inning, one-hitter to secure the win for Army.

The team followed up the Princeton win with a victory over Amherst by a score of 5–1. After losing to Penn State 7–3, they then ran off wins over Syracuse, Swarthmore, Bucknell, NYU before dropping their second game of the season against Fordham. Three days after defeating Union the team squared off against Navy in the biggest game of the year.

Nearly 14 years to the day from when he was expelled from West Point for academic reasons, Walter French returned to the school as its varsity baseball coach, May 15, 1939. (Courtesy of National Baseball Hall of Fame, and Museum)

The Army–Navy rivalry in baseball was every bit as heated as it was in football. The two schools first began playing baseball against one another in 1901 and coming into the 1937 game Army led the series 17–12. No games were played in 1917 and 1918 due to World War I and after the series resumed in 1919, Navy had won nine of the last 14 games.

Army jumped off to a quick 3–0 lead in Walter's first Navy game as the Army coach behind the strong pitching of Tom Davis. Davis retired all nine men he faced in the first three innings. Davis held Navy scoreless until the sixth inning when Navy's Ed Anderson hit a three-run home run to tie the score. Sensing that Davis was tiring Walter brought in Andy Lipscomb to pitch the seventh inning and he retired Navy easily in the top of the seventh inning. In the bottom of the seventh, led by Bob Griffin's second home run of the game, Army pushed across three runs. They would tack on two more in the eighth inning while Lipscomb was closing out the game. The final score was 8–3. Lipscomb had only given up one hit in the final three innings.

In the annual report of the Army Athletic Association it was noted that "in reviewing the season, much credit must be given to Walter E. French (ex-1924) for his excellent coaching and handling of the team."[2]

With his two star pitchers, Lipscomb and Davis, returning for the 1938 season, hopes for another good year were high. After being upset 4–2 by Williams in the first game of the season the team won nine of their next 11 games including a big win over Penn State to avenge their loss in 1937.

From the earliest days of their baseball programs, both Army and Navy tried to hire head coaches who had Major League experience and one story line leading up to the 1938 Army–Navy game involved the head coaches for the respective teams. After Navy baseball coach Marty Karow left the school to accept a position at Texas A&M, Navy hired Walter's old teammate from the Philadelphia Athletics, second baseman Max Bishop. Bishop was the same age as Walter and was from Waynesboro, PA. The two men had played together for the better part of six seasons, including the championship run of 1929. Bishop had played his last big-league game for the Boston Red Sox in 1935. After a few stops in the minor leagues and a stint as a scout, the Red Sox made him the manager of their Pocomoke City team in the Eastern Shore League. He jumped at the chance to take the Navy job, a position that he would hold for the next 25 years.

One of the umpires for the game was Ed Rommel, who also had been a teammate of both Walter French and Max Bishop for six years while he pitched for the Philadelphia Athletics. His best years were from 1922 through 1925 in which he averaged 21 wins per season. He pitched in game four of the 1929 World Series in which the A's came back from being down 8–0.

The three former teammates posed for a photograph together as the coaches presented their lineup cards.

The starting pitchers for the 1938 Army–Navy game were Jerry Bruckel for Navy and Tom Davis for Army. Army got off to a fast start when second baseman Jim Durbin led off the game with a single. In a very uncharacteristic mental error, Bruckel never looked over to first base to check on Durbin, who immediately broke for second and stole the base easily. Next up was centerfielder Al Weinnig, who hit a deep fly ball which advanced Durbin to third. Bob Kasper, the Army catcher, singled to centerfield scoring the game's first run. Bruckel remained calm and got the next two batters out, limiting the damage. That would be Army's only run of the game. Navy meanwhile recorded nine hits off of three different Army pitchers which when combined with six Army errors resulted in an easy 6–1 win for Navy.

The 1939 season was shaping up to be an exciting one for Army although the team was described as "inexperienced." The biggest loss to graduation was Andy Lipscomb, the team's best pitcher from the previous season. This left Tom Davis as the team ace.

The schedule had them playing 16 games, including their annual exhibition game against the New York Giants which took place on April 18 at West Point. Managing the Giants was future Hall of Famer Bill Terry. Terry played 14 seasons with the Giants and finished his career with a .341 lifetime batting average. In 1930 he hit .401. The *New York Daily News* reported that "Terry, fearful of the cold wind which whipped across the Plains, refused to take a chance with a regular hurler and permitted Jack Tansey, former Holy Cross moundsman, to pitch the complete game. He held the Cadets to five hits."[3]

Tom Davis started the game for Army and gave up four hits but only one run in his three innings of work. In the bottom of the fifth inning however, the "hybrid team of first- and second-string Giant players" went to work. Led my "Mercury" Myatt's double, the only extra base hit of the game, the Giants scored three runs to take a 4–2 lead. At this point the skies opened up and a steady rain began to fall and the game was called.[4]

The team's first collegiate opponent was the University of Vermont, who fell to the Cadets by a score of 7–1. This was followed by a loss to Lafayette in a tight 4–3 game. From that point on the team defeated Princeton, Rutgers, Georgetown, Syracuse, and Williams. Their losses came to Columbia, Duke, Yale, Penn, and Fordham.

On May 27, Walter French participated in his third Army–Navy game as the head coach of baseball. Although Walter had only played in two Army–Navy games as a cadet he clearly understood the importance beating Navy represented at West Point. In his first two seasons as coach, his teams had one win and one loss. Like everyone who has ever coached any sport at Army before him or since, he did not want to have a losing record against Navy. As the *Howitzer* observed, a victory over Navy "always marks the season as a success—no matter what has gone before."[5]

The game was played at West Point in front of 5,000 fans. Walter called on his ace Tom Davis to start the game for Army. The game was scoreless until the fourth inning when Navy scored one run but Davis, who gave up only six hits and one walk, shut the Middies out for the remainder of the game. In the meantime, Army scored two runs in their half of the fifth inning plus one in the seventh and eighth. In addition to being the pitching star of the game, Tom Davis, who was playing in his final game at West Point, had three hits in four trips to the plate, including a double which drove in one of Army's four runs.

Before the curtain would fall on the 1939 season there was one more game to be played. A post-season game against Colgate, to be held at Cooperstown, New York to commemorate what was believed to be the 100th anniversary of baseball's invention by Abner Doubleday, who was a West Point cadet when he supposedly "devised the game" on a farmer's field in 1839.

In 1905, a commission was formed, headed up by National League President Abraham Mills to determine the origin of the game of baseball. Two years later the Mills Commission issued their findings which credited Doubleday with creating the game. Since that time many researchers have debunked the notion that Doubleday, who became an Army Officer and was second in command at Fort Sumter at the start of the Civil War, was the inventor of the national pastime. It has been noted that in all his writings and correspondence he never once mentioned baseball or any role he played in the game's development. However, in 1939 the report of the Mills Commission was considered to be the definitive word on the subject.

Perfect weather and a holiday weekend brought a huge crowd to Doubleday Field in Cooperstown. The *Binghamton Press* reported that "some 7,500 persons … nearly filled the stadium surrounding the 'dream diamond' where baseball was first played 100 years ago." It was said to be the largest crowd to ever see a game in that part of New York. Army won the game easily by a score of 5–1. In summing up the game, the *Binghamton Press* wrote: "Yesterday belonged to the soldiers no matter how you look at it. Besides actually being Army Day, as well as Memorial Day, West Point honored a distinguished graduate Major General Abner Doubleday, creator of baseball, while the Cadet nine paid its own tribute by shelling Colgate."[6]

Before the game there was a ceremony and Major R. Ernest Dupuy, public relations officer at West Point, presented a painting of Doubleday to the National Museum and Hall of Fame scheduled to open in a few weeks. "Since Major General Doubleday was a cadet when he invented baseball, West Point is very proud to participate in this tribute,"[7] Dupuy said.

Once again, the *Howitzer* praised the job done by Walter French: "It would be fitting to close with a word about our fine coach Wally French. Wally was, some years back, heralded as the finest athlete to ever wear the Cadet grey. Unfortunately, yearling math proved a bit too complex and mysterious and Wally found himself a rookie with the Athletics. Professional ball he gave up to return to West Point as head baseball coach and coach-of-all-trades for the A.A.A. Year-after-year French turns out a team of which Army can be proud, and it is to him more than anyone else that we should give our thanks for our fine baseball record."[8]

In looking forward to the 1940 season Walter was unsure of what to expect from his team. They had been hit hard by graduation and would be a very inexperienced unit. On a positive note West Point teams, in all sports, had always given their utmost. It was true in Walter's day when he played for Hans Lobert and it was the case with this group as well. Of this Walter was sure.

The team may have hustled but 1940 marked the only losing season that Walter had as the West Point coach, with the team going 5–7. To make matters worse was the fact that the team got off to such a promising start, with three straight wins over Harvard, Princeton, and Brown. But their old nemesis Lafayette handed them their first defeat. That was followed up by losses to Penn State, Duke, and NYU. They also lost to all of their principal rivals Notre Dame, Fordham, and worst of all Navy.

In summing up the 1941 season *Howitzer* described it as one of "ups and downs with a record of eight victories and six defeats." The first win came against a team that, aside from Navy, might have been their most bitter baseball rival. Their 2–1 victory over Lafayette marked the first time that they had beaten the Leopards in 10 years. The game could have gone either way. Army scored the winning run following a walk, a passed ball and an error, but after a decade of futility Army was happy to finally get a win. Army then beat Harvard by a score of 7–2 and Amherst 11–5.

After the Amherst game the Army bats went to sleep as it seemed that every player was slumping at the same time. In the next three games against Pittsburg, Princeton, and Brown, all losses, the Cadets were outscored 31 to six. From there the Cadets went 5–3.

The game with Yale proved to be one of the best of the year. Pitching for West Point was Buck Tarver and he was opposed by Joe Wood, Jr. Although this game represented the best pitching performance that the Cadets had all season, Wood got the better of him in a 2–0 Yale victory. Wood struck out 10 batters in pitching a complete game shutout. Yale scored the only run they would need in the first inning and Tarver held them scoreless after that until the eighth inning when they scored an insurance run. Army's best chance to win the game came in the bottom of the ninth inning when they loaded the bases with one out, but they were unable to push any runs across the plate against Wood.

The *Hartford Courant* wrote that in "limiting Army to five hits, Joe Wood, Jr., captain of the Yale nine and son of its famous coach blanked Army 2 to 0, here today for the most impressive victory of his collegiate career."[9] The famous father referred to was "Smoky" Joe Wood, the same Joe Wood who had been embroiled with Ty Cobb and Tris Speaker in the Dutch Leonard Affair in 1926.

As always, the final game of the season was against Navy. Sporting a record of 14–5, with impressive wins against teams like Notre Dame, Virginia, Penn State, and Duke, Navy was considered a heavy favorite to win this, the thirty-fourth meeting of the two teams, held on May 29. A record turnout for an Army–Navy baseball game, packed the stands at West Point and included Robert Patterson, Under Secretary of War.

Also, on the same day at West Point the track teams from Army and Navy were squaring off in their annual meet. Meanwhile at Annapolis, the two schools' lacrosse, golf, and tennis teams were going head-to-head. To allow fans at each contest to follow the proceedings at the other events, a system was set up for spectators to be kept informed almost play-by-play. The Associated Press reported that "Periodic reports on the 'away' events will be broadcast to fans at the Army–Navy baseball game and track meet … The system will work both ways, since by means of a special direct telephone hookup, Annapolis fans also will be kept posted on what's happening at West Point."[10]

Cadet Eric De Jonckheere, pitching in his final game got off to a rough start when Navy touched him up for one run in the first inning and a pair in the second. However, he then settled down and shut out the Midshipmen the rest of the way.

Meanwhile Army scored two runs in their half of the third inning to pull them to within one run. Navy clung to a 3–2 lead until the bottom of the sixth inning when centerfielder Bill Garland slammed a triple which drove in two runs. De Jonckheere, who finished the game having given up only five hits and striking out eight, held Navy at bay over the last three innings to give Army a 4–3 hard earned victory.

In summing up the season the *Howitzer* explained that "With a few breaks Wally French might have coached a consistent winner in 1941. The team exhibited power in flashes with some excellent pitching. Practically the same power will be available next year with the exception of Dick Polk, the outgoing captain."[11]

Over the summer of 1941 Army hired former Cadet Earl "Red" Blaik, West Point class of 1920, to coach its football team. For the last six years Blaik had been the head coach at Dartmouth. The team got off to a great start winning their first four games and then playing in a college football classic against Notre Dame at Yankee Stadium before a crowd of 76,000 fans. The game ended in a 0–0 tie and the effort moved Army to number 11 in the national rankings. However, in the next two weeks they were beaten by Harvard and then Penn before beating West Virginia to set up their showdown with Navy on November 29. Navy held a record of 6–1 coming into the game and had shutout five of their opponents. Their only loss came against Notre Dame. Even more impressive was the fact that Navy had outscored their opponents 178–28 through that point of the season. The game was played at Philadelphia's Municipal Stadium in front of 98,924 fans. Although Army fought valiantly Navy came away with a 14–6 win.

At this time Walter French and his wife and two daughters were firmly established in the West Point community. After attending the Army–Navy game he returned home to Highland Falls, New York, a short distance from the West Point campus. He was looking forward to the 1942 baseball season and excited by the team's prospects with the number of key players he was expecting to return. However, eight days later everything changed.

John S. D. Eisenhower, the son of General and future President Dwight D. Eisenhower, was a plebe at the United States Military Academy on the weekend of December 7, 1941. Reflecting on that time years later he recalled that he was expecting it to be a quiet weekend. Everyone was still "smarting" over the loss to Navy the week before. "We had settled into our rigorous routine, anticipating the Christmas holiday."[12] On Sunday afternoons the Cadets, even the plebes, were able to enjoy some free time, and Eisenhower's favorite way to use that time was to catch up on some much-needed sleep. In the middle of the afternoon one of his classmates started shaking him awake. "The Japs are bombing Pearl Harbor," he shouted. Not believing that the Japanese would attack Hawaii, Eisenhower went back to sleep. "I finished my snooze in the late afternoon, about an hour before the Corps of Cadets was to march off to the evening meal. At that point, I came to realize that Toothman's alarm had been true; the Japanese Imperial Fleet had actually ventured as far east as

Hawaii and had bombed various military installations on Oahu. The naval base at Pearl Harbor and the Army Air Corps' Hickman Field were the most mentioned."[13]

He recalled that "every man was alone with his thoughts … This momentous event meant one primary thing to us all: Early Graduation."[14]

On Monday morning, December 8, 1941, a visitor to West Point would not have noticed anything different. Eisenhower recalled that "no visible changes, in fact occurred for months following. The authorities, however, were busy, and as of the next summer, 1942, the four-year curriculum had been shortened to three. The nation gained the services of one additional West Point class."

"In a way," Eisenhower recalled "the early morning Japanese attack on Pearl Harbor and Hickman Field would affect West Point cadets less than it did average American citizens, because the cadets were already in the Army when it occurred; they would not, therefore, be wrenched from home and family. On the other hand they paid dearly in casualties. Five hundred West Pointers died in the Second World War, and a large portion of those who gave their lives came from the ranks of these young men, all of whom graduated in the period between 1942 and 1943."

At some point in the next few months, feeling compelled to do his part for the war effort, Walter French made the decision that the 1942 season would be his last at West Point until after the war. At 43 years old, he would give up his dream job and re-enlist in the Army so that he could serve his country. He would eventually be commissioned a captain in the Army Air Corps in June but there was still one more baseball season to enjoy before he would be shipped off to his first post.

The 1942 Army baseball team turned out to be one of the school's best in more than a decade. The team which had several players returning from the 1941 overachieving team, got off to a fast start winning their first four games. Even the annual beating in the exhibition game against the New York Giants gave the Cadets a reason to smile. Despite ultimately losing the game by a score of 12–2, ace Bob Whitlow held the major league team to two runs for the first five innings and "Goose" Guckeyson crushed a fastball "out on Callum balcony" for a home run.

The team ended up with a record of 10 wins against four losses. The game against Syracuse ended in a tie. The signature wins at the end of the season against Yale and Navy by scores of 6–4 and 10–3 respectively were particularly sweet. However, as sweet as those wins were, the war must have been like a cloud hanging over every activity which in normal times would have been celebrated. Due to wartime regulations no members of the public, for example, were allowed to attend the Army–Navy baseball game, which the previous season had attracted thousands of fans. It is not hard to imagine what that last game must have felt like. The *Howitzer* in its summation of the 1942 season wrote "This team, like all of Army's will be hit hard by early graduation. Lost to the squad will be Stahle, Whitlow, Rebb, Benson, Prince, Glasgow, Frakes, Benedict, and Mazur. Therefore, the team will have to look to the plebes to fill the vacancies."[15] They also made note of Walter French's departure:

"Wally French, lost to Army baseball for the duration! It's a blow to West Point to lose Wally, but our loss is the country's gain. We know that no matter where he goes, he will look back on the 1942 edition of Army baseball with a glow of pride."[16]

A few weeks after the final game against Navy, it was publicly announced that Walter French was leaving his position as Army baseball coach and joining the Army Air Corps. The Associated Press announced that "Walter E. French, baseball coach at West Point for the last six years, has been appointed captain in the Army Air Force and ordered to report as an instructor in the Officers Candidate School in Miami Beach, Fla."[17]

Out of the view of the media, Walter had submitted a request to the Army Athletic Association for a leave of absence from his position as baseball coach for the duration of the war. His request was denied. The Board's position was that given that his contract was set to expire on June 30, 1942, that there would be no need to approve his request.

Selected to replace Walter as the Army coach was Paul Amen. Amen had been a multisport star at the University of Nebraska. Like Walter, Amen was hired to be the head coach of the baseball team and as an assistant coach for football. At some point he enlisted in the Army and was made a lieutenant and was preparing to start the season as both the coach and the military officer in charge of baseball. For each team at West Point, where the head coach is a civilian, there is a military officer assigned to the team to, among other things, handle any disciplinary action from a military standpoint. With Amen now an Army officer he could perform both functions.

However, in January of 1943, the Army Athletic Association voted to accept the offer of Brooklyn Dodgers' owner Branch Rickey which would allow them to use, free of charge, "Mr. Leo Durocher as Advisory Baseball Coach from March 1 to April 15." A few days later Rickey accompanied by what the Associated Press described as an "expedition of newspapermen" arrived on the West Point campus to make the unexpected announcement. With Durocher on the job, Amen's role would be that of the military officer in charge of the baseball team, while Durocher would coach the team. On April 15 or sooner if Durocher was drafted, Amen would once again assume both roles with the team.

After playing 17 years in the Major Leagues, Leo Durocher, nicknamed "the Lip" or "Lippy" because of his combative nature, was a successful manager with the Dodgers and Giants. When he finally retired at the age of 67, he ranked fifth, all-time, with 2,008 managerial victories. He was posthumously inducted into the Baseball Hall of Fame in 1994. Walter French had played against Durocher in the 1920s when he was a member of the Yankees.

CHAPTER 12

Captain French and the War Years

In July of 1942 Walter French packed up his wife and two daughters, now teenagers, and headed south to Miami Beach. Beginning in February of 1942, Miami Beach was transformed from being America's foremost resort area to a military training site and home to 78,000 enlisted men and officers. Under Secretary of War Robert P. Patterson, who had attended the 1942 Army–Navy baseball game, in announcing his plan to use Miami Beach's vast number of resort hotels for military training facilities declared that "The best hotel room is none too good for the American Soldier."[1] Oddly enough the hotel and apartment owners in the area quickly began to see the benefit in a lease arrangement with the U.S. Military. In the months leading up to the military takeover of Miami Beach, bookings had been down due to the government-imposed gas rationing and the fact that the beaches were stained from tar from German U-boat attacks on ships in the Atlantic. Having Uncle Sam as a tenant was a very attractive option. "Resort hotels became mess halls, bachelor officers' quarters and crowded army barracks over the course of the next year."[2] Eventually some 300 hotels and apartment buildings became military facilities, eventually servicing nearly half a million trainees.

Among those assigned to the Miami Beach training site were the movie actor Clark Gable and Franklin Roosevelt, Jr. the president's son. There were a number of famous athletes from the time that were also sent to Miami Beach, most notably the great baseball slugger, and future Hall of Famer, Hank Greenberg of the Detroit Tigers. Relying on his experience as an athlete, coach, and West Point Cadet, Walter French's job in Miami was that of a "physical instructor."

It was not until the start of World War II that the U.S. Army finally instituted a physical fitness test. Many of the men being called up to fight were not in the best of shape so the Army relied on men with a background like Walter's to put them through their paces and to prepare them for combat. To get the men into the best possible condition, the Army implemented a systematic physical development program as part of the Combat Basic Training course being offered at the Miami Training Center. "Soldiers marched on the beach, they marched on the golf courses, they marched down Lincoln Road and up Collins Avenue. Gas masks were used to peel onions. Airports stocked up on bomber jets. A mess hall could be anywhere from a grand art deco ballroom to a palm tree shaded park. Miami Beach was the center of basic training ops for hundreds of thousands of our brave boys, and we pulled it off in style."[3] Ocean swimming was also a key element of their training.

Walter and his family settled into an apartment on Alton Road, which was situated along the Biscayne Bay, and marked the western boundary of the area of Miami Beach being utilized by the military. Alton Road apartments were one of the areas in which officers with families were housed. One of their neighbors was Navy Captain Howard H. J. Benson and his wife. Benson had served in World War I, winning the Navy Cross, the branch's second highest award for valor. Also stationed at the Miami Training Center was Walter's friend and teammate from Rutgers and West Point, Don Storck.

Sports provided a needed diversion from the non-stop training activities taking place in Miami Beach. In September there was a baseball game scheduled, pitting a team from MacDill Field in Tampa against the home team made up of players stationed at the Air Forces Technical Training command. The pre-game festivities included "a platoon drill," the *Miami Herald* reported, "the platoon will be in formal dress, with white gloves and leggings. Officers believe that it will be one of the neatest exhibitions of the season. These pre-game ceremonies will be in the charge of Captain Walter French, former All-American football player at West Point, and an outfielder with the Philadelphia Athletics from 1923–1929."[4]

Walter's wife Beth kept busy while in Miami attending to her daughters as well as the social responsibilities expected of an officer's spouse. In October, the *Miami Herald* reported that "Mrs. James L. Kaufman, wife of the Rear Admiral began a series of 'diminishing bridge parties' this week to raise funds for Navy Relief. She invited three Army wives and two Navy wives, making a total of six. Each guest will in turn give a party for five and those five will entertain for four, etc. Mrs. Kaufman's guests from the Army were Mrs. Paul Wing, wife of General Wing, who was taken prisoner at Bataan, Mrs. Walter E. French, wife of Captain French, and Mrs. Henri DeSebour, wife of Captain DeSebour."[5] The *Miami Herald* also listed Beth among the officers' wives that had joined the St. Patrick's Guild which sponsored tea parties for newly arriving military wives to the Miami Training Center.

As for Walter's two teenage daughters, Mary Frances and Ann, it seemed like Christmas had come early. They were surrounded by thousands of young men, some just a little older than they were. The two young women spent their free time at the beach watching the soldiers go through their training regimen. *Life* magazine did a multipage story on the transformation of Miami Beach into a training site. Photos taken by Myron Davis and William Shrout "capture the juxtaposition between Miami's picture-postcard surroundings and the seriousness of the Army's mission. Soldiers cram into a baseball stadium stands, to take a course on chemical warfare.

Future mess hall cooks learn their trade in resort kitchens. Palm trees sway in the background as soldiers are pushed through the exercises meant to toughen them up for combat. The few pictures that might be mistaken for classic beach vacation photos are the ones of shirtless soldiers rushing into the water. In those shots, there is no hint of the hell they could be headed for once they were done in Miami."[6]

In April of 1943, Walter was reassigned to Basic Training Center No. 10, which had only opened the previous month in Greensboro, North Carolina. So he packed up his family once more and took them 800 miles north to yet another home.

As other training centers, such as No. 7 in Atlantic City, New Jersey, became overcrowded the Army built new facilities throughout the country. Trainees at the site typically were there from four to eight weeks and received training in weapons, drilling, physical fitness, and chemical warfare. From there the airmen would be sent to other bases for more advanced training before they were sent into combat.

After only seven months in Greensboro, the French family was on the move again, this time to Casper, Wyoming. The Casper Army Air Base was activated in September of 1942 and during its construction period, which was less than four months long, over 400 buildings were built. The base was the home to the training of bomber crews. Once their training was completed in Casper the men were given overseas assignments. Over 16,000 bomber crew members received their training at the Casper site.

For Walter's wife and daughters, Casper was a long way from the palm trees and ocean breezes of Miami Beach. John Goss, director of the Wyoming Veterans Memorial Museum, writing in an article on the history of the base for the Wyoming Historical Society described the site as a "high, flat, sage brush covered terrace located nine miles west of town on US Highway 20–26 and adjacent to the Chicago, Burlington, and Quincy Railroad."[7] Photos of the facility taken at the time show a place even more desolate than that described by Goss.

The French family's stay in Casper was brief. Three short months after his arrival he received orders sending him overseas to serve in Italy in January of 1944. He sat his family down at the kitchen table and broke the news of his new assignment to them and told them that they could live wherever they wanted while he was away. Without a second's hesitation both Mary Frances, who was 18 at the time, and Ann, who was 16, simultaneously blurted out "Highland Falls, New York." The West Point area was home to Walter's daughters. They had spent seven years there while their father was coaching the baseball team, which was a longer stay than any other place they had ever lived. Walter arranged for them to live in the Onodera Estates section of Highland Falls, which was the same neighborhood they lived in before moving to Miami in July of 1942.

Walter and his fellow officers boarded a B-24 for their trip to Italy. The flight was scheduled to make a stop in Brazil and then Africa before reaching their final destination. The U.S. military maintained a number of bases along the eastern

Walter had this photo taken of his wife and daughters and he carried it with him while serving in the Armed Forces during World War II and in the Korean War. Seated are his daughter Fran, age 18, on the left and her mother, Beth, on the right. Ann, age 16, is standing. (Courtesy of French Family)

portion of Brazil. Originally created as a defensive measure, these bases eventually became a major launching point for the South Atlantic airway to the fighting forces in Europe, however the airspace in and around Belem was particularly dangerous for the flight crews of the Army Air Corps. Engine failures, navigational errors, and the ever-present severe thunderstorms posed a constant threat. On the night of March 5, 1944, the Army B-24 with Walter, and his crew mates, was planning on stopping in Belem. The plan was for the plane to stop at the base to refuel before heading to Africa and to its eventual destination in Italy when it was caught in a thunderstorm. "The pilot battled the storm and fought the controls. For more than an hour the plane sailed on. Then the fuel ran out"[8] according to a *Philadelphia Inquirer* article written at the time. There were seven men on the flight, in addition to the pilot. Certain the plane was going down; the pilot ordered the men to bail out. One by one the men jumped from the plane landing in the tall jungle grass. Before jumping from the plane, the men made a plan to yell out when they hit the ground so they could meet up and await a rescue together. Walter recalled that when he hit the ground his "yell sounded more like a shriek."[9] Getting to his feet he felt a wetness in the vicinity of his shirt pocket. His immediate thought was that he had been injured and that the substance he was feeling was blood, however it turned out to be ink which had spilled out of a pen that he had in his pocket that snapped when he landed.

As he was making his way to meet his crew that he could hear off in the distance, he heard a rustling in the brush and he soon found himself surrounded by a group of machete-wielding locals. Walter discovered that he could communicate with them in French, which was one of his better subjects at West Point. He explained that he was an American and, with that, the men let down their guard. Walter met up with the rest of his crew and his new friends led them to their village where they spent the night.

None of the men were seriously injured in the jump, and remarkably the pilot even "found an open spot and contrived to land the plane,"[10] according to the *Philadelphia Inquirer*. The pilot made their whereabouts known, the search for the missing crew was called off and the Navy Airship K-114, a dirigible whose crew included Philadelphian Jack Glickstein was dispatched to pick up the men and a few days later they were back in the air headed to Italy.

The incident, reported to the local press by Walter's younger brother Cooper French, received a great deal of coverage. Walter's younger brother was a star football player at Penn State and in 1944 was the Athletic Director at Germantown Academy in Philadelphia. The headline in the *Philadelphia Inquirer* read: "Escape from Death in the Jungle … Captain Walter French 'Safe' in Italy." In the article the *Inquirer* incorrectly listed Penn State and West Point as the two schools attended by Walter French. A reader called the paper out, in a letter to the editor, for its inaccuracy. "In your story about Walter French's escape from death in the South American jungle," wrote Clarence Tucker, "you got him confused with his brother Cooper, giving his college as Penn State. But it was all right as I won $10 from a friend who insisted that Walter had not gone to Rutgers."[11] Even though he was far removed from his playing days, he was still front of mind to the sports fans of Philadelphia.

Walter served in Italy for approximately one year. His military records from this period were among those destroyed in a fire in 1973 at the National Personnel Records Center, so his specific role is unknown. However, throughout the war over 2.4 million men served in the Army Air Corps in Italy along with 80,000 aircraft. The primary function of the Air Force in Italy was the strategic bombing of enemy positions in Europe.

The war in Europe ended with the unconditional surrender of Germany in May of 1945. As Walter French, now a Major, was preparing to return to his family in Highland Falls, the Army Athletic Association Board, who earlier had rejected his request for a leave of absence, were meeting to determine his future at West Point. Coach Paul Amen, who succeeded Walter as the baseball coach when he re-enlisted in the Army in 1942 had coached Army to three very successful seasons. The Cadets had a record of 36–4 from 1943 to 1945 inclusive, including victories over Navy in 1944 and 1945. Amen was also only 29 years old in 1945, which made him 18 years younger than Walter. Over the three years that Amen had coached Army he also emerged as a leader in the coaching community and in 1945 he was a founding member of the American Baseball Coaches Association.

The Army Athletic Association's board, assuming that Walter would leave the Army once the war was over and he was released from active service, made the determination that they would not offer Walter his coaching position back.

In 1944, Congress passed, and President Franklin Roosevelt signed into law the Servicemen's Readjustment Act of 1944, also known as the GI Bill of Rights. The law was meant to prepare the nation for the return of thousands of soldiers and sailors, who would need medical care, education, and jobs. One of the most controversial parts of the bill was the provision which gave unemployment compensation to returning veterans for up to one year, to give them an opportunity to be retrained. Many felt that paying unemployment benefits would serve as a disincentive and keep people from seeking employment, but once in place only a small percentage of the funds that had been put aside for this benefit were ever used.

As the A.A.A. board deliberated the fate of Walter French, along with that of Fred Canausa, who had coached the Army golf team for 20 years, they considered "all moral obligations which may exist under the service man's bill of rights."[12] At their meeting on December 7, 1945 the board recommended that "these coaches now in the service be advised by letter that their services will not be required. The board recommends that in the above-mentioned letter it be suggested that Mr. French and Mr. Canausa, after their release from active service, come to West Point so that we may talk matters over with a view to making a substantial payment in recognition of past services."[13] The board was prepared to make the payment equal to a full year's pay which they felt would be comparable to the one-year unemployment payment called for in the Bill of Rights.

Walter would never see the one-year salary payment because he had already made the decision to stay in the military. Whether he took the rejection of his request for a leave of absence by the Army Athletic Association as a warning that they might go in a different direction after the war or he simply felt it was in his best interest to remain in the military he informed the officials at West Point that he intended to stay active.

While he was waiting for his next assignment Walter remained in the West Point area, living with his family in Highland Falls from March until August. He was granted official leave for this period and while he did not receive the year's pay being contemplated by the Army Athletic Association, he was paid, with "allowances" $2,350 over this period, which coincidentally was pretty close to what the year's pay would have been. It was also during this time that his two daughters were married to West Point graduates in the first "double ring" ceremony ever held in the chapel at West Point.

Over the next few years Walter French moved from station to station as a member of the Army Air Corps. In August of 1946, he was named director of training at the Army ground forces physical training school in Camp Lee, Virginia. It was while he was stationed at Camp Lee that Walter made a splash on the college football scene when he submitted a formal proposal to change the way college football games were being scored.

Walter felt that it was unfair for a team that held the lead by a small margin for three plus periods, to lose the game when the opponent scores a touchdown at the very end of the game and converts the extra point. He submitted a plan to Harvard Athletic Director, William Bingham, who was chairman of the intercollegiate rules committee, early in 1947 and asked for it to be considered at their next meeting. The Associated Press reported that under his plan "French would continue to give the boys six points for every touchdown they score and one point for a successful conversion but there is an added feature in this Army major's proposal."[14] Under Walter's plan a team would be awarded one point for each quarter in which it held the lead in the game and adding those points to those made by touchdowns and conversions. "French thinks this system would eliminate a lot of tie games," the AP reported, "and guard against 'fluke' plays which win games in the final seconds and provide more and faster action for the customers."[15] Walter was quoted as saying that "tie games are the plague of modern football and they have been the cause of much concern among those who are close to the modern-day grid games."[16] He concluded by saying that "such a system as I have proposed would keep the teams at their offensive best at all times and would place less emphasis on the presently all-too-important point-after-touchdown."[17] It was a testament to the fact that his standing in the sports world had not diminished in the years since he had been an active player and coach, that his proposal received so much coverage and serious consideration from the rules committee.

Bingham and his committee instituted seven rule changes in 1947 including moving of the hash marks, restrictions on the shift play, changes to the substitution rules, and others but Walter's proposal was not adopted.

Later that year Congress passed and the President signed into law the National Security Act of 1947. The act created the Department of Defense, which was composed of five military branches the Army, Navy, Marines, the Coast Guard, and the newly established Air Force, which replaced the Army Air Corps. Most of the men who were serving in the Army Air Corps, including Walter French, moved over to the new branch and over the next two years he worked at a few short-term stations, including one year overseas. However, in the fall of 1949 he was moved to a position, which must have seemed like a dream job, at Michigan State University. In November of 1949, he was made a member of the school's faculty as part of the

Air Force R.O.T.C. staff. The *Lansing State Journal* reported the new faculty member is "nationally known in the field of athletics having starred in football, baseball and basketball and played pro-baseball with the Philadelphia Athletics in 1929, the year they won the World Series."[18] His specific role was that of the public information officer, a position he held until 1953.

In 1954, Walter, who had been promoted to Lieutenant Colonel, was required to complete a Department of Defense form 398. DD398 is a personal history statement used to screen individuals seeking to obtain a specific security designation so that a person could be "allowed access to classified information, sensitive areas, or permitted assignment to sensitive national security."[19] Over the next few years, he would serve in a variety of locations throughout the world, including Korea. Although the specifics of his assignments were lost in the fire at the National Personnel Records Center in 1973, his role at this time was later described in newspaper stories about Walter as an intelligence officer.

This much we know, after serving in Korea in 1954 he was transferred to Tokyo, Japan, to serve on the staff of General Earle Everard "Pat" Partridge, who was the Commander of Far East Air Forces. "Pat" Partridge was Walter's classmate at West Point. When Walter called Beth to see if she would like to join him in Japan, according

Lt. Col. Walter French serving in the Far East, circa 1954. (Courtesy of French Family)

to their daughter Ann, she told him "That noise you hear in the background is the sound of me packing." Oddly enough, Beth French, even though her husband was an officer in the Air Force, was deathly afraid of flying. She traveled to Japan by boat to join her husband.

While he and Beth were in Japan, his old classmates from the West Point class of 1924 were gathering for their thirtieth-class reunion. Included in the book published for the event, which profiled all of the members of the graduating class, was Walter French. His former classmates had agreed to make him an honorary member of the class. "West Point classes don't often make honorary members of their foundlings" the program read and "it is a rare mark of esteem and affection that has to be deserved. In Fritz's case, he's always been something special to us … from the first day of Beast Barracks. When he lost his two-year feud with the English Department, it left a gap in the Herd that we remedied the only way we could … Fritzie French and the years 1920–1922 in West Point sports history are indivisible. He was already a finished athlete when he came in and won three major sports 'A's with the ease and grace of a natural. On the football field and baseball diamond especially, he did much to lift the Academy out of the bushes and into the big leagues. As one of our most successful grandparents, Fritz is getting small pleasure from this, immolated in the Far East, but hopes by now that his Beth will at least help fill the gap by joining him over there. Despite his head start with an 'early graduation', he refused to get the jump on his classmates and waited to join the benedicts until '24. Both his boys being girls has not prevented him from continuing the Long Gray Line he loves, both of them married classmates of '46 in a double ceremony at the Chapel. Come home soon Fritzie and catch up on your babysitting."[20]

Over the next five years, Walter and Beth moved to a variety of stations, both foreign and domestic. One of his roles near the end of his military career was helping soldiers returning from the Korean War who were suffering from what was described as "battle fatigue" which was what we would today call Post-Traumatic Stress Disorder.

In 1959, Lt. Col. Walter French announced his retirement from the military. He and Beth settled in La Selva Beach, California, which is located along the Pacific Ocean in Santa Cruz County.

After leaving the Air Force, Walter took a job as a security guard at the local Lockheed Martin facility near La Selva. It was while working at Lockheed that he first began to experience dizzy spells and hearing loss that was later diagnosed as Ménière's disease. The spells come and go without warning and while no single cause has ever been identified for this condition, in his case, likely culprits are the concussions he sustained playing for Rutgers and later with the Maroons, combined with his exposure to loud noises while in the military.

In retirement Walter kept in touch with some of his old teammates. His daughter, Ann, recalled that her parents visited Ty Cobb at his lodge on Lake Tahoe on a number of occasions. He also corresponded with Joe Zacko, who was keeping the fight alive to restore the 1925 NFL Championship to the Pottsville Maroons. In February of 1963 Zacko wrote to Walter to invite him to a team reunion taking place in June of that year back in Pottsville. Walter wrote back and declined saying "There is nothing I would rather do than to say 'yes I will be at the reunion in June,' but I just can't afford such a trip, I'm retired and though I work, I have to watch my pennies every month. I don't just live around the corner. Thanks for the reunion program—it arrived today." He concluded, referring to Zacko's crusade to have the title restored to the Maroons by saying "Sure hope your efforts are successful." Later in that same month, Zacko wrote Walter to let him know that the date of the reunion had been pushed back to which he replied "Sorry but the change in dates does not change my situation. I appreciate all the efforts you and your committee is putting forth. I'll probably be east in 1964 and if my trip materializes, I will make it a point to drop in on you." After he came across an article in the *Washington Post* by Dave Brady making the case for the restoration of the Maroons' title in 1965, he clipped the article and sent it to Joe. Like the other surviving members of the Maroons, he was still smarting over the stolen title some 40 years later, writing "Maybe our luck will change one of these days."

He also continued to stay in contact with his classmates from West Point. He attended Army–Navy football games with Dennis Mulligan, who was the captain of the Army football team in the years Walter played, as well as other former teammates like Sam Smithers, George Smythe, and Don Storck.

After living such an active life for over 60 years Walter settled down to a slower pace in retirement. He took up gardening and enjoyed growing fruits and vegetables.

He also took up golf, and as with every other sport he tried, he became an accomplished player. He played at the golf course located at Fort Ord in Seaside California which was located about 30 miles from his home in La Selva. The original 18-hole, challenging course, was built in 1954 and was described as "as mean as can be." A decade later another 18-hole course was built on the site. The courses are now known as the Bayonet and Black Horse golf courses. Typically, Walter would make the trip over to Fort Ord three days a week to play golf and had two holes in one to his credit on the difficult course. One of his golfing buddies was retired Brigadier General William N. Gilmore, who was in the class behind Walter at West Point and his teammate on the 1921 Army football team. Among other roles in which Gilmore served, he was the Commanding General of the 101st Airborne Division during World War II. The two former teammates played golf together three times a week starting in 1963. "The money bet was small, but the competition was hot," Gilmore later recalled.

When his older brother William passed away in 1972 Walter became the last surviving member of his immediate family. His sister Esther died in 1952 and his brother, Penn State football star Cooper, as was the case with his brother Joseph, took his own life in 1962. Walter became the patriarch of the French family and was a hero to his grandchildren and many nephews and nieces. His niece, Mary Jo Walsh, the daughter of Esther French, once wrote about him that "he was my hero, no doubt about it … When thinking about marriage I made a list of the things I was looking for in a husband and realized the perfect person would be just like Uncle Walter."

In 1973, while helping members of a church, to which he and Beth belonged, build a drainage system, he suffered a heart attack. He recovered and was soon back out playing golf, although now making use of a golf cart. However it was in 1979, while playing golf at the Fort Ord course that he suffered his second, and this time nearly fatal, heart attack. Once again, he recovered and was soon back to his old routine. On days when he was not playing golf, he made it a point to walk two or three miles to stay in shape and was proud of the fact that he never gained one pound above what he weighed in his playing days.

In 1980, shortly after recovering from his second heart attack, he reported, in a letter to a friend, "I shot my age in golf last week—80." Often described as the toughest accomplishment for the average golfer, shooting one's age, is just that, shooting a score that is equal to or less than the player's age. It is estimated that for every million rounds of golf that are played, only nine will result in the player shooting his or her age.

His interest in baseball never waned in his later years. His granddaughter recalled how she would see him reading the newspaper's sports section, while listening to one ball game on the radio, and watching another game on television, during her visits. He provided a scouting report on the 1980 St. Louis Cardinals, to a friend who was a big fan of the team writing "Now as to your first love, the 'Cards', their pitching must be pretty terrible for they sure have the hitters. Maybe the change in managers will help. It seems to be for a short period." He was referring to the fact that the Cardinals had just replaced Manager Ken Boyer with Whitey Herzog. In August of 1982, he wrote a letter to syndicated columnist Murray Olderman to complain about the way balls and strikes were being called in the majors, especially against the San Francisco Giants and their manager Frank Robinson. After laying out his bona fides on the subject, that is having played for the Athletics from 1923 to 1929, he went on to say "there are three or four National League umpires that have it in for Frank Robinson. His beefs at San Diego—and Johnny Lemaster's called third strike and Sixto Lezcano's third strike that wasn't called were legit … too bad they don't have some old-time umpires to call strikes on pitches six-to-eight inches above the belt." Always getting the last word in his columns Olderman wrote "I can't buy any theory of prejudice against the San Francisco Giants' Robinson.

You never win any arguments on balls and strikes anyway. Also, the strike zone has become smaller since French was playing baseball."

There was one practice that is common for old, retired ballplayers in which Walter French refused to engage. He found it off-putting when old-timers spent their time reminiscing about how things were better "back in their day." It was so evident that he felt this way to his children and grandchildren, that they never asked him anything about his playing days. He would be more than happy to discuss his golf game, and remark on the accomplishments of current day athletes but that was the extent of it.

Over time the damage caused by his heart attacks began to take a toll on him and eventually he and Beth decided to move to Arkansas to be near his daughter Ann and her husband C. F. Horton, who lived in Oakland, Arkansas, where Horton, after retiring from the military, was a fishing trip guide. Just a few days after settling into their new home, Walter got up in the middle of the night to use the bathroom and not wanting to wake up his wife kept the lights off. After feeling his way along the hallway leading to the bathroom instead of stepping through a doorway he turned the wrong way, ran into a wall, took a bad fall, and broke his hip. A reoccurrence of Ménière's disease, for which he was successfully being treated, was ruled out as a cause and it appeared that he just got disoriented in his new surroundings. He was taken to the hospital and operated on for his broken hip.

The risk for pneumonia for people of Walter's age hospitalized for a fractured hip, especially for someone with his history of heart problems is significant. Several studies, conducted well after Walter's accident, have shown that lower respiratory tract infection is the primary cause of death in elderly patients with hip fractures.

On Sunday, May 13, 1984, three weeks after his fall, Walter French passed away at the age of 84. The cause of death was listed as pneumonia.

When he died, Walter was the last surviving member of the "Team That Time Forgot," the 1929 World Series Champion Philadelphia Athletics. His passing also left Russ Hathaway as the lone surviving member of the 1925 Pottsville Maroons.

Epilogue

On May 17, 1984, an article appeared in the *Gettysburg Times* under the headline "Pottsville Still Wants its Title Back after more than 50 Years." Seemingly unaware of Walter's passing only a few days before, Walter Kraus, recalling the 1925 championship game with the Chicago Cardinals, wrote in the article that "Walter French, who played in the offseason as an outfielder for Connie Mack was credited as the chief source of the grief for the Cardinals. He was here, there, and everywhere, gaining yardage, breaking up Cardinal plays, bucking lines, hurling deadly passes, and running … displaying skill in every move. French also accounted for one of the three touchdowns."[1]

One of the favorite pastimes of baseball enthusiasts is to speculate on "what if" scenarios. What impact would have allowing Black players to participate in the major leagues decades before they were, have had on the various records? What if Walter Johnson was pitching today, would he still be considered the fastest pitcher? What if Babe Ruth was never a pitcher and played 150 games each year in his early days, how many home runs would he have hit? What if Babe Ruth's entire career was played in the live ball era? What if World War II and the Korean War had not interrupted the illustrious career of Ted Williams in its prime for five years? How many more records would he have set? What if the powerful Pittsburgh Pirates' shortstop Honus Wagner had played in the live ball era, is it not almost certain that he would have finished his 21-year career with more than 101 home runs? Each day on social media, and on radio sports talk shows, these debates, and others like them, play out among sports fans, but they almost always involve trying to place old time ballplayers into a more modern era.

In the case of Walter French, however, speculation goes in the opposite direction. What would his career have been like if he had come along in the 1890s and had played in the dead ball era where speed, making contact, stealing bases, and scoring runs were the skills that teams coveted? What if he played in an era when the ability to reach first base, steal two bases, and subsequently score on a sacrifice fly, was valued as much as hitting a home run? Walter's career began just as the rule changes ushered in during the 1920s brought an end to the "dead ball" era. In the years after the changes were instituted the number of home runs hit per game more than doubled while the number of stolen bases went into a three-decade decline.

In an article announcing French being named the Most Valuable Player in The Southern League in 1933, James C. Isaminger observed "French entered the majors at a bad time for one of his size. He was a bullet for speed, could bunt in the most scientific fashion, and would rip off his share of singles, but he was no giant. In those days baseball managers did not want fast little fellows with a scientific attack. The cry was for the beefy stalwart who might hit the wall or over it. This was rough for French. The Babe Ruth influence was working and managers instructed their scouts not to bring anyone but giant gardeners who hit for distance. Earlier in the century, when baseball styles were different, French could not have been crowded off of any major league club he joined. Connie Mack frankly admitted that he was playing in the wrong era."[2]

When Walter was playing for the Knoxville Smokies, the Athletics came to town to play them in an exhibition game. When Walter saw Connie Mack, before the game, holding court with reporters in what was to be the Athletics' dugout he stopped catching flyballs and jogged in to greet his old manager, who was now 73 years old. One newspaper reported that "after French and Mack finished their chat in Knoxville yesterday the 73-year-old satrap of baseball turned to a friend and said 'that young man was in baseball in the wrong era. In the nineties he would have been a second Willie Keeler but he entered the majors when baseball was homerun mad. If an outfielder could not hit the wall or drive the ball out of the park like Ruth, he never had a chance.'"[3]

But without going back to a previous era, Walter French, as a versatile two-sport star in the Golden Age of Sports, left his mark. He finished his major league baseball career with a lifetime batting average of .303 in 981 at bats. Had he not been injured at the end of his 1924 season with Shreveport and had he come up to the A's as was the plan he would have undoubtedly finished his career with over 1,000 at bats which would have made him eligible for *The Baseball Almanac*'s listing of the best lifetime averages in the history of the game. His .303 would have placed in in the top 150 players of all time.

He was one of only 25 men to have played in baseball's Major Leagues and the National Football League in the same season and only a handful have done it since he and Charlie Berry accomplished the feat in 1925. Moreover when he died, he was one of only two men who could legitimately claim to have played for a World Series winner and an NFL Championship team.

In 1925, the *Record American* newspaper, published in the Wilkes-Barre, PA area was asked by a fan "who was the fastest ball carrier we ever saw"? The paper responded that the three fastest running backs in the country were Walter French, Red Grange, and Fritz Pollard, in that order. "It happened our questioner was a Grange rooter" the paper reported, "and we had to explain at length why the West Point brilliant was faster than the Wheaton iceman. And we told him—simply because he is. There is no argument to it at all. We made no effort to compare the men in football ability or ball-carrying ability, judging only by the speed we saw flashed by both men. We saw Grange lead a pack down the field, saw them streaming behind him, saw him putting open water, as the yachters say, between himself and the nearest tackler. When we saw men who know Walter French take after the little mite—well, they didn't bother to chase him. They stood by and enjoyed him running as much as the fan in the bleachers. To us, the sight of French about to dodge a man is as pretty as anything we have seen in football. There he goes, the little legs working like pistons, and without any apparent effort, running as fast as the fastest ordinary player on the field. That's to keep his footing when he dodges. Once he dodges, he starts to run and then it is hopeless to think of even trying to catch him. And once we saw Grange dropped from behind. French, to us, is the fastest we have seen. He has three speeds—fast, faster, and then fastest."[4]

His natural athletic gifts, his speed and great hand–eye coordination went a long way to making him a successful athlete at the highest levels of football and baseball, but there was something else about him that endeared him to fans wherever he played and helps explain a Navy man remembering having seen him play when he was only a boy so many years later. Walter never stepped on the playing field, be it a diamond, court, or gridiron without giving it his all. The *Knoxville Journal* summed up what made Walter a fan favorite "Wally French never lays down on the job. Loafing is not according to the creed of these West Pointers. They give their all as long as there is an ounce of energy left. It was drilled into them. That may account for Walter French's continued stay at the top of the heap."[5]

The *Knoxville Journal* was right. Walter French was inexorably linked to the United States Military Academy at West Point. The one place to which he was most connected was the one that had expelled him. Almost every one of the countless newspaper stories about Walter French made mention of his time at West Point. In fact, it was not unusual to see him incorrectly referred to as a "West Point graduate," and it is hard to imagine him being more closely tied to the academy if, in fact, he had graduated from the school.

Paul Robeson

After graduating from Rutgers University, Paul Robeson played three seasons of professional football before entering Columbia Law School. Upon graduating from law school, he joined a New York City law firm but was soon disenchanted by the racial tension he witnessed. He was subjected to a variety of insults, starting with the office he was assigned which was a converted broom closet, to the secretary that refused to type for him. Eventually, his wife Eslanda convinced him to leave his position and to seek work as an actor. In the 1920s he appeared in a number of Broadway productions including Eugene O'Neill's *All God's Chillun Got Wings* and *The Emperor Jones* in 1924 and 1925 respectively. He was originally cast in the role of Joe in the Rodgers and Hammerstein production of *Showboat* but delays with the show's opening made him unavailable. He did, however, appear in the London premiere and the show's Broadway revival in 1936. He also played the part in the 1936 film version. His rendition of the song "Old Man River" was a highlight of the show. Brooks Atkinson, noted critic at the time, described Paul's performance as "a touch of genius."

From 1943 to 1944, Robeson played the title role in *Othello* on Broadway, which remains the longest running Shakespeare production in Broadway history. He soon became an international sensation.

Before becoming the host of the most famous variety show of all time, Ed Sullivan was a sports and entertainment writer for the *New York Daily News* and the *Chicago Tribune*. In 1943 he wrote a column about Robeson as his *Othello* performance was hitting the peak of its popularity. He recalled how Robeson was an All-American on the great Rutgers team in 1918 and how those teammates must be proud of him: "Down in Miami Beach, FL. LTC Don Storck one of the heads of the O.C.S. will read this column on Robeson with great delight, for Storck played on that team too as did Judge Paul Duffy, Dr. Mike Whitehill, Army's Walter French, Rutgers coach Harry Rockafeller, New Jersey State Senator John Summerill, US Rubber executive Cliff Baker are some of the teammates who have cheered Robeson every step of the way since he left the famed university at New Brunswick ... because Paul Robeson, Class of '19 is one of the all-time idols of his school."[6] Sullivan went on to write this of Robeson's performance as Othello, "Robeson's performance caused the dramatic critics to whoop and holler with delight ... this, they said, was the Moor that Shakespeare had in mind when he wrote the play ... physically, vocally and emotionally, Robeson brought the character to life as no other actor could establish the reality of the Moor ... and it is a tribute to Robeson's artistry that as Iago tortures him with innuendos, the 6 foot 3 giant seems to shrink and become a little man ... Of such is the magic of make-believe compounded."[7]

Robeson also continued to speak out on social issues, mainly against fascism overseas and racism at home. He numbered among his friends Eleanor Roosevelt, W. E. B. Du Bois, Joe Louis, and Harry Truman. Eventually his positions, and refusal to sign an affidavit swearing that he was not a member of the Communist Party, placed him in the crosshairs of the House Un-American Activities Committee. Extraordinary measures were taken to silence him. Lloyd Brown, one of his biographers, wrote that "Paul Robeson was the most persecuted, the most ostracized, the most condemned black man in America, then or ever."[8] W. E. B. Du Bois writing in his autobiography said, "The persecution of Paul Robeson by the government has been one of the most contemptible happenings in modern history."[9]

Eventually he was stripped of his passport for an eight-year period which meant that he could not travel abroad to perform and participate in the causes in which he believed. By the time his passport was reinstated the ordeal had sent him into bouts of depression. He also realized that he no longer had his powerful singing and speaking voice so he decided to retire and live out of the public eye with his sister on Walnut Street in Philadelphia, which he did until his death in 1976. The home he shared with her is now the Paul Robeson House & Museum. In 1995, Paul Robeson was posthumously inducted into the College Football Hall of Fame.

Knute Rockne, George Gipp, the Big Game

After Notre Dame's win over Army in 1920, Knute Rockne would coach in 10 more games between the two schools before he was tragically killed in a plane crash in March of 1931. He was traveling from South Bend to Los Angeles for a speaking engagement when the plane, in which he was a passenger, according to an eyewitness, suddenly exploded. At the time of his death, Rockne had coached Notre Dame for 13 seasons and led them to six national championships in that span. He finished with five teams that were undefeated and untied, and his winning percentage of .881 remains the best of any coach in the college or professional game. In 1951 he was inducted into the College Football Hall of Fame.

Both Knute Rockne and George Gipp would be portrayed in a feature film, *Knute Rockne, All American* which came out in 1940 from Warner Brothers. The movie was directed by Lloyd Bacon and starred Pat O'Brien in the title role and future president Ronald Reagan as George Gipp.

In 2007, a woman named Ellen Easton, who believed that she might be George Gipp's granddaughter, encouraged by a publicity-seeking author, successfully petitioned the authorities in Laurium to exhume Gipp's body, buried for 87 years, to perform a DNA test. The belief was that Gipp had fathered a child with Easton's grandmother, then an 18-year-old girl in 1920, the year he died and the year of his greatest game against Army. A crew from ESPN was dispatched to film the process which angered the Gipp family and the local community. The DNA samples were tested and no match was found.

Although, as an annual game, the Army vs. Notre Dame football series ended after the 1947 matchup, the two teams did meet 17 more times, with the last meeting in 2016. In the leadup to the 1943 game Grantland Rice, in his syndicated column "The Sportlight" said this about the rivalry: "Looking back some thirty years the top rivalries in football include Harvard and Yale, Princeton and Yale, Cornell and Pennsylvania, Stanford and California, Michigan and Minnesota, Army and Navy, Dartmouth and Harvard, Colgate and Syracuse, to suggest just a few. Then one Saturday afternoon Notre Dame went east to meet Army at West Point. There was no particular reason why this shouldn't have been just another football game. But it clicked from the start. As a result, Army and Notre Dame make up one of the keenest rivalries that football has ever known … and so it happens that even in the middle of the world's biggest war their next meeting will bring together two of the finest squads either side has sent to the field." Rice wrote that Notre Dame's winning margin in the series results from a "remarkable flow of backs year after year ... Gus Dorias, Ray Eichenlaub, George Gipp, the Four Horsemen, Marty Brill, Marchy Schwartz, Frank Carideo, Joe Savoldi, Angelo Bertelli, etc. It might also be suggested that Army has had her full share of great backs over most of this period ... the fast-flying Walter French, Chris Cagle, Light Horse Harry Wilson, now a star flier in the Far East, young Monk Myers, K. H. Murrel, Jack Buckler."[10]

Grantland Rice

Although he first came to prominence during the Golden Age of Sports, Grantland Rice remained the dean of American sportswriters for another quarter of a century. Many stars in the world of sports continued to credit Rice and his writing for part of their fame during this period. He was ringside at Yankee Stadium in June of 1954 for the heavyweight championship fight between Rocky Marciano and Ezzard Charles. It would be the last big sporting event he would cover because a few weeks later he suffered a stroke and died on July 13, 1954. His last column, written on the day of his death, was about a 23-year-old centerfielder who had reversed the fortunes of the New York Giants, by the name of Willie Mays. Tributes poured in from the world of sports, but most prominent were those from the decade of the 1920s including boxing legend Jack Dempsey and golfing great Bobby Jones who said that "the thing that made him great as a writer was that he was a great human being." Jimmy Crowley, speaking on behalf of the "Four Horsemen" called him a "true friend and master craftsman."[11]

Hans Lobert

Hans Lobert left his coaching position at West Point in 1928. Over the next 20 years he served as a coach for several major league teams including the New York Giants, Cincinnati Reds, and the Philadelphia Phillies. He managed the Phillies for one season in 1942. In 1953 Hans, like Rockne and Gipp, was depicted in a feature film. *The Big Leaguer* starred Edward G. Robinson as Hans Lobert, who acted as a technical advisor on the project. Robinson's Lobert character is visited by his niece at spring training in Florida as players try out for the team. She is attracted to one of the team's prospects.

The real Hans Lobert, however, would fall on hard times. When author Lawrence Ritter met with Lobert to interview him for his book on the early days of baseball *The Glory of Their Times*, in 1966, he found him living in a cheap "fleabag" hotel in Philadelphia by himself. Ritter recalled that Lobert had been seriously injured when he was struck by a car and his insurance company refused to pay all of his claims. After the interview was completed, Ritter went out and bought Hans a small 14 inch black and white television so he could watch baseball games. Shortly after his interview with Ritter, Hans suffered a heart attack and although he initially recovered, he succumbed to a variety of ailments in September of 1968.

Don Storck

Don Storck, who played baseball and football with Walter French at both Rutgers and West Point was awarded the Legion of Merit in 1943 for his role in establishing the first officer training school of the U.S. Army Air Corps in Miami, Florida. He married Broadway actress Winifred Lawshe with whom he lived for 60 years in Bronxville, New York, along with their three children. When he passed away in 1987 after a long battle with cancer his obituary noted that "before entering West Point, he played football at Rutgers University with actor and singer Paul Robeson and enjoyed telling friends about his friendship and experiences with Robeson."[12]

General Douglas MacArthur and Louise Cromwell Brooks

Pershing made good on his promise and sent MacArthur and his wife to the Philippines in 1922. In 1925, MacArthur was promoted to the rank of Major General and at the age of 45 he was the youngest person to reach that rank. After his promotion he was transferred back to the U.S. serving in Washington, D.C. He and Louise moved into her family's estate located between Baltimore and the nation's Capital.

Although Louise would later claim that the three years she spent with MacArthur in the Philippines to be the happiest of her life, indications are that the marriage was a rocky one. Responding to Louise's complaints about her husband, her mother wrote her a letter in November of 1923 stating that "Your letters have made me sick with distress and sympathy ... that you should be so unhappy and Douglas is such a cruel disappointment to you. Your quarrels and his striking you are dreadful to me. I don't know what to advise you to do. I do not advise you to divorce him ... I do not think you were made to marry."[13] But in 1929, divorce him she did. She soon had taken up with an actor named Lionel Atwill. The press speculated that the cause of the tension in the MacArthur's marriage was Louise's desire to have her husband leave the military and enter the business world. She adamantly denied that she had ever pressured him to change professions. On the contrary, she claimed that she wanted him to remain in the Army because it was "so much a part of him." In an interview she gave to society columnist Betty Beale, at the time of MacArthur's death in April of 1964, she claimed that "it was an interfering mother-in-law who eventually succeeded in disrupting our married life."[14] After divorcing MacArthur, Louise married and divorced two additional husbands.

At MacArthur's funeral she sent a floral basket made up of white roses and forget-me-nots which is what he would send her during happier times. She passed away from a heart attack one year later on May 30, 1965.

Fritz Pollard

Fritz Pollard, like Walter French, played on a number of professional football teams in the same season over a period of years. In 1921, while playing for the Akron Pros, one of the original NFL teams, he earned the distinction of becoming the first African American head coach, when he was named co-coach of the team along with Elgie Tobin. In addition to playing for Gilberton in 1923, where he teamed up with Walter French, he also played for the Hammond Pros. In the 1925 season, he once again was the co-coach of this team, this time with Doc Young. He also played for the Akron Indians and the Providence Steamroller in that season in which he played a total of 23 games for the three teams.

In 1926, the NFL owners made a "gentlemen's agreement" not to allow Black players to play on any of their teams. This was made formal in 1933 when African Americans were officially banned from the league. In 1928, Pollard organized a team made up of African American players. Based in Chicago, the team went by the name of the Chicago Black Hawks. The team went on a barnstorming tour of the United States where they played other professional teams in sold out stadiums. The Black Hawks were particularly popular on the West Coast. Pollard was the team's owner, coach, and star player. When attendance at the games began to drop during the Great Depression, the team was forced to disband in 1932.

In 1935, a Harlem sports promoter by the name of Herschel "Rip" Day, organized the Harlem Brown Bombers, and hired Pollard to be the team's coach. He held the position for two seasons before stepping down before the start of the 1938 season.

In 1936, Pollard's son, Fritz Pollard, Jr. won a bronze medal at the Berlin Olympics, in the 110-meter hurdles.

After his football days were over, Pollard had a successful second career in the newspaper business and as a producer in the entertainment industry. He was elected to the College Football Hall of Fame in 1954. He passed away on May 11, 1986, in Silver Spring, MD. He was posthumously elected to the Pro Football Hall of Fame in 2005.

Connie Mack and the Philadelphia Athletics

After winning the championship in 1929, the Athletics followed it up with an equally impressive season in 1930 winning 102 games and defeating the St. Louis Cardinals in the World Series in six games. Although they lost to the Cardinals in the 1931 Series in seven games, they won more games, 107, than they did in 1929. However, even fielding what many people believe to be the greatest team of all time, the Athletics could not defeat the Great Depression.

Even before the stock market crash, unemployment in Philadelphia was at 10 percent but by 1932, 60 percent of the city's workforce was either entirely unemployed or able to obtain only part-time work. Attendance at games began to plummet. In 1929, the team drew 839,176 fans but by 1932 after two years of a steady substantial decline, the team drew only 405,500 fans. In 1933 that number dropped to 297,138.

For his team to survive, Connie Mack began to sell off his best players. He sold Al Simmons and Jimmy Dykes to the Chicago White Sox for $100,000 in 1932. The following year he sold Lefty Grove to the Boston Red Sox and Mickey Cochrane to the Detroit Tigers. Finally, in 1936, he sent Jimmie Foxx to join Grove in Boston. With the departure of the team's great stars the Athletics soon became one of the worst teams in the American League. In 1935 the A's finished in last place and over the next 10 seasons they finished last seven times and in seventh place twice.

Connie Mack continued to manage the team into his eighties until his players and coaches noticed that he was making strange decisions, even calling the name of a player long gone from the team to pinch hit or come in to pitch. Finally in 1950, Mack's sons, Roy, Earl, and Connie Jr. persuaded their father to make coach Jimmy Dykes the "assistant manager" of the team. Dykes soon began making all the in-game decisions for the Athletics. Finally in 1951, Mack retired.

As the team's financial situation began to worsen, pressure began to build for the Athletics to be sold. The Yankees were pushing for the sale to Chicago businessman Arnold Johnson, who had recently purchased Yankee Stadium. When attempts to sell the team to a group from Philadelphia was rejected by the owners, Connie Mack agreed to sell the team to Johnson for $1.5 million. Johnson immediately proposed moving the team to Kansas City and the other owners agreed. Connie Mack came out swinging against the league and even his own son Roy who sided with the Johnson group. He issued a statement that was read by his wife Katherine to the newsmen concluding that Connie was "terribly disappointed."[15]

Later that year Mack fell, broke a hip, and was confined to a wheelchair. In February of the next year Connie Mack passed away at the age of 93. The Associated Press reported that Ty Cobb "broke down and cried today when told of the death of Connie Mack in Philadelphia." "I loved Mr. Mack," Cobb was reported to have said "you know, a man can love another man. I am pretty old myself, but I just can't help crying at hearing that he is gone."[16]

Almost as if somehow the team knew that one day they would be leaving, in their 55 years in the City of Brotherly Love, the Athletics never had the word "Philadelphia" on any of their uniforms, home or away. Every other team would have their city's name on their road uniform. Not so with the Athletics. Their uniforms either depicted a large "A's" or the "White Elephant logo" which, as the story goes, was adopted by Mack after critics said he was building a "white elephant."

When the A's got to Kansas City, it became clear why the Yankees pushed so hard for Johnson to be awarded the team. The Kansas City Athletics soon became a glorified farm team for the Yankees, who were the beneficiaries of 15 lopsided trades with Kansas City. None of the trades could top the one they made in December of 1959, when they traded Roger Maris to the Yankees for Don Larsen, Hank Bauer, Marv Throneberry, and Norm Siebern, all of whom were way past their prime. Maris would be the league MVP in 1960 and again in 1961 when he broke Babe Ruth's record of 60 home runs in a single season.

When Arnold Johnson died in 1960 the team was purchased by businessman Charles Finley and in 1968, he moved the team to its current home in Oakland, California.

Pottsville Maroons

After the Maroons were reinstated at the end of 1925, most of the Maroons' star players returned for the 1926 season including Charlie Berry, Tony Latone, Frank Butcher, Duke Osborn, Frank Racis, Herb Stein, and Barney Wentz. The team played a 14-game schedule, winning 10 and losing two, with two ties. That put them in third place. In 1927, however, the team finished with a record of five wins against eight losses. They were outscored by their opponents 163 to 80. Things were even worse in 1928, when the once great Maroons finished with only two wins and eight losses. In 1929, the team was moved to Boston where they became the Boston Bulldogs. From the original team only Ernst, Latone, Racis, and Dick Rauch played for Boston. The Bulldogs finished the season with a 4–4 record in what was their first and only season in Boston. The team folded after that.

Over the years the people of Pottsville have kept the story of the Maroons alive and have on numerous occasions petitioned the NFL to award the Maroons the 1925 championship. In each case the league owners, with the exception of the owners of Pennsylvania's two teams, the Philadelphia Eagles, and the Pittsburgh Steelers, have been reluctant to strip the title from the Cardinals, now in Arizona.

The Chicago Cardinals won the NFL championship, without controversy, when they beat the Philadelphia Eagles in 1947. It has turned out to be the last championship that the Cardinals have won and giving them the distinction of having the longest title drought of any team in any sport. There are those who believe that the team is cursed and that the fortunes of the Cardinals will not improve until they give the 1925 title to its rightful owner, the Pottsville Maroons. In January of 2022, in the days preceding the start of the NFL playoffs, Pottsville Mayor Dave Clews received an email from an Arizona radio producer asking to have the curse removed. The mayor declined.

Charlie Berry

After his playing days were over, Charlie Berry was hired by Connie Mack to be a coach with the Athletics and in 1940 he became the manager of the A's affiliate the Wilmington Blue Rocks in the Interstate League. During the offseason he began to take jobs officiating high school and college football games. In 1941 he was named the head linesman for the National Football League. He enjoyed officiating so much that he left his position as manager of the Blue Rocks and began umpiring baseball games, first in the Eastern League, and then later in the American League. He would go on to be a successful baseball umpire and football referee. He umpired five All-Star games and five World Series. He was the head linesman in the 1958 NFL Championship game between the New York Giants and the Baltimore Colts, which was won by the Colts in overtime. The 1958 championship game is considered by many to be the greatest professional football game ever played and did a lot to propel the NFL forward.

In a poll of writers conducted by the *Sporting News* in 1961, Charlie Berry was named the best umpire in the American League. Later he went to work for the American League as the supervisor of umpires, and also did some work for the NFL evaluating their officials. In June of 1972, at the age of 70, he suffered a stroke at his home in New Jersey. He was in the process of making a recovery, when on September 6, he suffered a major heart attack and died. Today, the shoe that Charlie wore to kick the winning field goal against the Four Horsemen team, is bronze plated and on display at the Schuylkill County Historical Society.

Dutch Leonard

After the controversy of 1926, Dutch Leonard never pitched again. Instead, he continued to work on his grape farm near Fresno, California. His careful management of the 2,500-acre business had turned it into a multi-million-dollar operation and made him a very wealthy man. He and his wife Sybil Hitt, a vaudeville dancer who went by the name of Muriel Worth, lived a lavished lifestyle until they were divorced in 1931. Living comfortably on his own, Dutch remained in good health until 1942, when he suffered a heart attack. He lived another 10 years until he was struck by a cerebral hemorrhage. He died on July 11, 1952, and left an estate worth $2.1 million, which would be equal to $22.3 million in 2022.

Smoky Joe Wood

Smoky Joe Wood's 20-year coaching tenure at Yale ended with his dismissal, along with two other coaches due to economic considerations caused by World War II. Wood moved to California and opened a golf driving range with his brother. Not only did Wood survive his involvement in the Dutch Leonard Affair, keeping his job at Yale, but also in 1985 Bart Giamatti, then President of Yale University, bestowed an honorary doctorate degree on Wood, who was 95 years old at the time. Giamatti, ironically, would become baseball commissioner four years later and would be best known for banning Pete Rose from the game for life for gambling on baseball.

A few months after receiving his Yale degree, Wood, who was living in a convalescent home in New Haven, CT, passed away.

Ty Cobb

In September of 1958, Ty Cobb appeared on the television game show *I've Got a Secret*, where a panel of blindfolded celebrities ask questions of the guest, in an effort to guess that person's secret. In Cobb's case, his secret was "I have the highest lifetime batting average in baseball." When the panelists had exhausted their questions, they were no closer to discovering the "secret." To make matters worse, when the panelists removed their blindfolds, they were still unable to recognize one of the game's greatest players, Cobb had so dropped from the consciousness of sports fans in the 30 years since his retirement. After the show's host Gary Moore listed off all of Cobb's records one of the panelists chimed in with the comment "he spiked a lot of second basemen too," a reference to the long-held belief that Cobb was a dirty player who went out of his way to injure opposing players. After accepting a carton of cigarettes for being on the show Cobb stopped to shake hands with the panelists while exiting the set. He can be seen speaking with the panelist who made the "spiking" comment and while what was said can't be heard, the man seems to have been made very uncomfortable by whatever it was that Cobb said to him. Cobb was offended by the fact that none of the panelists recognized him and felt worse about the fact that the first thing that came to mind for one of the panelists, once his identity was revealed, was that he had been a dirty player.

To set the record straight Cobb began to reach out to book publishers to sell one of them on the idea of publishing his autobiography. Doubleday and Co. agreed to his terms and assigned a ghost writer, a hack newspaperman by the name of Al Stump. After spending a few days with Cobb, Stump began to work on the book in which he makes Cobb out to be a racist, gun waving, belligerent, drunkard who could barely function on his own. When Cobb finally got a copy of the manuscript to review, he immediately began writing letters to the publisher threatening a lawsuit if the book was not scrapped, however he died in July of 1961 before the book was published.

In 2016, Charles Leerhsen, who had been an editor at *Sports Illustrated* and who had written for years at Newsweek, took another look at Cobb's life in his biography *Ty Cobb: A Terrible Beauty*. Leerhsen's research paints a whole new picture of Cobb. Cobb, he writes, was not a racist as previous biographies had contended but rather descended from a long line of Georgia antislavery activists who refused to fight for the Confederacy during the Civil War. He was not despised by his teammates, did not ignore letters from young fans, and although his playing style was intense, opponents never thought of him as a dirty player.

Tris Speaker

After the 1928 season, his last in the major leagues as a player, Tris Speaker became the player-manager of the Newark Bears of the International League in 1929 and again in 1930. He then embarked on a career as a broadcaster with the White Sox and Cubs in 1931. He followed that up with a stint as part owner and manager of the Kansas City Blues of the American Association and when that did not work out, he returned to the broadcast booth, this time with the Cleveland Indians. He also cashed in on his name as he became a popular guest on the banquet circuit. He branched out into the business world establishing Tris Speaker Inc., a wine and liquor distributor. In 1937, he along with Nap Lajoie and Cy Young, were members of the second class to be inducted into the Baseball Hall of Fame.

He returned to uniform one last time in 1947 at the request of Bill Veeck of the Cleveland Indians. The Indians were signing second baseman Larry Doby, to be the second man to break baseball's color barrier and they were looking to convert him to an outfielder. Who would better tutor him in the art of playing the outfield than the best to ever do it?

On December 8, 1958, while helping a friend pull up a boat onto a dock after a day of fishing, Tris Speaker suffered a fatal heart attack. He was 70 years old.

Carolina League

By 1938, the contraction in the number of minor league teams in organized baseball was beginning to reverse itself, presenting more opportunities, especially for the most talented, younger ballplayers that had gravitated to the outlaw league. In order to keep players from jumping to organized baseball, the owners increased the free spending and one-upmanship for which they were known. In time even the higher salaries couldn't keep the best players from leaving for the minor leagues, and as this happened fan interest began to wane. Eventually teams either folded or became part of the organized minor leagues, making 1938 the league's final season. When the league folded Judge Bramham's player blacklist was forgotten.

Tom Davis and Andy Lipscomb

Two of the best players that played for Army during Walter French's coaching tenure were Tom Davis and Andy Lipscomb. After graduating from West Point in 1939 Tom Davis was commissioned into the Coast Artillery Corps and volunteered for duty in the Philippines. Davis was serving as the commander of Battery Geary on the island of Corregidor located in Manila Bay. Corregidor was the last stronghold for the U.S. Army and its allies after the Japanese had taken over the rest of the Philippines. When Corregidor eventually fell, Davis was taken prisoner and subjected to torture. After he was initially held on Luzon he was transported aboard a "hell ship" to the Japanese mainland and held at the Sendai Camp #8 and forced to work in the mines there and smelting copper for a Japanese construction company. He was held there until he and his fellow soldiers were rescued on September 11, 1945. He remained in the Army after the war and retired as a colonel.

After graduating from West Point in 1938 and meeting his Army obligations, Andy Lipscomb signed with the Pittsburgh Pirates, but he soon decided that the military was the career he wanted to pursue. In World War II, he commanded the Third Infantry Battalion in the Rhineland, Germany, Belgium, and Holland and served occupation duty in Europe when the war ended. He later served as an aide to President Harry S. Truman. He served in Vietnam and rose to the rank of Brigadier General. He was awarded the Silver Star, the Soldiers Medal, and a Bronze Star for his service during the Vietnam War. In 1971, he made the news when he was called as a witness in the trial of General Oran Henderson, who was accused of covering up and downplaying the My Lai Massacre.

Acknowledgements

Many people have helped me with this project in a variety of ways. On the top of my list of people to thank are the members of Walter French's family who shared their memories and treasures with me. They include his daughter, Ann French Christie, now in her 96th year, his granddaughters Debbie Cowles, Marsha Cook, and Kathy Berheim, grandson Ed Christensen, and niece Mary Jo Walsh.

There are a number of people affiliated with the United States Military Academy at West Point whose assistance I very much appreciated. This includes Neima Nelson and the staff with the Archives and Special Collections section of the USMA library, West Point Historian Sherman Fleek, Brigadier General (Ret.) Lance Betros, former chairman of the History Department at West Point, and LTC Alan Van Saun.

The team at the Pottsville Free Public Library were helpful to me and patient with my lack of microfilm machine skills. The same goes for the folks at the Schuylkill County Historical Society. I would also like to thank Erica Gorder at the Rutgers University Library as well as John Horne and the staff at the Library and Research Center at the National Baseball Hall of Fame in Cooperstown, NY. Thanks too to Stephen Casper, PhD, for sharing his wisdom about the history of sports related concussions.

From closer to home many thanks to Dave Townsend of the South Jersey Baseball Hall of Fame and John Watson of the Historical Society of Moorestown.

Thanks to my friend Bill Tharion for reading an early draft and for making some excellent suggestions.

Last but not least thanks to Connie Mack biographer, Norman L. Macht, for taking the time to speak with me about Walter French some 15 years ago, and for providing me with needed encouragement.

Endnotes

Chapter 1

1 Bohn, Michael K., *Heroes and Ballyhoo: How The Golden Age of the 1920s Transformed American Sports*, Potomac Books, Inc., 2009, Page 1.
2 Ibid.
3 Ibid.
4 Rice, Grantland, "The Four Horsemen," *New York Herald*, October 18, 1924.

Chapter 2

1 French, Howard Barclay, *Genealogy of the Descendants of Thomas French*, Philadelphia, PA, 1913, Privately Printed.
2 *Courier-Post Newspaper*, November 17, 1929, Page 35.
3 *Pennington Life* 1918 Edition, Page 26, The Senior Class.
4 *Trenton High School Is Deserving of Three Men On All-State Ghost Team*, Trenton Times, Trenton, NJ.
5 *Pennington Life* 1918 Edition, Page 30, Basketball.
6 *Big Ten Fixes New Schedule, November Only*, Associated Press, Indianapolis Star, Indianapolis, IN, Page 13.
7 Robeson, Paul, *Here I Stand*, Beacon Press, Boston, MA, 1971.
8 Ibid.
9 Robeson, Paul, Jr. *The Undiscovered Paul Robeson: An Artists Journey, 1898–1939*, John Wiley & Sons Inc., New York, NY, 2001.
10 Ibid.
11 "All-American Football Elevens Named By Camp," *New York Herald*, New York, NY, January 1, 1919, Page 15.
12 "Football Gossip," *Trenton Evening Times*, Trenton, NJ, September 18, 1918, Page 13.
13 Ibid.
14 "Rutgers Eleven In Opening Game of Season Defeats Ursinus College in One-Sided Game By a Score of 66–0," *New Brunswick Sunday Times*, New Brunswick, NJ, September 29, 1918, Page 8.
15 "Scarlet Eleven Defeats Pelham Bay Team in Exciting Game on Neilson by a 7-0 Score," *The Central New Jersey Home News*, October 20, 1918, Page 8.
16 Cook, Harvey, "Rutgers Failed to Score a Single Point in Game with Fast Syracuse Team Yesterday," *The Central New Jersey Home News*, New Brunswick, NJ, December 1, 1918, Page 8.
17 Baker, Cliff, *1919 Rutgers University Yearbook*, New Brunswick, NJ.
18 Robeson, Paul, *1919 Rutgers University Yearbook*, New Brunswick, NJ.
19 Ibid.

20 O'Neill, Harold E., "French and Gardner Are Dazzling Brilliant in Rutgers 19–0 Victory Over Univ. of North Carolina: Visitors Make but Two First Downs," *New Brunswick Sunday Times*, October 5, 1919, Page 8.
21 Ibid.
22 Ibid.
23 Ibid.
24 O'Neill, Harold E., "Rutgers Loses to Lehigh," *New Brunswick Sunday Times*, New Brunswick, NJ, October 11, 1919, Page 10.
25 "Princeton and Rutgers Lose Football Players," *The Trenton Times*, Trenton, NJ, October 13, 1919, Page 10.
26 "Gridiron Gossip," *Trenton Evening Times*, Trenton, NJ, October 14, 1919, Page 17.
27 Harrison, Emily, "The First Concussion Crisis: Head Injury and Evidence in Early American Football," *American Journal of Public Health*, April 9, 2014, Page 2.
28 Harrison, "The First Concussion Crisis: Head Injury and Evidence in Early American Football."
29 Ibid.
30 Ibid.
31 Ibid.
32 O'Neill, Harold E., "Rutgers Outplays Crack Boston College Team That Defeated Yale," *The Central New Jersey Sunday Times*, New Brunswick, NJ, November 9, 1919, Page 10.
33 O'Neill, Harold E., "Rutgers Yields to Wonderful Forward Passing of the West Virginians, After Taking the Lead in the First Half on French's Brilliant Run For Score, Crowd of 8,000 Sees Spectacular Game, Featured by Vivid Offenses," *The Central New Jersey Home News*, November 16, 1919, Page 10.
34 Ibid.
35 O'Neill, Harold E., "Rutgers Gives Her Greatest Exhibition of Football Power in Crushing Strong Northwestern Eleven 28–0, Before Assemblage of 15,000; Westerner's Defense Spreads Before French's Speed and Gardner's Power," *The Central New Jersey Sunday Times*, New Brunswick, NJ, November 22, 1919, Page 9.
36 *The Central New Jersey Home News*, New Brunswick, NJ, March 1, 1920, Page 10.
37 "Here are the Rutgers Players Who Will Contest for The National Title," *The Central New Jersey Home News*, New Brunswick, NJ, March 3, 1920, Page 10.

Chapter 3

1 Fleek, Sherman L., *The Pointer View*, "June 12, 1919: The Arrival of Douglas MacArthur as Supe," United States Military Academy, June 13, 2019.
2 Perret, Geoffrey, *Old Soldiers Never Die: The Life of Douglas MacArthur*, Random House, New York, NY, 1996, Page 115.
3 "West Point's Round-Up of College Football Players Includes Walter French, Rutgers Star Halfback," *The Daily Home News*, New Brunswick, NJ, August 30, 1920, Page 10.
4 "Numerous Towering and Massive Freshman Give Indication of Another Formidable Rutgers Eleven Despite Loss of Some Veterans," *The Central New Jersey Home News*, September 5, 1920, Page 6.
5 Ibid.
6 Ibid.
7 Manchester, William, *American Caesar: Douglas MacArthur 1880–1964*, Little-Brown and Company, New York, NY, 1978, Page 121.
8 Perret, Geoffrey, *Old Soldiers Never Die: The Life of Douglas MacArthur*, Random House, New York, NY, 1996, Page 122.

9   "Army Team in Light Work," *New York Times*, October 12, 1920, Page 13.
10 "French Passes Through," *The Central New Jersey Home News*, October 25, 1920, Page 9.
11 Rice, Grantland, "The Sportlight," *Buffalo Evening News*, November 1, 1943, Page 26.
12 "Notre Dame Open Play Amazes Army," *New York Times*, November 2, 1913, Page 33.
13 Gekas, George, *The Life and Times of George Gipp*, And Books, South Bend, Indiana, 1988.
14 Sperber, Murray, *Shake Down the Thunder: The Creation of Notre Dame Football*, Henry Holt and Co., New York, NY, 1993, Page 106.
15 Houk, Phil, *In Search of George Gipp—Part 1*, 247 Sports, May 9, 2020.
16 Sperber, Murray, *Shake Down the Thunder: The Creation of Notre Dame Football*, Page 107.
17 Sperber, Murray, *Shake Down the Thunder: The Creation of Notre Dame Football*, Page 108.
18 Cavanaugh, Jack, *The Gipper: George Gipp, Knute Rockne, and The Dramatic Rise of Notre Dame Football*, Skyhorse Publishing, New York, NY, 2010, Page 148.
19 Rice, Grantland, "The Sportlight," *Buffalo Evening News*, November 1, 1943, Page 26.
20 Cavanaugh, Jack, *The Gipper: George Gipp, Knute Rockne, and The Dramatic Rise of Notre Dame Football*, Skyhorse Publishing, New York, NY, 2010, Page 149.
21 Beech, Jim and Moore, Daniel, *The Big Game: Army vs. Notre Dame, 1913–1947*, Random House, New York, NY, 1948, Page 56.
22 Chelland, Patrick, *One For The Gipper: George Gipp, Knute Rockne, and Notre Dame*, Henry Regnery Co., Chicago, IL, 1973.
23 "Army Defeated By Notre Dame," 27–17, *New York Times*, New York, New York, October 31, 1920, Page F-1.
24 Ibid.
25 "Army Seeks to Keep Tickets From Speculators," *New York Times*, New York, New York, November 11, 1920.
26 Hanna, William B., "Navy Will Keep an Eye on French," *New York Herald*, November 24, 1920, Page 12.
27 "Navy Beats Army in Close Battle," *New York Times*, November 28, 1920, Page 102.
28 "Poor Kick Paves the Way For Army's Defeat," *New York Times*, November 28, 1920, Page 103.
29 "Army Gives Navy Credit For Stopping Fleet French," *New York Tribune*, November 29, 1920, Page 12.
30 "1921 Basketball Review," *The Howitzer* 1921, United States Military Academy Library Digital Collection, Page 390.

Chapter 4

1   Perret, Geoffrey, *Old Soldiers Never Die; The Life of Douglas MacArthur*, Random House, New York, NY, 1996.
2   "75,000 See Yale Beat Army 14–7," *Philadelphia Inquirer*, October 23, 1921, Page 19.
3   "1921 Football Review," *The Howitzer* 1921, United States Military Academy Library Digital Collection, Page 381.
4   "75,000 See Yale Beat Army 14–7," *Philadelphia Inquirer*, October 23, 1921, Page 19.
5   Ibid.
6   "Football Throngs Leave Washington," *New York Times*, November 26, 1921.
7   Ibid.
8   "Army's Work Handicapped," *New York Times*, November 24, 1921.
9   "Army Announces Lineup," *New York Times*, November 25, 1921.
10 "Navy's Victory Is Well Earned," *New York Times*, November 27, 1921.
11 Ibid.

12 "1921 Football Review," *The Howitzer* 1921, United States Military Academy Library Digital Collection, Page 381.
13 Ibid., 385.
14 Ibid., 386.
15 Manchester, William, *American Caesar: Douglas MacArthur 1880–1964*, Little-Brown and Company, New York, NY, 1978, Page 127.
16 Ibid., 130.
17 Ibid., 121.
18 Bailey, Jim, "One of a Kind but One of Many," *Arkansas Gazette*, August 12, 1979, Page 38.

Chapter 5

1 Riley, Don, "Three Players Report Today," *The Baltimore Sun*, Baltimore, Maryland, October 23, 1922, Page 8.
2 "Marines Win Over Third Army Corps," *The Pittsburgh Press*, Pittsburgh, PA, December 3, 1922, Page 19.
3 *The Central New Jersey Home News*, New Brunswick, New Jersey, Page 13.
4 "Walter French to Coach YMHA Basketball Team," *Washington Times*, District of Columbia, October 12, 1922, Page 30.
5 Graham, Frank, "Walter French," *New York Sun*, March 9, 1939.
6 Mack, Connie, *My 66 Years in the Big Leagues*, Dover Publications, Inc., Mineola, New York, Page 19.
7 Riley, Don, "Walter French, Athletic Star, Gets Discharge From Army," *The Baltimore Sun*, April 10, 1923, Page 13.
8 "W. S. French, Who Married Selma Girl, Dies at His Home in Mooretown," NJ, *The Selma Times-Journal*, Selma, Alabama, March 21, 1923, Page 5.
9 "Mackmen Win and Tie Sox For Sixth," *The Philadelphia Inquirer*, Philadelphia, PA, September 21, 1923, Page 24.
10 Ibid.
11 Ibid.
12 *The Houston Post*, Houston, Texas, April 13, 1924, Page 20.
13 *The Houston Post*, Houston, Texas, April 28, 1924, Page 8.
14 "French as Coach: Walter French Coach of Riverside Eleven," *The Morning Post*, Camden, New Jersey, September 3, 1924, Page 4.
15 Ibid.
16 Macht, Norman L., *Connie Mack: The Turbulent and Triumphant Years, 1915–1931*, University of Nebraska Press, Lincoln, NE, Page 361.
17 Ibid.
18 *The Philadelphia Inquirer*, Philadelphia, Pennsylvania, March 1, 1925, Page 26.
19 Baumgartner, Stan, "Sluggers Are Impotent Against Young Twirler; French Speedy," *The Philadelphia Inquirer*, Philadelphia, Pennsylvania, March 11, 1925, Page 20.
20 Ritter, Lawrence S., *Lost Ballparks: A Celebration of Baseball's Legendary Fields*, Viking-Penguin Books, New York, NY, Page 179.
21 Evans, Billy, "Walter French To Front," *The Evansville Press*, Evansville, Indiana, January 20, 1926, Page 8.
22 Harrison, James G., "Jones Gets Two Hits As Yanks Win 3-1," *New York Times*, New York, NY, Page 20.

23 Evans, Billy, "Walter French To Front," *The Evansville Press*, Evansville, Indiana, January 20, 1926, Page 8.

Chapter 6

1   Graham, Frank, "Walter French," *New York Sun*, March 9, 1939.
2   Costello, Doug, "City Sent a Celestial Message to the NFL In '24," *Pottsville Republican*, Pottsville, PA, Page 13.
3   Ibid.
4   Hodon, Sara, "The Pottsville Maroons Cheated Again and Again," *Pennsylvania Heritage Magazine*, Volume XXXVII, Number 4, Fall 2011.
5   "Potts Squad is Crippled," *Pottsville Evening Republican*, October 4, 1925, Page 16.
6   "Walter French to Get Going," *Pottsville Evening Republican*, October 8, 1925, Page 15.
7   "Game Recap," *The Pottsville Evening Republic*, Pottsville, PA. Page 18.
8   "Striegel Will Take Over Team," *The Pottsville Evening Republic*, Pottsville, PA, October 15, 1925, Page 20.
9   "Maroons To Providence," *The Pottsville Evening Republic*, Pottsville, PA, October 15, 1925, Page 20.
10 "Game Recap," *The Pottsville Evening Republic*, Pottsville, PA, October 18, 1925. Page 15.
11 Ibid.
12 "Maroons Beat Columbus 20–0," *The Pottsville Evening Republic*, Pottsville, PA, November 2, 1925, Page 10.
13 Fleming, Dave, *Breaker Boys: The NFL's Greatest Team and the Stolen 1925 Championship*, ESPN Books, George Kenneally Interview with Maroons Reunion Committee, 1963.
14 "Pottsville Backs Maroons To Limit," *The Morning Call*, Allentown, Pennsylvania, November 13, 1925, Page 31.
15 Ibid.
16 Ibid.
17 Ibid.
18 "Frankford Crushes Pottsville Before A Huge Throng," *The Philadelphia Inquirer*, Philadelphia, PA, November 15, 1925, Page 62.
19 "Maroons Trip Rochester in Pro League Tilt," *The Record American*, Mahanoy, Pennsylvania, November 16, 1925, Page 4.
20 Fleming, Dave, *Breaker Boys: The NFL's Greatest Team and the Stolen 1925 Championship*, Page 156.
21 "Maroons Crush Frankford In Game of Sensations By a Big Score of 49–0," *The Pottsville Republican*, Pottsville, PA, November 30, 1925, Page 7.
22 Fleming, Dave, *Breaker Boys: The NFL's Greatest Team and the Stolen 1925 Championship*, Page 167.
23 Ibid., 169.
24 Ibid at 22.
25 "Cardinals Add Ex-Husker for Title Game," *The Chicago Tribune*, Chicago, Il, December 3, 1925, Page 21.
26 "Professional Football Title at Stake in Game," *Journal Gazette and International News Service*, Chicago, Illinois, December 5, 1925, Page 7.
27 "Cardinals Play Pottsville For Pro Title Today," *The Chicago Tribune*, Chicago, Illinois, December 6, 1925, Page 32.
28 Schreiber, Frank, "Pottsville Wins Over Cards and Takes Pro Title," *The Chicago Tribune*, Chicago, Illinois, December 7, 1925, Page 29.
29 Ibid.

210 • PLAYING WITH THE BEST

30 Ibid.
31 "Maroons Conquer Cards, Take Crown," *The Philadelphia Inquirer*, Philadelphia, PA December 7, 1925.
32 "Proud And Happy Maroons Enroute Home," *The Pottsville Republican*, Pottsville, Pennsylvania, December 7, 1925, Page 1.
33 Ibid.
34 Mackay, Gordon, "Pottsville Defeats the Four Horsemen," *The Philadelphia Inquirer*, Philadelphia, PA, December 13, 1925, Page 78.
35 Fleming, Dave, *Breaker Boys: The NFL's Greatest Team and the Stolen 1925 Championship*, Page 229.

Chapter 7

1 "Athletics Will Make Only Pair of Changes Now," *The Miami News*, Miami, Florida, January 7, 1926, Page 23.
2 Macht, Norman L., *Connie Mack: The Turbulent and Triumphant Years, 1919–1931*, University of Nebraska Press, Lincoln, Nebraska, Page 401.
3 Ibid., 393.
4 Isaminger, James, "Pithy Tips From The Sport Ticker," *The Philadelphia Inquirer*, Philadelphia, Pennsylvania, March 28, 1926, Page 60.
5 Evans, Billy, *Evansville Press*, January 20, 1926, Page 8.
6 Harrison, James, "Yanks Hit Barrage Lays Low Rommel," *New York Times*, New York, NY, April 28, 1926, Page 30.
7 Harrison, James, "Poole's Bat Deals Blow to Yankees," *New York Times*, New York, NY, July 1, 1926.
8 Ibid.
9 Kahanowitz, Ian S., *Baseball Gods in Scandal, Ty Cobb, Tris Speaker and The Dutch Leonard Affair*, Summer Game Books, South Orange, NJ, 2019.
10 Ibid.
11 Ibid.
12 Ibid.
13 "Rests His Case," United Press International, *The Boston Globe*, Boston, MA, December 22, 1926, Page 14.
14 "Cobb Charges Leonard With Blackmail," United Press International, *The Dayton Herald*, Dayton, OH, December 24, 1926, Page 1.
15 "Leonard Refused to Go to Chicago, Fearing He Would Be 'Bumped Off'," Associated Press, *The Boston Globe*, Boston, MA, December 22, 1926, Page 1.
16 "Senator Warren Has Confidence in Cobb and Other Players," United Press International, *The Dayton Herald*, Dayton, OH, December 24, 1926, Page 1.
17 "Cobb and Speaker Deny Plot Charges," *Chicago Daily Tribune*, Chicago, IL, December 22, 1926, Page 1.
18 Ibid at 9.
19 Hunt, Marshall, "Not Guilty Verdict For Ty, Tris," *New York Daily News*, New York, NY, January 28, 1927, Page 140.
20 Macht, Norman L., *Connie Mack: The Turbulent and Triumphant Years, 1919–1931*, University of Nebraska Press, Lincoln, NE, Page 440.
21 Ibid., 393.
22 Ibid., 440.
23 Ibid., 441.

Chapter 8

1. Duffy, Don Q., "Athletics 1927," *The Evening Herald*, Pottsville, PA, 21 February 22, 1927, Page 9.
2. Rigby, Elwood R., "Galloway Shows Improvement," *The Morning Call*, Allentown, PA, March 10, 1927, Page 21.
3. Ibid.
4. Walsh, Davis J., "Walter French May Beat Ty Cobb For A's Berth," International News Service, *The Evening News*, Wilkes-Barre, PA, March 18, 1927, Page 21.
5. Ibid.
6. Evans, Billy, "Billy Evans Says," *The Evening Journal*, Wilmington, DE, April 12, 1927, Page 28.
7. Ibid.
8. Macht, Norman L., *Connie Mack: The Turbulent and Triumphant Years*, University of Nebraska Press, Lincoln, NE, 2012, Page 461.
9. Ibid., 463.
10. Isaminger, James C., "With Al and Ty in the Game, Macks Come Back to Life," *The Philadelphia Inquirer*, Philadelphia, PA, May 11, 1927, Page 24.
11. Isaminger, James C., "Mackmen Divide Twin Bill with Washington," *The Philadelphia Inquirer*, Philadelphia, PA, June 22, 1927, Page 25.
12. Isaminger, James C., "Macks Win Two From Yanks," *The Philadelphia Inquirer*, Philadelphia, PA, June 26, 1927, Page 41.
13. Ibid.
14. "Star Outfielder Injured and Must Rest For 3 Weeks," Associated Press, *The Wilkes-Barre Record*, Wilkes-Barre, PA, July 26, 1927, Page 17.
15. Isaminger, James C., "Mack Shorts On Local Diamond," *The Philadelphia Inquirer*, Philadelphia, PA, August 10, 1927, Page 18.
16. "Walter French Earned 'Break' At Catasauqua: Stayed Late and Missed His Bus Which Later Figured in Crash," *The Morning Call*, Allentown, PA, August 13, 1927, Page 16.
17. "A's Vicious Swing Almost Disastrous," *The Philadelphia Inquirer*, Philadelphia, PA, September 8, 1927, Page 22.
18. Macht, Norman L., *Connie Mack: The Turbulent and Triumphant Years*, University of Nebraska Press, Lincoln, NE, 2012, Page 475.
19. "Quits Pro Football," *The Journal Gazette*, Mattoon, IL, October 31, 1927, Page 5.
20. *Dayton Daily News*, Dayton, OH, February 5, 1928, Page 39.
21. *Sioux City Journal*, Sioux City, IA, February 5, 1928, Page 30.
22. Macht, Norman L., *Connie Mack: The Turbulent and Triumphant Years*, University of Nebraska Press, Lincoln, NE, 2012, Page 480.
23. Ibid., 481.
24. Ibid., 445.
25. Ibid., 447.
26. Isaminger, James C., "Connie Expects Cobb To Sign In a Few Days," *The Philadelphia Inquirer*, Philadelphia, PA, February 27, 1928, Page 14.
27. Lathrop, Greg, "The Life and Times of Walter Edward French," *Santa Cruz Sentinel*, Santa Cruz, CA, March 28, 1929, Page 15.
28. "Walter French To Quit Game," *Chester County Times*, Chester, PA, November 1, 1928, Page 15.
29. Burr, Harold C., "Dream Hastened French's Return To Connie Mack," *The Brooklyn Daily Eagle*, Brooklyn, NY, September 29, 1929, Page 40.

30 "Czar Reinstates French," Associated Press, *The Knoxville Journal*, Knoxville, TN, March 29, 1929, Page 23.
31 "Baseball Season Begins Tuesday," *New York Times*, New York, NY, April 14, 1929.
32 Mack, Connie, *My 66 Years in the Big Leagues*, Dover Publications, Inc., Mineola, NY 2009 (originally published 1950), Pages 47–48.
33 Ibid.
34 Nack, William, "Lost In History," *Sports Illustrated*, August 19, 1996, Page 81.
35 Ibid.
36 Getty, Frank, "Ehmke Mows Down Heaviest Hitters in Opener," United Press International, *The Herald Press*, Chicago, IL, October 9, 1929, Page 9.
37 Mack, Connie, *My 66 Years in the Big Leagues*, Dover Publications, Inc., Mineola, New York 2009 (originally published 1950), Pages 48–49.
38 Getty, Frank, "Root Opposes Quinn in Fourth Series Game," United Press International, *The Daily Times*, New Philadelphia, Ohio, October 12, 1929, Page 1.
39 Burns, Edward, "Here That Din? It's From the Cubs Dressing Room," *The Chicago Tribune*, Chicago, Illinois, October 12, 1929, Page 23.
40 Nack, William, "Lost In History," *Sports Illustrated*, August 19, 1996, Page 82.
41 Ibid., 81.
42 Baumgartner, Stan, "Connie Calls Game Greatest Thrill," *The Philadelphia Inquirer*, Philadelphia, PA, October 13, 1929, Page 1.
43 Macht, Norman L., *Connie Mack: The Turbulent and Triumphant Years*, University of Nebraska Press, Lincoln, NE, 2012, Page 551–552.
44 Runyon, Damon, "Damon Runyon Says He Can Prove A's Scored Ten Runs In That Seventh Inning; Even Though It Sounds Like a Fairy Tale," *The Morning Call*, Allentown, PA, October 13, 1929, Page 14.
45 Burns, Edward, "Athletics Rout Cubs, 10–8," *Chicago Tribune*, Chicago Illinois, October 13, 1929, Page 1.
46 Ibid.
47 Nack, William, "Lost In History," *Sports Illustrated*, August 19, 1996, Page 81.
48 McLinn, Stoney, "French, Pinch-Fanner in 1929 Series, To Play in 1931 Little World Classic," *Philadelphia Evening Ledger*, Philadelphia, PA, September 15, 1931.
49 Foxx, Jimmie, "Knew We'd Do It," *Morning Call*, Allentown, Pennsylvania, October 15, 1929, Page 29.
50 Nack, William, "Lost In History," *Sports Illustrated*, August 19, 1996, Page 81.
51 Baumgartner, Stan, "Macks Tell What They're Going To Do With Dough," *The Philadelphia Inquirer*, October 15, 1929, Page 24.

Chapter 9

1 Baumgartner, Stan, "Macks Tell What They're Going To Do With Dough," *The Philadelphia Inquirer*, October 15, 1929, Page 24.
2 Bailey, Jim, "One of a Kind but One of Many," *Arkansas Gazette*, August 12, 1979, Page 38.
3 "Mr. and Mrs. Walter French Will Make Their Home in Prattville," *The Prattville Progress*, Prattville, AL, December 5, 1929, Page 7.
4 *The Birmingham News*, Birmingham, AL, December 12, 1929, Page 18.
5 King, Sid, *Eugene Guard*, Eugene, OR, April 11, 1929, Page 9.
6 "A Horsehide Goes Out At Night," *Los Angeles Times*, September 7, 1930.
7 Bailey, Jim, "One of a Kind but One of Many," *Arkansas Gazette*, August 12, 1979, Page 38.

8   "Walter French With Little Rock Travelers," *Associated Press*, Pottsville Republican, Pottsville, PA, March 27, 1931, Page 9.
9   "Walter French Stars," *The Birmingham News*, Birmingham, AL, May 17, 1931, Page 30.
10   *The Birmingham News*, Birmingham, Alabama, June 18, 1931, Page 14.
11   Ibid.
12   *The Birmingham News*, Birmingham, Alabama, August 26, 1931, Page 13.
13   Newman, Zipp, "French To Take Moore's Place In Center," *The Birmingham News*, Birmingham, AL, September 8, 1931, Page 12.
14   Newman, Zipp, "Milan Inserts French Into Lineup, Hoping to Get Batting Punch Back," *The Birmingham News*, Birmingham, AL, September 19, 1931, Page 7.
15   *The Birmingham News*, Birmingham, AL, September 20, 1931, Page 2.
16   *The Birmingham News*, Birmingham, AL, September 26, 1931, Page 7.
17   Ibid.
18   Bailey, Jim, "One of a Kind but One of Many," *Arkansas Gazette*, August 12, 1979, Page 38.
19   "Two 'Moonshine' Nines In Southern Association," Associated Press, *The Boston Globe*, Boston, MA, April 14, 1932, Page 21.
20   Bailey, Jim, "One of a Kind but One of Many," *Arkansas Gazette*, August 12, 1979, Page 38.
21   Murphy, Bob, "Knoxville Obtains Walter French," *Knoxville Journal*, Knoxville, Tennessee, May 14, 1931, Page 13.
22   Ibid., 1.
23   Murphy, Bob, "Knoxville Obtains Walter French," *Knoxville Journal*, Knoxville, Tennessee, May 19, 1931, Page 9.
24   Ibid.
25   Murphy, Bob, "Knoxville Honors French," *Knoxville Journal*, Knoxville, Tennessee, August 6, 1931, Page 1.
26   Isaminger, James C., "Walter Of Moorestown's Famous Athletic House of French, Named Southern Loop's Outstanding Player," *Philadelphia Inquirer*, Philadelphia, PA, December 6, 1933.
27   Thompson, Marvin, "Walter French, Smoky Outfielder, Bids for Most Valuable Player Award Again," *The Knoxville Journal*, Knoxville, TN, August 12, 1934, Page 11.
28   Rainey, Chris, *Bob Allen*, Society of American Baseball Research Biography Project.

Chapter 10

1   Army Athletic Association Meeting Minutes, United States Military Academy, May 1935.
2   Army Athletic Association Meeting Minutes, United States Military Academy, June 1935.
3   Army Athletic Association Meeting Minutes, United States Military Academy, September 1935.
4   Army Athletic Association Meeting Minutes, United States Military Academy, November 1935.
5   "Walter French To Coach Baseball at West Point," *Knoxville Journal*, Knoxville, TN, November 28, 1935, Page 11.
6   Utley, Hank and Verner, Scott, *Diamond Outlaws: Piedmont North Carolina's Early Challenge to the Professional Baseball Monopoly*, McFarland Press, Jefferson, NC, 1998, Pages 2–3.
7   Wade, Jake, "Conover Fails In Effort To Buy Club," *Charlotte Observer*, Charlotte, North Carolina, May 18, 1936, Page 14.
8   Utley, Hank and Verner, Scott, *Diamond Outlaws: Piedmont North Carolina's Early Challenge to the Professional Baseball Monopoly*, 1998, Page 2–3.
9   Utley, Hank and Verner, Scott, *Diamond Outlaws: Piedmont North Carolina's Early Challenge to the Professional Baseball Monopoly*, 1998, Page 8.

10　Utley, Hank and Verner, Scott, *The Independent Carolina Baseball League*, MacFarland Press, Jefferson, NC, 1999, Page 75.
11　"French Stars," *The Charlotte News*, Charlotte, North Carolina, June 14, 1936, Page 29.
12　Utley, Hank and Peeler, Tim, *Outlaw Ballplayers: Interviews and Profiles from the Independent Carolina League*, MacFarland Press, Jefferson, North Carolina, 2005, Page 106.
13　Ibid.
14　Utley, Hank and Peeler, Tim, *Outlaw Ballplayers: Interviews and Profiles from the Independent Carolina League*, MacFarland Press, Jefferson, NC, 2005, Page 55.
15　Utley, Hank and Verner, Scott, *The Independent Carolina Baseball League*, MacFarland Press, Jefferson, NC, 1999, Page 126.

Chapter 11

1　*The Howitzer*, United States Military Academy, Yearbook of the United States Corps of Cadets, West Point, NY, 1938, Page 327.
2　Army Athletic Association Annual Report, 1937, United States Military Academy, West Point, NY.
3　"Giants Triumph Over Army," *Daily News*, New York, New York, April 18, 1939, Page 636.
4　Ibid.
5　*The Howitzer*, United States Military Academy, Yearbook of the United States Corps of Cadets, West Point, New York, 1940, Page 323.
6　"Cadets Whip Colgate, 5–1," *Press and Sun Bulletin*, Binghamton, New York, May 31, 1939, Page 19.
7　Ibid.
8　*The Howitzer*, United States Military Academy, Yearbook of the United States Corps of Cadets, West Point, New York, 1940, Page 336.
9　"Joe Wood Hurls Yale To Shutout Over Army, 2–0," *The Hartford Courant*, Hartford, Connecticut, May 22, 1941, Page 15.
10　"They'll Know What Squads Are Doing," Associated Press, *St. Louis Dispatch*, St. Louis, Missouri, May 29, 1941, Page 14.
11　*The Howitzer*, United States Military Academy, Yearbook of the United States Corps of Cadets, West Point, New York, 1941, Page 316.
12　Eisenhower, John, "Pearl Harbor Day at West Point, 1941," *Special to the Star Democrat*, Easton, Maryland, December 7, 2011, Page 1.
13　Ibid., 2.
14　Ibid.
15　*The Howitzer*, United States Military Academy, Yearbook of the United States Corps of Cadets, West Point, New York, 1942, Page 442.
16　Ibid., 414.
17　"West Point Coach Sent to New Post," Associated Press, *The Herald Statesman*, Yonkers, NY, June 23, 1942, Page 9.

Chapter 12

1　*Miami Beach Hotels*, Museum of Florida History, Page 1.
2　Ibid.
3　McCaughan, Sean, "Miami in WWII was a City-Sized Bootcamp in Paradise," *Curbed Miami*, May 26, 2015.

ENDNOTES • 215

4   "Pre-Game Drills," *The Miami Herald*, Miami, FL, September 20, 1942, Page 20.
5   *The Miami Herald*, Miami, FL, October 4, 1942, Page 17.
6   *Life Magazine*, December 18, 1942.
7   Goss, John, *Aerials to Zephyrs: A Brief History of the Casper Army Airbase*, Wyoming Historical Society.
8   Morrow, Art, "Escape From Death in the Jungle: Capt. Walter French 'Safe' in Italy," *The Philadelphia Inquirer*, Philadelphia, PA, April 27, 1944, Page 22.
9   Ibid.
10 Ibid.
11 "This and That," *The Philadelphia Inquirer*, Philadelphia, PA, May 4, 1944, Page 17.
12 Army Athletic Association Meeting Minutes, December 7, 1945.
13 Ibid.
14 Ore, Robert, "Ex-Army Halfback Has Plan To Stop Point-After-Touchdown," Associated Press, *Durham Morning Herald*, Durham, North Carolina, March 10, 1947, Page 6.
15 Ibid.
16 Ibid.
17 Ibid.
18 *Lansing State Journal*, Lansing, MI, November 13, 1949, Page 50.
19 Department of Defense Personal Security Questionnaire, Office of Management and Budget Definition.
20 30th Class Reunion Program, West Point Class of 1924.

Epilogue

1   Kraus, Walter, "Pottsville Still Wants its Title Back After More Than 50 Years," Associated Press, *The Gettysburg Times*, Gettysburg, PA, May 17, 1984, Page 27.
2   Isaminger, James C., "Walter Of Moorestown's Famous Athletic House of French, Named Southern Loop's Outstanding Player," *The Philadelphia Inquirer*, Philadelphia, PA, December 6, 1933.
3   "Old Sports Musings," *Philadelphia Evening Ledger*, Philadelphia, PA, 1934.
4   *The Record American*, Mahanoy City, PA, December 10, 1925, Page 4.
5   *The Knoxville Journal*, Knoxville, TN, August 12, 1934, Page 11.
6   Sullivan, Ed, "Little Old New York," *Daily News*, New York, NY, October 31, 1943, Page 108.
7   Ibid.
8   Bourne, St. Clair, *Paul Robeson: Here I Stand*, PBS American Masters, 1999.
9   Du Bois, W. E. B., *The Autobiography of W. E. B. Du Bois*, International Publishing Company, New York, NY, 1968, Page 396.
10 Rice, Grantland, "The Sportlight," *Buffalo Evening News*, Buffalo, NY, November 1, 1943, Page 6.
11 "Rice Wrote 50 Years and Made No Enemies," *The Boston Globe*, Boston, MA, July 14, 1954, Page 27.
12 "Don Storck, veteran; was columnists father," *The Philadelphia Inquirer*, Philadelphia, PA, March 24, 1987, Page 37.
13 "First Mrs. MacArthur Gives Divorce Reason," *Pensacola News Journal*, Pensacola, Florida, April 20, 1964, Page 2.
14 Ibid.
15 "Connie Mack Raps Son Roy as 'Real Fly in the Ointment' Hits Barring of the Philadelphia Group," *The Philadelphia Inquirer*, Philadelphia, PA, October 30, 1954.
16 "Baseball Great Mourn Mack, Cobb in Tears," Associated Press, *The New York Daily News*, New York, NY, October 9, 1956, Page 147.

Bibliography

Allen, Frederick Lewis, *Only Yesterday: An Informal History of The Nineteen Twenties*, Harper and Brothers, New York, NY, Originally published in 1957.
Beach, Jim and Moore, Daniel, *The Big Game: Army vs. Notre Dame 1913–1947*, Random House, New York, NY, 1948.
Betros, Lance, *Carved From Granite: West Point Since 1902*, Texas A&M University Press, College Station, TX, 2012.
Bohn, Michael K., *Heroes and Ballyhoo: How the Golden Age of the 1920s Transformed American Sports*, Potomac Books, Dulles, VA, 2009.
Brown, Lloyd, *The Young Paul Robeson: On My Journey Now*, Basic Books, New York, NY, 1998.
Cavanaugh, Jack, *The Gipper: George Gipp, Knute Rockne, and The Dramatic Rise of Notre Dame Football*, Skyhorse Publishing, New York, NY, 2010.
Chelland, Patrick, *One for The Gipper: George Gipp, Knute Rockne, and Notre Dame*, Panoply Publications, 2016.
Danzig, Allison and Brandwein, Peter, *Sports Golden Age*, Harper and Row Publishers, New York, NY, 1948.
Fleming, David, *Breaker Boys: The NFL's Greatest Team and The Stolen 1925 Championship*, ESPN Books, New York, NY, 2007.
Gekas, George, *The Life and Times of George Gipp*, And Books, 1988.
Kahanowitcz, Ian S., *Baseball Gods in Scandal: Ty Cobb, Tris Speaker, and The Dutch Leonard Affair*, Summer Game Books, South Orange, NJ, 2019.
Macht, Norman, *Connie Mack: The Turbulent and Triumphant Years 1915–1931*, University of Nebraska Press, Lincoln, NE, 2012.
Mack, Connie, *My 66 Years in the Big Leagues*, Dover Publications, Mineola, NY, Originally published 1950.
Manchester, William, *American Caesar: Douglas MacArthur 1880–1964*, Little, Brown & Co., Boston, MA, 1978.
Pellowski, Michael, *Rutgers Football: A Gridiron Tradition in Scarlet*, Rutgers University Press, New Brunswick, NJ, 2008.
Perret, Geoffrey, *Old Soldiers Never Die: The Life of Douglas MacArthur*, Random House, New York, NY, 1996.
Ritter, Lawrence, *Lost Ballparks: A Celebration of Baseball's Legendary Fields*, Viking Studio Books, New York, NY, 1992.
Robeson, Paul, *Here I Stand*, Beacon Press, Boston, MA, 1998.
Robeson, Paul Jr., *The Undiscovered Paul Robeson: An Artists Journey 1898–1939*, John Wiley and Sons, Inc., New York, NY, 2001.
Sperber, Murray, *Shake Down the Thunder: The Creation of Notre Dame Football*, Henry Holt, New York, NY, 1993.

Utley, Hank and Peeler, Tim with Peeler, Aaron, *Outlaw Ballplayers: Interviews and Profiles From The Independent Carolina Baseball League*, McFarland Press, Jefferson, NC, 2005.

Utley, Hank and Verner, Scott, *The Carolina Baseball League, 1936–1938*, McFarland Press, Jefferson, NC, 1999.

Index

Academic Board, 27, 56, 58, 59, 62, 167
All-American selectors, 12, 46
All-American team, 12, 46
Allen, Bob, 155–7
Amateur Athletic Union, 22, 24, 64, 89
Amen, Paul, 175, 182
American League, 64–5, 73, 78, 99, 101–3, 105–6, 108–9, 114, 116–9, 123, 125, 128–9, 131–3, 156, 197, 199
Anderson, Eddie, 41–2, 92
Anderson, Hunk, 39, 43
Annapolis, MD, 43, 57, 172
Anthracite Association, 80, 91, 160
Archdeacon, Maurice, 79
Army Athletic Association, 28, 35, 37, 44, 159, 169, 175, 181
Army Football, 3, 28, 44, 46, 56, 84, 131, 186

Baker, Cliff, 13–5, 17, 21, 192
Baltimore Orioles, 63, 73, 125
Barley, George, 164
Basic Training Center No. 10, 179
Bazemore, Elizabeth, 65–6
Belem, Brazil, ix, 180
Benzoni, Ed, 22–5
Berry, Charlie, 79, 81–9, 92, 94–5, 97, 190, 198–9
Besas, Doc, 13, 18, 23–4
Bidwill, Charles, 96
Bingham, William, 183
Birmingham Barons, 150, 156
Bishop, Max, 73, 101, 103, 113–5, 122, 126, 131, 133, 137–9, 143, 168
Black Tuesday, 145
Blaik, Earl, 34, 173
Boley, Joe, 113, 115, 120, 129, 137, 139, 140, 142
Boston College, 27, 33, 43, 53

Boston Red Sox, 50, 75, 106–7, 162, 169, 197
Bramham, W. G., 238, 244, 293
Breidster, Fritz, 40
Brooklyn Dodgers, 175
Brown University, 10, 68
Bucher, Frank, 82
Buffalo Bisons, 82

Cagle, Chris, 29, 194
Caldwell, Ray, 151–3
Camp, Walter, 10, 12, 14, 16, 46, 55, 68, 79
Canausa, Fred, 182
Cann, Howard, 23
Canton Bulldogs, 3, 83
Carolina League, 161–2, 164–6, 201
Carolina Textile League, 160, 162
Carr, Joe, 80–1, 94–5
Chapman, Ray, 146–7
Charlotte Hornets, 162–3, 165
Chicago Bears, x, 14, 88, 90, 95
Chicago Cardinals, 14, 87, 90–2, 95, 97, 189, 198
Chicago Cubs, 49, 130, 134, 141, 147
Chicago White Sox, 67, 75, 77, 91, 99, 105–6, 111, 118–9, 121–3, 125, 129, 133, 137, 197, 201
Cincinnati Reds, 49, 146, 194
Cleveland Indians, 75, 105, 107, 116, 123, 146, 152, 201
Cobb, Ty, x, 3, 76, 105, 107–16, 119–20, 122–3, 125–7, 129, 130, 172, 186, 197, 200
Cochrane, Mickey, 65, 73–4, 99, 101, 114, 120–3, 126, 131, 133, 137, 140, 142–3, 197
Collegians, Moorestown, 7
Collins, Eddie, x, 65, 110, 113–5, 117, 120, 124, 135, 156

Columbus Tigers, 85–6, 90, 93
Concord Weavers, 162, 166
concussions, 18, 19, 185
Coolidge, Calvin, xi, 1, 53
Corps of Cadets, 46, 52, 173
Cotter, Bill, 34, 36
Cromwell, Henrietta, 54, 58, 195
Cronin, Jimmy, 145–6, 149
Cuyler, Kiki, 136–9, 142

Daly, Charlie, 32–3, 38, 46, 55–6
Danford, Robert, 51
Davis, Tom, 168–170, 201
Dead Ball Era, 49, 147, 189
Dean, Dizzy, x, 151–3, 165
Dempsey, Jack, 3, 125, 194
Dent, Martha, 93
Department of Defense, 183–4
Detroit Tigers, 67, 73, 99, 105, 107–8, 120, 122–3, 177, 197
Dorias, Gus, 36, 194
Doubleday, Abner, 170–1
Drennan, Mike, 64
Dreyfuss, Barney, 49
Driscoll, Paddy, 14, 91, 93
Durocher, Leo, 175
Dykes, Jimmy, 64, 67, 73, 101, 120–1, 126, 128, 132, 137–40, 142, 156, 197

Earnshaw, George, 132, 134–6, 138
Edison, Thomas, x, 100
Eisenhower, John, 173–4
Emke, Howard, 102, 120, 135–7, 142
English, Woody, 136–9, 140, 142
Ernst, Jack, 81, 86–9, 91, 94–5, 142
Ewen, Eddie, 44–5

Fenway Park, 19
Fitzgerald, F. Scott, 66
Flanagan, Hoot, 82–4, 88–9, 91–3, 97
Fort Myers, 72–3, 100, 127
Fort Ord, 186–7
Four Horsemen, 3, 4, 88, 94–5, 97, 193, 199
Foxx, Jimmie, x, 64, 123, 133, 136–40, 142–3, 156, 197
Frankford Yellow Jackets, 68, 81, 83, 85–90, 92

French, Walter,
 ancestors, 5
 baseball coach at West Point, 167–8, 170, 173–5
 cadet, 29–32, 36, 38, 40–4, 46, 50, 54–7, 59, 63–5
 death, 188
 during the Great Depression, 145, 148–56, 163, 166
 military service, 177, 181, 183, 184
 at Pennington, 8
 with the Philadelphia Athletics, 64–5, 70–2, 74, 76–8, 100–5, 110, 115–9, 122–5, 127–133, 135, 141–2
 with the Pottsville Maroons, 79, 81, 82–5, 87–9, 91–2, 94, 97
 retirement, 185–6
 at Rutgers, 10, 12, 14–17, 20–2, 24–5
Frisch, Frankie, 113

Gable, Clark, 177
Galloway, Chip, 73, 76, 101, 103, 113, 115
Gardner, Turk, 13, 16–7, 20
Gehrig, Lou, 103–4, 118, 122, 124, 127, 155
Gilberton Catamounts, 68, 80, 196
Gilmore, William, 186
Gipp, George, 37, 39–43, 46, 53, 61, 192–4
Gleason, Kid, 99–101, 116, 144
Glickstein, Jack, ix, x, 181
Goettge, Frank, 63
Goslin, Goose, 102, 118, 125
Graham, Ray, 71
Grange, Red, 3, 20, 89–90, 93, 95–7, 190–91
Great Depression, 145, 147–8, 154, 156, 160–1, 196–7
Green Bay Packers, 80, 88
Greenberg, Hank, 177
Grimm, Charlie, 136–40, 142
Grove, Lefty, x, 73–4, 100, 102–5, 115, 122–3, 126, 134–6, 138, 140, 156

Haas, Mule, 127–30, 133, 137–9, 141, 143
Hagan, Walter, ix
Halas, George, 14, 88, 90
Hall, Art, 22, 24–5
Harper, Jesse, 35–7
Harris, Bucky, 101–2
Hartnett, Gabby, 136, 138, 140

INDEX

Hathaway, Russ, 82, 86, 93, 188
Hay, Ralph, 3
Hayes, Philip, 37, 44
Heisman, John, 35
Herrington, Arthur, 17
Highland Falls, New York, 43, 173, 179, 181–2
Hill, Frank, 21–4
Hinson, Baron, 162
Hite, Clay, 20
Hornsby, Rogers, 113, 134, 136–40, 143
Houston Buffaloes, 150–1
Howley, Dan, 112
Hoyt, Waite, 103, 115, 122

Jacobson, "Baby Doll", 104
Johnson, Walter, 76–7, 102–3, 118, 125, 152, 189
Jones, Bobby, xi, 3, 194

Kannapolis Towelers, 161–5
Keeler, Willie, 74, 190
Kelly, Frank, 11, 13, 61
Kiley, Roger, 40–2
Knight, Bobby, 57
Knoxville Smokies, 155–6, 190
Koehler, Ben, 45

La Selva, 185–6
Lajoie, Napoleon, 65, 201
Lamar, Bill, 70, 74, 101, 116–20, 125
Lambeau, Curley, 80, 88
Landis, Kennesaw Mountain, 91, 108–13, 134, 141
Lardner, Ring, 37, 39
Larson, Ojay, 40
Latone, Tony, 69, 80–1, 83–91, 93–5, 97, 198
Lawes, Lewis, 165
Lawrence, Charlie, 40
Lazzeri, Tony, 103–4, 156
Leahy, Frank, 34
LeConey, Alfred, 84
Leonard, Dutch, 106–11, 117, 172, 199–200
Lipscomb, Andy, 167–69, 201–2
Little Rock Travelers, 149, 154–55
Lobert, Hans, 49–50, 100, 171, 194
Loomis, Harold, 35
Lyons, Ted, 77

MacArthur, Douglas, 27–8, 31–3, 37, 46, 51, 54, 56, 58–9, 195–6
Mack, Connie, 64–6, 70, 72–80, 86, 99–104, 111–20, 123–40, 142–45, 156, 190, 196–98
Major League All-Star game, 156
Malone, Pat, 134, 138, 140, 142
Maranville, Rabbit, 114
Mays, Carl, 146–7
McCabe, Dick, 152
McCarthy, Joe, 134, 136–40, 142
McCormick, Moose, 159–60, 168
McEwen, John, 39
McGraw, John, 49
Medwick, Joe, 151–53
Memphis Chicks, 154
Merchantville, NJ, 122
Meury, Calvin, 22–4
Meusel, Bob, 103
Miami Beach, 175, 177–79, 193
Milan, Clyde, 150, 152–3
Milburn, Deveraux, 125
Miller, Bing, 70, 74, 99, 101, 104, 125, 127–30, 133, 137–40, 142–3
Mills, Abraham, 170–1
Minersville Park, 82, 88
Mohardt, Johnny, 40–2
Moorestown, NJ, 4–8, 24, 65, 71–2, 74, 84, 86
Mulligan, Dennis, 186
Murphy, Danny, 67

National Football League, 4, 14, 61, 68, 79–81, 92, 114, 190, 199
Navy, 28, 30, 33, 43–6, 50–1, 53–7, 167–70, 172–4, 178, 182
NCAA, 16, 19, 20, 36, 46
Neale, Earl, 12
Negro League, 147, 165
New Haven Independents, 68
New York–Penn League, 66, 165
New York Giants,
    baseball, 49, 58, 99, 113, 141, 143, 159, 170, 174, 194
    football, 63, 87–8, 96, 199
New York Yankees, 68, 73, 75–7, 97, 103–5, 111, 115–16, 118–34, 141, 146, 151, 164, 175, 197–8

Northwestern University, 14–15, 21
Notre Dame, 14, 32–43, 45–46, 53, 55–56, 88, 90, 93–95, 172, 193
Noyes, Vic, 44–45
NYU, 23, 57, 167, 171

O'Neill, Harold, 16–19, 21
O'Shea, Joseph, 47
Ochs, Adolph, xi
Oliphant, Elmer, 28, 38
Onodera Estates, 180
Orr, Billy, 70–1

Pacific Coast League, 73, 145–8
Partridge, Earle, 184
Patterson, Francis, 121
Pearl Harbor, 173–4
Pegler, Westwood, 3
Pennington Seminary, 7–9
Pennock, Herb, 162
Pennsylvania Carlisle Indian Industrial School, 36, 65
Perry, Lawrence, 29, 46
Pershing, John, 58, 195
Philadelphia, 4, 24, 43, 61–66, 73, 78, 81, 86, 89, 93–4, 97, 112, 119, 121, 144, 173, 192, 197
Philadelphia Athletics, x, xi, 64, 70, 75, 99–100, 113–15, 124, 130, 132, 141, 169, 178, 184, 188
Philadelphia Phillies, 65, 100, 106, 135, 140, 149, 194
Pitts, Edwin, 165
Pittsburgh Pirates, 49, 127, 134, 189, 202
Plain, the, 33, 39, 43, 51, 170
Pollard, Fritz, 10, 68, 190, 196
Polo Grounds, 4, 14, 19, 43–4, 53, 58, 143
Poole, Jim, 104
Portland Beavers, 216, 219, 220
Pottsville Maroons, 68, 79–98, 114, 185–6, 198
Prattville, AL, 145, 150
Princeton University, 8, 10, 22, 33, 44, 167, 193
Providence Steam Roller, 82, 84
Pyle, Charles, 96–7

Quinn, Jack, 121, 134, 138–9

Rauch, Dick, 81–3, 88–9, 91, 95, 198
Rhem, Bethel, 164
Rice, Grantland, xi, 3, 34, 76, 126, 152, 194
Richards, Richard, 72
Riverside "Big Green", 72
Robeson, Paul, 11–17, 24, 61, 68, 132, 192–3, 195
Robinson, Frank, 187
Rochester Jeffersons, 87
Rockne, Knute, 34, 36–7, 41–2, 56, 92, 193
Rodgers, Ira, 20–1
Rommel, Eddie, 73, 101–3, 122, 139, 168
Roosevelt, Theodore, 36
Root, Charlie, 134, 137–9
Roper, Harry, 160
Rotogravure, xi, 148
Royle, Shep, 81, 86, 90, 93
Runyon, Damon, 3
Ruppert, Jacob, 107
Rutgers University, x, 8–24, 29–30, 33, 61, 63, 88, 91, 132, 150, 178
Ruth, Babe, xi, 3, 49, 90, 103–5, 115, 122–4, 127, 156, 190

Sanford, George Foster, 10–15, 24, 61, 63
Sayre, Zelda, 66
Schuerholz, Bill, 63
Schuylkill County, 79, 199
Shaney, Struttin Bud, 164
Shibe, Ben, 64, 74
Shibe Park, 74, 75, 77, 94
Shreveport Gassers, 70–1, 74
Simmons, Al, x, 64, 74–7, 99, 101, 102, 104, 114–7, 119–120, 122–33, 136–40, 143, 157, 197
Sladen, Fred, 59
Smithers, Sam, 186
Smythe, George, 51, 55–6, 58, 186
Southern League, 146, 150–1, 154, 156, 190
Spanish flu, 9, 13, 15
Speaker, Tris, x, 105–12, 127–30, 146, 152, 201
St. Louis Browns, 67, 76, 104–5, 112, 120, 125, 130–1, 133
St. Louis Cardinals, 99, 105, 114, 130, 152, 188, 196
Stagg, Amos Alonzo, 16, 35
Stauffer, Beezer, 123

Stein brothers, 68, 91, 84–5, 91, 95
Storck, Don, 17, 30, 40, 45, 50–1, 57–8, 132, 178, 187, 192, 195
Striegel, Doc, 81, 86, 89, 90, 93–4, 96
student service payments, 16
Sullivan, Ed, 192
Sylvester, Joey, 105
Syracuse University, 9, 14–5, 19, 22, 34, 50, 167, 175

Tacony Athletic Club, 68
Taliaferro, Leland, 22, 24
Talman, Howard, 61
Taylor, Zach, 64, 138–40, 142
Terry, Bill, 170
Texas League, 70, 72, 150–1, 153
Thayer Method, 56
The Sporting News, x, 150, 157, 199
Thomas, Ira, 70, 74
Thorpe, Jim, 21, 36, 49, 80
Torpey, James C., 9
Tunney, Gene, xi

United Mine Workers, 85
United States Military Academy, 6, 28, 30, 37, 56, 59, 61, 167, 173, 192
University of California, 24
University of Georgia, 23
University of Utah, 23

Vidal, Gene, 63

Wagner, Honus, 49, 189
Walberg, Rube, 73, 133–5, 139, 142–3

Warner, Pop, 36, 68, 82
Washington Football Club, 62
Washington Senators, xi, 64, 72, 75–8, 101–3, 112–13, 118, 120, 122, 124–5, 128, 132–3, 147, 152
Waterfield, Luke, 24
Weissmuller, Johnny, xi, 3
Wentz, Barney, 82–6, 89, 92, 94–5, 198
West Point, x, 24–33, 37, 39, 42–3, 46–7, 51–9, 61–5, 74, 77, 86, 92, 100, 104, 144, 159, 160–2, 166–68, 170–5, 177, 178, 179, 182–3, 185–86, 188, 190–91
Western Carolina Textile League, 160
Wheat, Zach, 113–4, 116
Wilkes-Barre (PA) Panthers, 68
Willhide, Glenn, 40, 49, 56
Williamsport Billies, 66–7
Wilson, Harry, 29, 194
Winder, Ray, 155
Wood, Joe, 106, 108, 110–1, 172, 199
World War I, 1–4, 7–8, 14–15, 23, 27–8, 31, 33, 43, 56, 168, 177–8
World War II, 177, 180, 186, 189
Worsham, L. D., 159–60
Wynne, Chet, 40–42

Yale University, 10, 16, 19, 35, 44, 51–3, 125, 167, 170
Yanigans, 74
Young Men's Hebrew Association, 63
Young Men's Organization of Detroit, 23

Zacko, Joe, 186